Power Eating

Second Edition

Susan M. Kleiner, PhD, RD
High Performance Nutrition
Mercer Island, Washington

with

Maggie Greenwood-Robinson, PhD

Human Kinetics

Library of Congress Cataloging-in-Publication Data

Kleiner, Susan M.

Power eating / Susan M. Kleiner, with Maggie Greenwood-Robinson.–2nd ed.

p. cm.

Includes bibliographical references and index.

ISBN 0-7360-3853-1

1. Athletes–Nutrition. 2. Bodybuilders—Nutrition. I. Greenwood-Robinson, Maggie. II. Title.

TX361.A8 K595 2001 2001024193

613.2'024'796–dc21

ISBN: 0-7360-3853-1

Acquisitions Editor: Martin Barnard
Developmental Editor: Leigh LaHood
Copyeditor: Judith Wolken
Proofreader: Sue Fetters
Indexer: Betty Frizzéll
Graphic Designer and Graphic Artist: Judy Henderson
Photo Manager: Clark Brooks
Cover Designer: Jack W. Davis
Photographer (cover): Wilmer Zehr
Photographer (interior): Tom Roberts unless otherwise noted
Printer: Bang Printing

Human Kinetics books are available at special discounts for bulk purchase. Special editions or book excerpts can also be created to specification. For details, contact the Special Sales Manager at Human Kinetics.

Printed in the United States of America 10 9 8 7 6 5 4 3 2

Human Kinetics
Web site: www.humankinetics.com

United States: Human Kinetics
P.O. Box 5076
Champaign, IL 61825-5076
800-747-4457
e-mail: humank@hkusa.com

Canada: Human Kinetics
475 Devonshire Road, Unit 100
Windsor, ON N8Y 2L5
800-465-7301 (in Canada only)
e-mail: orders@hkcanada.com

Europe: Human Kinetics
Units C2/C3 Wira Business Park
West Park Ring Road
Leeds LS16 6EB, United Kingdom
+44 (0) 113 278 1708
e-mail: hk@hkeurope.com

Australia: Human Kinetics
57A Price Avenue
Lower Mitcham, South Australia 5062
08 8277 1555
e-mail: liahka@senet.com.au

New Zealand: Human Kinetics
P.O. Box 105-231, Auckland Central
09-523-3462
e-mail: hkp@ihug.co.nz

Contents

Preface

Power Eating was the book I always wanted to write. From the time that I did my doctoral research on bodybuilders in 1983, it took 15 years until there was a book's worth of valid scientific information on nutrition for strength training. But in only the past three years the science of nutrition and strength training has moved forward so rapidly that it gave us the opportunity to write a bigger and better *Power Eating!*

If you are a new *Power Eating* reader, you will find the latest and most accurate scientific and practical advice on eating for strength and power. If you have already been following the *Power Eating* program, you will find new and expanded sections on fueling, proteins, fluids, supplements, herbs, timing of eating, diet plans, menus, and recipes. And there are new success stories from famous athletes and everyday people interested in staying strong and performing at their best.

I know that *Power Eating* will teach you what you can't learn anywhere else. My Power Eating diet plans will get your body where you want it to be when you want it to be there and keep you healthy, safe, and legal. You *can* have it all! Train hard and POWER EAT!

Acknowledgments

To my coauthor, Maggie Greenwood-Robinson, thank you again. You are the best. Many thanks to Martin Barnard, our acquisitions editor, who got this important revision off the ground ahead of the scheduled publication date. A special thank you to Dr. Scott Murdoch for your expertise in herbal supplements, and to Erica Zuieback for your research assistance. A number of the revisions to *Power Eating* occurred as the result of working with athletes and clients dedicated to excellence. Thank you for your invaluable contributions. To Jeff, Danielle, Ilana, and Mom, you are all part of this book. Thanks for the teamwork.

Part I

Foundation

Nothing is more important than a good foundation. A house must be built on a strong foundation to remain sturdy and structurally sound for many years. A child needs a good academic and emotional foundation to develop independence and go out into the world as a happy and productive individual. And an athlete must be anchored by a strong, scientifically-based foundation of nutrition, training, and experience to stay in peak health and to perform successfully throughout life.

This is your introduction to your nutrition foundation. This section will translate the science of nutrition for strength training into the nuts and bolts of what you need to eat, day in and day out, to be a healthy, high-performing individual. Build a strong nutrition foundation, and muscular fitness, strength, and performance will follow.

1 Fueling for Strength Training

Think about how you'd like to look and feel. Imagine yourself with a body that's fit and firm with just the right amount of muscle. Imagine the joy of high strength and energy that give you the power to perform, day in and day out.

Keep those images in your mind's eye. This book will show you how to achieve them with a few nips and tucks in one of the most important fitness factors of all—nutrition. But not just any type of nutrition. This is a book for people who strength train—to stay in shape, compete in strength-training sports, or improve their athletic ability. In other words, you're a "strength trainer" if you lift weights a few times a week or train for competition. As a strength trainer, you have very specific nutritional needs, depending on your type and level of activity.

So, what kind of strength trainer are you? Are you a bodybuilder, powerlifter, Olympic lifter, an athlete who strength trains for conditioning, or someone who works out with weights to stay in shape? Granted, all these activities have different physical demands and different nutritional requirements. That's why you will find several individualized strength-training diets in chapters 11 through 14. But the common denominator is that all strength-training athletes, from competitors to recreational exercisers, are interested in the same thing: building lean muscle.

What Builds Muscle?

Most certainly, strength training builds muscle. But for this construction to take place, you have to supply the construction material: protein, carbohydrates, and fat. In a process called metabolism, the body breaks down these nutrients and uses the products to generate the energy required for growth and life.

During metabolism, proteins are broken down into amino acids. Cells use amino acids to make new proteins based on instructions supplied by DNA, our genetic management system. The DNA provides specific information on how amino acids are to be lined up and strung together. Once these instructions have been carried out, the cell has synthesized a new protein.

On the basis of this process, logic would tell you that the more protein you eat, the more muscle your body can construct. But it doesn't work that way. Excess protein is converted to carbohydrate to be used for energy or converted to fat for storage.

The way to make muscles grow is not by gorging on protein but by demanding more from it—that is, by making it work harder. The muscles will respond by taking up the nutrients they need, including amino acids from protein metabolism, so that they can grow. If you work your muscles hard, muscle cells will synthesize the protein the muscles need.

What Fuels Muscles?

To work your muscles hard, you have to provide the right kind of muscle fuel. Muscle cells, like all cells, run on a high-energy compound known as adenosine triphosphate (ATP). One of the energy molecules, ATP makes muscles contract, conducts nerve impulses, and promotes other cellular energy processes. Muscle cells make ATP by combining oxygen with nutrients from food, mainly carbohydrate. Fat is also used for fuel by muscles, but fat can be broken down only when oxygen is present. Muscle cells really prefer to burn carbohydrate, store fat, and use protein for growth and repair.

Your cells generate ATP through any one of three energy systems: the phosphagen system, the glycolytic system, and the oxidative system.

The phosphagen system rebuilds ATP by supplying a compound called creatine phosphate (CP). Once ATP is used up, it must be replenished from additional food and oxygen. During short intense bursts of exercise such as weight training or sprinting, available oxygen is exhausted by the working muscles. At that point, CP kicks in to supply energy for a few short seconds of work. CP can help create ATP when ATP is depleted.

Any intense exercise lasting for 3 to 15 seconds will rapidly deplete ATP and CP in a muscle; they must then be replaced. Replenishing ATP and CP is the job of the other energy systems in the body.

The glycolytic system makes glucose available to the muscles, either from the breakdown of dietary carbohydrates during digestion or from the breakdown of muscle and liver glycogen, the stored form of carbohydrate. In a process called glycolysis, glycogen is disassembled into glucose in the muscles and, through a series of chemical reactions, ultimately converted to more ATP.

The glycogen reserve in your muscles can supply enough energy for about two to three minutes of short-burst exercise at a time. If sufficient oxygen is available to the muscle cell, a lot of ATP will be made from glucose. If oxygen is absent or in short supply, the muscles produce a waste product from glucose called lactic acid. A buildup of lactic acid in a working muscle creates a burning sensation and causes the muscle to fatigue and stop contracting. Lactic acid exits the muscle when oxygen is available to replenish CP and ATP. A brief rest period gives the body time to deliver oxygen to the muscles, and you can continue exercising.

The third energy system in your body is the oxidative system. This system helps fuel aerobic exercise and other endurance activities. Although the oxidative system can handle the energy needs of endurance exercise, all three energy systems kick in to some degree during endurance exercise. The phosphagen and glycolytic energy systems dominate when you are strength training.

Oxygen is not a direct source of energy for exercise; it is used as an ingredient to produce large amounts of ATP from other energy sources. The oxidative system works as follows: You breathe in oxygen, which is subsequently taken up from your lungs by the blood. Your heart pumps oxygen-rich blood to tissues, including muscle. Hemoglobin, an iron-containing protein of the blood, carries oxygen to the cells to enable them to produce energy. Myoglobin, another type of iron-containing protein, carries oxygen primarily to muscle cells. Inside muscle cells, carbohydrates and fats are converted into energy through a series of energy-producing reactions.

Your body's ability to produce energy by means of any one of these three systems can be improved with the right training diet and exercise program. The result is a fat-burning, muscle-building metabolism.

Nutrition Principles for Strength Trainers

If you are serious about improving your physique and your strength-training performance, you'll do everything you can to achieve success.

Unfortunately, advice given to strength trainers today is a hodgepodge of fact and fiction. What I'd like to do is separate one from the other by sharing several basic principles with you—principles that all strength trainers can follow to get in shape and achieve their personal best in performance. These principles are the same ones I have advocated for world-class athletes, Olympic contenders, and recreational strength trainers for more than 15 years. Let's review them here.

1. Vary Your Diet

You have probably admired the physiques of bodybuilders in magazines. And for good reason. They are muscular, well defined, and in near-perfect proportion. The picture of health, right? Wrong—in many cases. The first study I ever conducted investigated the training diets of male competitive bodybuilders. What I found was that they ate a lot of calories, roughly 6,000 calories a day or more. The worrisome finding about this study was that they ate, on average, more than 200 grams of fat a day. That's almost as much fat as you'd find in two sticks of butter! Short term, that's enough to make most people sick. Eaten habitually over time, such an enormous amount of fat will lead to heart disease.

Bodybuilding diets, especially precontest diets, tend to be monotonous, with the same foods showing up on the plate day after day. The worst example I've ever seen was a bodybuilder who ate chicken, pepper, vinegar, and rice for three days straight while preparing for competition. The problem with such a diet is that it lacks variety, and without a variety of foods, you miss out on loads of nutrients essential for peak health.

Bodybuilders, on average, don't eat much in the way of fruit, dairy products, and red meat. Fruit, of course, is packed with disease-fighting, health-building antioxidants and phytochemicals. Dairy products supply important nutrients like bone-building calcium. And red meat is an important source of vital minerals like iron and zinc.

When such foods are limited or eliminated, potentially serious deficiencies begin to show up. In studies I've done, and in studies others have done, the most common deficiencies observed are those of calcium and zinc, particularly during the precompetition season. In fact, many female bodybuilders have dangerous shortages of these minerals, and they may have the shortages year round. A chronic short supply of calcium increases the risk of osteoporosis, a crippling bone-thinning disease. Although a woman's need for zinc is small (8 milligrams a day), adequate zinc is an impenetrable line of defense when it comes to protecting women from disease and infection. In short, deficits of these minerals can harm health and performance. But the good news is that some skim milk, red meat, and dark meat poultry added back into the diet will help alleviate some of these problems. A three-ounce portion of lean sirloin beef has about six milligrams of zinc; nonfat, 1, or 2 percent milk has about one milligram of zinc in one eight-ounce glass; and three ounces of dark meat turkey have about four milligrams of zinc.

Another nutritional problem among bodybuilders is fluid restriction. Just before a contest, bodybuilders don't drink much water, fearing it will inflate their physiques to the point of blurring their muscular definition. Compounding the problem, many bodybuilders take diuretics and laxatives, a practice that flushes more water, plus precious minerals called electrolytes, from the body. Generally, bodybuilders compete in a dehydrated state. In one contest, I saw two people pass out on stage—one because of severe dehydration, the other because of an electrolyte imbalance.

After a competition, bodybuilders tend to go hog wild. There's nothing wrong with this, as long as it's a temporary splurge. But such dietary indulgence over a long time can lead to extra fat pounds you surely don't want.

Bodybuilders, however, do a lot of things right, especially during the training season. They eat several meals throughout the day—a practice that nutritionists recommend to the general public.

2. Follow a High-Energy Diet

It's well known, too, that most athletes, strength trainers included, don't eat enough carbohydrates, the primary fuel food. Most athletes eat diets in which only half of their total daily calories come from carbs, when seven to nine grams per kilogram of body weight daily should be consumed as carbs. Lots of bodybuilders practice low-carbohydrate dieting because they believe it promotes faster weight loss. The problem with these diets is that they deplete glycogen, the body's storage form of carbohydrate. Once available glycogen stores are emptied, the body starts burning protein from tissues (including muscle tissue) to meet its demand for energy. You lose hard-earned muscle as a result.

Fitness-minded people, athletes, and others shy away from carbs, particularly breads and pastas. They think these foods will make them fat—a food myth that is partially responsible for the lopsided proportion of carbohydrate, fat, and protein in strength-training diets, which are typically too high in protein.

Carbs are probably the most important nutrient for losing fat and building muscle. By the time you finish this book, you'll be convinced of this truth!

3. Consume Enough Calories

A key to feeling energized is to eat the right amount of calories to power your body for hard training. A lack of calories will definitely make you feel like a wet dishrag by the end of your workout.

A diet that provides less than 1,600 calories per day generally does not contain all the vitamins and minerals you need to stay healthy, prevent disease, and perform well. Very low-calorie diets followed for longer than two weeks can be hazardous to your health. Nor do they provide the Dietary Reference Intakes (DRI) of enough of the nutrients needed for good health.

Historically, the recommended dietary allowances (RDA) were the national standard for the amount of carbohydrate, protein, fat, vitamins,

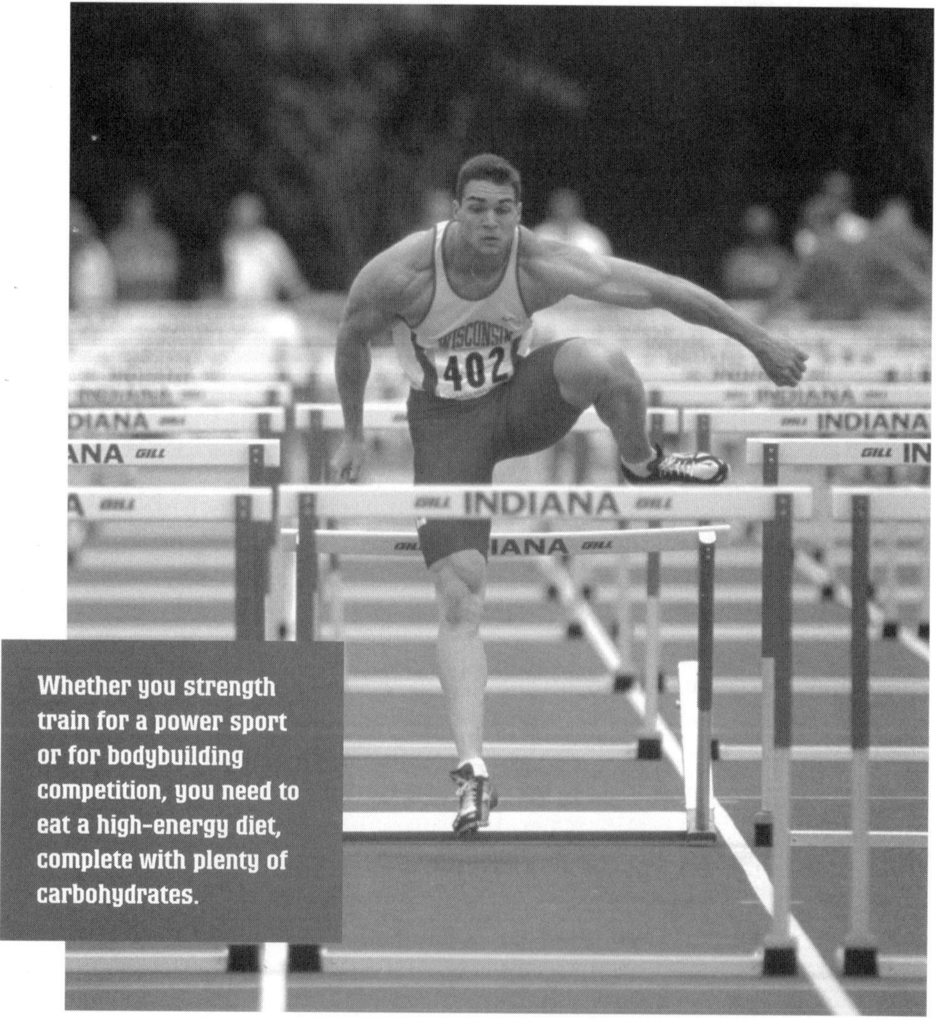

Whether you strength train for a power sport or for bodybuilding competition, you need to eat a high-energy diet, complete with plenty of carbohydrates.

and minerals we need in our diets to avoid deficiency diseases and maintain growth and health. Recently the DRIs were established to update the RDAs based on more functional criteria rather than criteria based on deficiency diseases. But under certain conditions—stress, illness, malnutrition, and exercise—we may require a higher intake of certain nutrients. Studies have shown that athletes, in particular, may have to exceed the DRI of many nutrients. Some competitive bodybuilders have estimated their caloric intake to be greater than 6,000 calories a day during the off-season—roughly three times the DRI for the average person (2,000 calories a day for a woman and 2,700 calories a day for a man).

How much you need of each nutrient depends on a number of factors, including your age and sex, how hard you train, and whether you are a competitive or recreational strength trainer, among other considerations. Generally, we find that strength trainers need to eat more carbohydrates and may be wise to supplement with antioxidants and certain minerals. You'll learn more about these issues as you read this book. If you are trying to gain muscle and lose body fat, eating enough calories and taking in enough nutrients will make the difference between success and failure.

4. Time Your Food and Nutrients

To achieve superb shape and maximum performance, forgo the usual "three squares a day" approach to meals. Active people must fuel themselves throughout the day. That means frequent small meals and snacks every two to three hours.

There are numerous research-confirmed benefits to eating small, frequent meals and snacks. For example, eating multiple meals (four or more a day) increases "thermogenesis," the production of heat by the body as it digests and absorbs food. During thermogenesis, metabolism steps up, and your body processes nutrients more efficiently. Increased meal frequency also stimulates fat burning, improves the body's use of protein, preserves lean muscle, and reduces appetite.

Another advantage of multiple meals is mental performance. Regular, timed meals help you think and process information more effectively, increase your attention span, and boost your mood.

So, the question is: What should you eat and when? The key is to time your meals around your workout schedule. In a nutshell, exercise and food intake work in concert to build lean muscle. Table 1.1 provides a step-by-step look at how to time your meals properly and the benefits of doing so. The supplements listed in the table are discussed in detail elsewhere in this book.

5. Stop Megadosing

A writer in a popular bodybuilding magazine once wrote: "Bodybuilders seem to believe that nothing succeeds like excess. That if something is good for you, twice as much is even better. That too much is never enough."

In many ways, this statement prevails as a motto in strength-training nutrition, particularly when it comes to protein and supplements. Thus, strength trainers and bodybuilders tend to megadose on supplements and foods, thinking that the more they take or eat, the more muscle they'll build. Nothing could be further from the truth. You require a specific amount of nutrients for muscle building, based on your individual needs. Eat more food than you need and it turns to unsightly fat. And if you megadose on supplements, the surplus is excreted or can be toxic to your body.

Protein, Strength, and Muscle Building

For generations, athletes have believed that a high-protein diet will increase strength. This myth can be historically traced to a famous Greek athlete, Milo of Crotona, in the sixth century B.C. One of the strongest men in Greece, Milo was the wrestling victor in five Olympic Games and in many of the other sacred festivals. As the legend goes, he applied progressive resistance training by lifting a growing calf daily, and when the calf was four years old, he carried it the length of the Olympian stadium, killed, roasted, and ate it. It is written that his normal daily intake of meat was about 20 pounds.

In the sixties and seventies, protein was thought to be a miracle food, because muscle magazines hyped it so much. Thus, bodybuilders and other athletes would follow diets made up mostly of meat, milk, and eggs. The raw egg milkshake was particularly popular, thanks to Rocky Balboa. Why would anyone want to swill such a concoction? Answer: misinformation. Articles and advertising from those days continue to falsely communicate the notion that the protein from raw foods, and eggs in particular, is more available to our bodies for building muscle compared with cooked foods.

Not only is this notion absolutely untrue, it is dangerous to believe. A protein molecule is a string of amino acids connected together like a strand of pearls. If two strands of pearls were wound together and then twisted to double up on each other, they would resemble a protein molecule.

Heating or cooking the protein molecule unwinds the string of amino acids, straightens it out, and finally separates it into smaller pieces. This is the process of heat denaturing, which is similar to the process of chemical denaturing, otherwise known as digestion. Cooking food protein can begin the digestive process and can actually decrease the net energy that the body must expend during digestion.

Table 1.1 Timing Meals

Throughout the day
Fluids: At least 8–12 glasses a day; at least 5 should be water.
Breakfast: Never skip this meal, because it improves physical and mental performance and helps regulate weight.
Meals: Small, frequent protein/carbohydrate meals and snacks every 2 to 3 h.
Before exercise
Fluids: At least 8 oz. before exercise.
Pre-exercise meal: At least 4 h before exercise so that the body properly assimilates carbohydrates for use by muscles.
Pre-exercise snack: 30 to 90 min before exercise. Snack should include 50 g of a slow-release carbohydrate, plus 5 to 10 g protein. Snack can be food or meal-replacement supplements. These will provide additional energy for prolonged stamina and help decrease exercise-induced breakdown of muscle protein.
During exercise
Fluids: 7–10 oz. every 10–20 min.
Glucose electrolyte sport drinks: Sipping these during a workout has been shown to extend endurance.
After exercise
Fluids: Replace each pound of fluid lost with 16–24 oz. of water or sport drink.
Carbohydrates: Consume 1.5 g/kg of fast-release (or high glycemic index) carbohydrate within 30 min after exercise and again 2 h later for increased muscle glycogen resynthesis.
Protein: Consume 0.5 g/kg protein with carbohydrate to encourage muscle growth. Postexercise snacks can be in the form of meal-replacement beverages with 1.5 g/kg simple carbohydrate (dextrose/maltodextrin/sucrose) and 0.5 g/kg protein. Follow this by a meal within 2 h of exercise containing lots of carbohydrate and high-quality protein sources (fish, lean meats, low-fat dairy products, eggs, etc.).
Recovery supplements: Consume these with your meal replacement: creatine (2–5 g); glutamine (4–10 g); vitamin C (up to 500 mg); zinc (up to 25 mg/d); echinacea if you feel a cold or flu coming on. (Do not supplement with echinacea if you have hay fever; the herb may cause an adverse reaction.)

Power Profiles

Calories are certainly important in building muscle mass; however, the source of those calories is key if you want to maximize muscle and minimize body fat. Case in point: a professional rookie football player who wanted to lose weight to improve his speed on the field. Unless he trimmed down, his chance to be on the team was in jeopardy, so he needed a dramatic nutritional rescue.

This football player was eating slightly more than 7,000 calories a day. Broken down, those calories figured out to 17 percent protein, 32 percent fat, and about 49 percent carbohydrate. In daily fat grams, he was consuming a whopping 250 grams a day. The composition of his calories was an impediment to losing fat. I reconfigured his diet to 5,680 calories a day, with 12.5 percent of those calories coming from protein, 25 percent from fat, and 62.5 percent from carbs. That mix would slash his fat grams to a healthier 142 grams a day.

He was eating a lot of hidden fat in foods like fried chicken, whole milk, and fast foods. For the high-fat foods, we substituted skinless chicken breasts, 1 percent milk, and fast-food choices such as salads and frozen yogurt that were lower in fat. In addition, we modified some of his favorite dishes such as sweet potato pie into lower fat versions. He also began to load up on complex carbs like rice, pasta, bread, and vegetables. Plus, he cut his meat allotment down to about eight ounces a day.

The upshot of these dietary changes was that he lost the weight, made the team, and had a great season. He is still a professional football player.

Eating raw eggs is a hazardous practice, because eggs may be contaminated with the microorganisms that cause salmonella poisoning. Cooking eggs destroys bacteria, eliminating the risk of contracting this serious foodborne illness. Clearly, the idea of eating raw eggs to build muscle size and strength is a food myth. Raw eggs should be avoided completely.

Today, amino acid supplements—a modern twist on the high-protein myth—are promoted to increase lean body mass and improve muscular performance.

Sport nutrition research has debunked all these protein myths. We now know that the most important dietary factor influencing muscle growth and strength is a carb-rich diet. Strength-training athletes do need more protein than the general population, but it's not as much as you may think. In my many years of working with strength trainers, I've never seen anyone who was protein deficient, not even a vegetarian!

The Scoop on Supplements

In the past several years, sales of dietary supplements have zoomed, according to the *Nutrition Business Journal*, an independent research and publishing company based in San Diego, California. In 1996, for example, Americans spent more than $6 billion annually on supplements. Today, that figure is more than $14 billion a year—and climbing.

That means that a lot of us are spending much more than the average, because these statistics only cover what we call essential nutrient supplements—the commonly recognized vitamins and minerals we must consume in our diets to stay healthy and avoid deficiencies. Typically, the only disease a vitamin or mineral will cure is one caused by a deficiency of that vitamin or mineral. It is preferable to consume these nutrients as food. But when you don't eat enough in your diet, supplementation with a daily multiple vitamin and mineral pill may be an important way to get what you need.

Nonessential supplements are chemicals or compounds that don't cause classical signs of deficiency diseases if they are absent from the diet. Put another way, these supplements aren't required to maintain health or boost performance. We can certainly perform without nonessential supplements like medium-chain triglyceride (MCT) oil or chromium picolinate, but many strength trainers wouldn't be without them. Could we reach new levels of performance if we included some nonessential supplements in our diets?

It's hard to say for sure, although the links between diet and performance are becoming clearer all the time. We have also come to realize that these links are more complex than we thought. Every day we read about new research discoveries relating to some factor in food that promises to boost energy or prevent disease. Sometimes these discoveries tell us that some factor previously considered nonessential may be very important in helping improve health and energy.

Such information is all that supplement manufacturers need to hear. Once one small piece of evidence surfaces—even in a single rat study—that a certain food factor may be helpful in preventing disease, building muscle, or enhancing performance, the next place you see that factor is in a supplement.

Unfortunately, supplement manufacturers don't have to follow the same rigorous review process that is required for new drugs. Supplements are legally considered food, not drugs. The United States Food and Drug Administration (FDA) expects the same kind of truth in labeling with supplements as it does with food. But in contrast to drugs, supplements do not have to be proven to work before they are placed on the market.

Unless someone gets sick from taking a supplement and reports it to the FDA, supplement manufacturers rarely have to prove their claims. So consumer beware. There may be no truth, part truth, or full truth to the claims for the use of a supplement. Before you believe everything that you read on a supplement label or advertisement, try to get some facts.

Where Do You Stand Now?

Analyze your present diet now to see exactly what you're eating, particularly in terms of the three energy nutrients. You should also analyze how much water you're drinking, because water is a critical nutrient. This analysis will make the following chapters more relevant and interesting to you. For example, when you're reading about protein, you may wonder how much protein you're eating now. With this analysis handy, you can find out quickly.

Using the chart provided in table 1.2, record everything you eat over the course of three days. Choose days that best represent your typical diet. Be as accurate as you can in terms of the amount of food you eat. Use a food composition guide, either in book or software format, to help you figure out nutrients and calories. Table 1.2 is a simple form you can use to record your food and analyze your diet.

Sport Nutrition Fact vs. Fiction: Are Carbs Fattening?

Researchers investigating diet, weight loss, chronic disease, and diet and exercise have debunked the myth that breads and starchy foods (high-carbohydrate foods) are fattening and should be avoided. On the contrary, starchy foods are low in calories, and the most healthful diet for weight loss, disease prevention, and physical performance is a high-carbohydrate diet.

The problem with eating high-carb foods like breads, noodles, and potatoes is not the foods themselves, but what we put on them. The myth that starchy foods are fattening should be changed to the truism that the butter, spreads, creams, and sauces on starchy foods are fattening. High-fat foods are high-calorie foods. By replacing regular butter, spreads, and sour creams with their new low-fat and nonfat versions, we can eliminate most of the high-fat, high-calorie fare that often accompanies these low-fat, low-calorie, high-carbohydrate foods.

Table 1.2 Three-Day Food Record

Food	Amount	Protein (g)	Carbs (g)	Fat (g)	Calories
Day 1					
Totals					
Day 2					
Totals					
Day 3					
Totals					

Sport Nutrition Fact vs. Fiction:

Organic Foods—Are They Better for You?

With the amount of food strength trainers eat, many are opting to go organic to avoid the chemical fertilizers, pesticides, and additives used in many foods. Do you get an advantage in buying organic foods?

In general, organically grown foods are grown in soil enriched with organic fertilizers, rather than synthetic fertilizers, and treated only with nonsynthetic pesticides. Organic farms use a soil-building program that promotes vibrant soil and healthy plants, usually including crop rotations and biological pest control. At present, the job of regulating the organic farming industry is left up to the states. The states vary in their enforcement of regulations and their oversight of organic farming, and not all states have instituted organic programs or statutory definitions. In 1990, Congress passed a law defining a federal standard for organic farming methods. The bill has created much controversy and has not yet been implemented.

Advocates of organic foods claim that they are more nutritious and present fewer of the health hazards associated with pesticide contamination. In general, this argument does not seem to hold up. Some surveys find similar pesticide levels in both organically and conventionally grown foods. Even when organic foods are grown according to certification standards, contaminated runoff water, contaminated shifting soil, and airborne pesticides may still result in pesticides being present on food.

Organically grown food does not have greater nutritive value than food grown with conventional methods. The soil nutrients from natural fertilizers are no different from the nutrients in chemical fertilizers made in factories. The genetic makeup of the food will also determine that particular food's nutrient content and needs.

The freshness of organic foods may also be questionable. In many states, an efficient production, distribution, and retail sales system is not in place for organic produce, and the slow movement of the produce from field to market may permit wilting and nutrient losses.

Organically grown produce costs much more than its conventionally grown counterpart. Depending on supply and demand, this difference can be quite significant.

According to Miles McEvoy, program manager for the Washington State Department of Agriculture Organic Food Program, organic foods are not safer, and they are not better. His reason for promoting organic farming is that it is "a more environmentally benign way of producing food."

Organic farming methods are less harmful to the environment than conventional methods. The use of natural products helps to improve the soil. Organic pest control generally relies on preventive measures such as crop rotation and biological controls. These methods place little to no stress on the earth or its wildlife inhabitants.

Another reason to choose organic foods: There is a difference in the pesticide content of produce grown outside the United States. Their regulations are not at all like ours, and we hardly have enough inspectors at the borders (especially for food imported from Mexico and Central and South America) to catch everything that doesn't meet our standards.

Also, I think that organic produce often tastes better. Here in Seattle, where I live, lots of organic food is grown locally. Consequently, the produce is very fresh, because it doesn't have to be transported in.

In the end, the choice is yours. Purchasing organic foods is not just a nutritional issue but a political and social issue as well. Nutritionally speaking, it's clearly important to eat a variety of foods to ensure a balanced nutrient intake and to lessen pesticide contamination from any one source. Despite the use of pesticides, populations that eat large amounts of fruits and vegetables have lower rates of cancer than populations eating few fruits and vegetables.

You'll pay more for organic produce, so if your pocketbook is light, buy fresh conventional produce and follow these guidelines for reducing pesticide residues in foods:

- Wash fresh produce in water. Use a scrub brush, and rinse the foods thoroughly under running water.
- Use a knife to peel an orange or grapefruit; do not bite into the peel.
- Discard the outer leaves of leafy vegetables such as cabbage and lettuce.
- Peel waxed fruit and vegetables; waxes don't wash off and can seal in pesticide residues.
- Peel vegetables such as carrots and fruits such as apples when appropriate. (Peeling removes pesticides that remain in or on the peel but also removes fibers, vitamins, and minerals.)

2 Manufacturing Muscle

Inside your body a marvelous process of self-repair takes place, day in and day out, and it all has to do with protein, the nutrient responsible for building and maintaining body tissues.

Proteins are present everywhere in the body—in muscle, bones, connective tissue, blood vessels, blood cells, skin, hair, and fingernails. These proteins are constantly being lost or broken down as a result of normal, physiological wear and tear and must be replaced. For example, about one half of the total amount of protein in muscle tissue is broken down and replaced every 150 days.

The mechanism by which this occurs is really quite amazing. During digestion, protein in food is dismantled by other proteins (enzymes) into subunits called amino acids. In this form, amino acids can enter cells, where other enzymes, acting on instructions from DNA, put them back together as the new proteins needed to build and repair tissue. No other system in the world repairs itself so wonderfully. Every day, this process goes on and life continues.

Under any condition of growth—childhood, pregnancy, muscle building—the body manufactures more cells than are lost. From an energy source such as carbohydrate or fat, the body can manufacture many of the materials needed to make new cells. But to replace and build new proteins, it must have protein from food. Unlike carbohydrates and fat, protein contains nitrogen, and nitrogen is required to synthesize new proteins.

Protein, therefore, is absolutely necessary for the maintenance, replacement, and growth of body tissue. But protein has other uses, too. The body uses protein to regulate hormone secretion, maintain the body's water balance, protect against disease, transport nutrients in and out of cells, carry oxygen, and regulate blood clotting.

Protein and Muscle Building

Protein is a key player in the repair and construction of muscle tissue after exercise. By lifting weights, you force your muscles to lengthen when they want to contract. This action causes microscopic tears in your muscle fibers (the reason for the muscle soreness you feel a day or two after your workout). In response, your body makes muscle fibers bigger and stronger to protect against future insults.

The construction material for this process comes primarily from dietary protein, which is broken down in digestion into amino acids. As previously explained, amino acids enter the bloodstream and are transported to cells to be synthesized into body proteins. Your muscle cells use amino acids to create more muscle protein. There are two major types of muscle protein, actin and myosin. During muscular contraction, these muscle proteins slide over each other like two pieces of a telescope. When you build muscle, you're basically increasing the amount of actin and myosin in your muscles. This makes the muscle fibers increase in diameter, get stronger, and contract more powerfully.

Protein and Strength-Training Performance

It would seem that the more construction material (protein) you supply your body, the more muscle you would build. At least that's the train of thought strength athletes have followed for ages. But it doesn't quite work that way. In other words, eating twice as much protein won't make your muscles twice as big. Furthermore, one problem with eating too much protein is that the excess can be stored as body fat.

To build muscle, you must be in a positive nitrogen balance. Nitrogen leaves the body primarily in the urine. Nitrogen lost by excretion must be replaced by nitrogen taken in from food. Protein contains a fairly large concentration of nitrogen. Generally, healthy adults are in a nitrogen equilibrium, or zero balance—that is, their protein intake meets their protein requirement. A positive nitrogen balance means that the body is retaining dietary protein and using it to synthesize new tissue. If more nitrogen is excreted than was consumed, the nitrogen balance is negative. The body has lost nitrogen—and therefore protein. A negative nitrogen balance over time is dangerous, leading to muscle wasting and disease.

Achieving a positive nitrogen balance doesn't necessarily mean you have to eat more protein. Muscle cells take up the exact amount of nutrients (including amino acids from dietary protein) they need for growth. And strength training helps them make better use of the protein that's available.

This fact was clearly demonstrated in 1995 by a group of Tufts University researchers led by Wayne W. Campbell. The researchers took a group of older men and women (ages 56 to 80) who had never lifted weights before, placed them on either a low-protein diet or a high-protein diet, and measured their nitrogen balance before and after participation in a 12-week strength-training program. The low-protein diet was actually

Strength training helps muscle cells make better use of the protein that's available to them.

based on the RDA for protein (0.8 grams per kilogram of body weight daily). The high-protein diet was twice the RDA (1.6 grams per kilogram of body weight daily). The researchers wanted to see what effects each diet had on nitrogen balance during strength training.

What they found out was interesting. Strength training enhanced nitrogen retention in both groups—in other words, protein was being retained and used to synthesize new tissue. However, in the low-protein group, there was even better use of protein. Strength training caused the body to adapt and meet the demand for protein—even when the bare minimum requirement for protein was eaten each day. This shows how marvelously the body adjusts to what is available and how strength training makes muscle cells more efficient at using available protein to synthesize new tissue.

So exactly how much protein should you eat for maximum performance and results? That is a question that has been hotly debated in science for more than 100 years and by athletes since the time of the ancient Greeks. It has been difficult for nutrition scientists to reach a consensus on protein intake for several reasons. One has to do with the type of exercise you do and how frequently you do it. In endurance exercise, for example, protein can act as kind of a spare fuel tank, kicking in amino acids to supply fuel. If protein is in short supply, the endurance athlete can peter out easily. In strength sports, additional dietary protein is needed to provide enough amino acids to synthesize protein in the muscles.

For generations, strength trainers have looked to protein as the nutritional panacea for muscle building. Is there any scientific basis to this belief? Possibly. Some exploding new research proves that as a strength trainer, you may benefit from eating some extra protein.

Protein Benefits Older Strength Trainers

It's no secret that as you age, you can lose muscle mass, strength, and function, partly because of inactivity. One way to reverse the downhill slide is by strength training. Study after study has shown that you can make significant muscle gains well up into your nineties if you strength train.

Now scientific research indicates that senior strength trainers can get a real boost from additional protein. At Tufts University, researchers gave supplemental protein to a group of elderly strength trainers, while a control group took no supplements. The result? Based on CAT scans of muscle, the supplement group gained much more muscle mass than the control group did.

Protein Benefits Younger Strength Trainers, Too

But what if you're not yet in your golden years? Can you get the same benefits from extra protein? Many studies say yes. Two groups of young bodybuilders following a four-week strength-training program followed the same diet, but with one exception. One group ate 2.3 grams of protein per kilogram of body weight (a very large amount) compared with 1.3 grams of protein per kilogram of body weight in the other group. By the end of the study, both groups had gained muscle. But those eating the higher amount of protein had gained five times more muscle!

How High Can You Go?

At Kent State University, researchers divided strength trainers into three groups: (1) a low-protein group on a diet of 0.9 grams of protein per kilogram of body weight, which approximates the 0.8 grams per kilogram protein recommendation for sedentary people; (2) a group eating 1.4 grams of protein per kilogram of body weight; and (3) a group eating 2.4 grams of protein per kilogram of body weight. Control groups with both sedentary subjects and strength-training subjects were also included.

Two exciting findings emerged. First, increasing protein intake to 1.4 grams triggered protein synthesis (an indicator of muscle growth) in strength trainers. There were no such changes in the low-protein group. Second, upping protein intake from 1.4 grams to 2.4 grams produced no further protein synthesis. This latter finding suggested that a plateau had been reached, meaning that the subjects got more protein than they could use at 2.4 grams.

The research appears to indicate that if you strength train and eat more protein, you are going to enhance muscle development and preservation. But does this mean you should start piling protein on your plate? Not necessarily. Studies should always be interpreted with caution. Let's talk about how much protein you really need for your individual activity level.

Your Individual Requirements

As a strength trainer or bodybuilder, you do need more protein than a less active person. In fact, your requirement is higher than the current DRI of 0.8 grams of protein per kilogram of body weight a day, which is based on the needs of nonexercisers. But it's only slightly higher. (Don't forget; your body can work with a protein intake that meets the DRI.) Plus, individual protein requirements vary, based on whether you're in a muscle-building phase, doing aerobic exercise on a regular basis, or dieting for competition. Here's a closer look.

For Muscle Building

With increases in training intensity, you need additional protein to support muscle growth and increases in certain blood compounds. On the basis of the latest research with strength trainers, I recommend that you eat 1.6 grams of protein per kilogram of body weight a day. Here's how you would figure that requirement if you weigh 150 pounds or 68 kilograms (a kilogram equals 2.2 pounds):

$$1.6 \text{ g of protein per kg of body weight} \times 68 \text{ kg} = 109 \text{ g of protein a day}$$

If you also engage in regular aerobic exercise, consume 1.8 grams of protein per kilogram of body weight daily. Strength trainers living in high altitudes need even more protein: 2.2 grams per kilogram of body weight daily. And, vegan vegetarians should take in 2.0 grams of protein per kilogram of body weight a day to make sure their diets are providing all the amino acids their bodies require.

Are you a brand new strength trainer? If so, you may need to eat more than a veteran strength trainer typically consumes—as much as 40 percent more.

If You're Doing Aerobic Exercise, Too

On average, most strength trainers and bodybuilders perform an hour or two of intense weight training daily, plus five or more hours a week of aerobic exercise. If you are in this category, your protein needs are further elevated. Here's why.

During aerobic exercise lasting 60 to 90 minutes, certain amino acids—the so-called branched-chain amino acids (BCAAs)—are used for energy in small amounts, particularly when the body is running low on carbohydrates, its preferred fuel source. One of the BCAAs, leucine, is broken down to make another amino acid called alanine, which is converted by the liver into blood sugar (glucose) for energy. This glucose is transported to the working muscles to be used for energy. The harder you work out aerobically, the more leucine your body breaks down for extra fuel.

Given this special use of amino acids as an energy source, you should increase your protein intake if your training program includes aerobics.

You may require as much as 1.8 grams of protein per kilogram of body weight. With the preceding example, you would calculate your requirements as follows:

1.8 g of protein per kg of body weight × 68 kg = 122 g of protein a day

When Dieting for Competition or to Trim Fat

When cutting calories to lean out for looks or for competition, you risk losing body-firming muscle. Because muscle is the body's most metabolically active tissue, losing it compromises the ability of your body to burn fat. What's more, no bodybuilder wants to lose muscle before competition. One way to prevent diet-related muscle loss is to consume adequate protein while you're preparing for competition. Dieting bodybuilders need between 1.8 and 2.0 grams of protein per kilogram of body weight a day. For example:

2.0 g of protein per kg of body weight × 68 kg = 136 g of protein a day

For more information on getting cut for competition, see chapter 9.

The Benefits of Properly Timing Your Protein Intake

Let's say you've just finished a super-intense strength-training workout. If you could zoom down to the microscopic level of your muscles, you'd be astounded by the sight. There are tears in the tiny structures of your muscle fibers and leaks in muscle cells. Over the next 24 to 48 hours, muscle protein will break down, and additional muscle glycogen will be used up.

These are some of the chief metabolic events that occur in the aftermath of a hard workout. And although they might look like havoc, these events are actually a necessary part of "recovery"—the repair and growth of muscle tissue that take place after every workout.

During recovery, your body replenishes muscle glycogen and synthesizes new muscle protein. In the process, muscle fibers are made bigger and stronger to protect themselves against future trauma.

You can do much to enhance this recovery process—including the consumption of protein after your workout. According to research conducted with active people, you can jump-start the glycogen-making process by eating 0.5 grams of protein per kilogram of body weight, along with a high-glycemic index carbohydrate such as dextrose, maltodextrin, sucrose, or even honey, within 30 minutes of exercise. That equates to 34 grams of protein if you weigh 150 pounds.

When protein is consumed along with carbs, there's a surge in insulin. Biochemically, insulin is like an acceleration pedal. It races the body's glycogen-making motor—in two ways. First, it speeds up the movement of glucose and amino acids into cells, and second, it activates a special enzyme crucial to glycogen synthesis.

There's more: Additional research shows that a carbohydrate/protein supplement ingested after exercise triggers the release of growth hormone in addition to insulin. Both are conducive to muscle growth and recovery.

Also, the availability of essential amino acids (see table 2.1) after exercise encourages the rate of muscle protein resynthesis in the body. On the basis of these findings, I recommend that you consume 1.5 grams per kilogram of a high glycemic index carbohydrate with 0.5 grams of a protein food or a quality protein supplement—preferably one that contains all the essential amino acids. (See table 3.4 on page 56 for a glycemic index of foods.)

Table 2.1 Essential, Conditionally Essential, and Nonessential Amino Acids

Essential	Conditionally essential	Nonessential
Isoleucine*	Arginine	Alanine
Leucine*	Cysteine (cystine)	Asparagine
Lysine	Glutamine	Aspartic acid
Methionine	Histidine	Citruline
Phenylalanine	Proline	Glutamic acid
Threonine	Taurine	Glycine
Tryptophan	Tyrosine	Serine
Valine*		

*Branched-chain amino acid

Adapted from M.G. Di Pasquale. 2000. Proteins and amino acids in exercise and sport. In J.A. Driskell and I. Wolinsky (eds). *Energy-Yielding Macronutrients and Energy Metabolism in Sports Nutrition.* CRC Press, pp.119-162.

Beware of High-Protein Diets

High-protein diets promising quick weight loss continue to be the rage. These diets let you fill up on beef, chicken, fish, and eggs, with little emphasis on other foods like vegetables and grains.

What's wrong with such a diet? To begin with, high-protein diets are high in fat. The protein in animal foods is often coupled with large amounts of saturated fat and cholesterol. Excess dietary fat can make you gain body fat and is damaging to your heart.

High-protein diets are often low in fiber, too. Without enough bulk to move things along, your whole digestive system slows down to a crawl. That can lead to constipation, diverticulosis, and other intestinal disorders.

Adding insult to injury, high-protein diets can also flush too much calcium from the body. High-protein diets cause an increase in calcium loss in the urine. Over a lifetime, this loss can be unhealthy, particularly for women who need adequate levels of calcium to protect against the bone-thinning disease osteoporosis.

There's more: Excess dietary protein is rough on the kidneys. The kidneys process the nitrogen wastes generated by protein metabolism. A system overloaded with protein interferes with the kidneys' ability to properly eliminate these wastes, possibly setting the stage for kidney disease.

High-protein diets are also dehydrating. Within the first week on a high-protein diet, you can lose a lot of weight, depending on your initial weight and body fat percentage. You get on the scale, see an exhilarating weight loss, and feel wonderful. But most of this loss is water. You could be very dehydrated as a result. That spells trouble. A mere three-pound water weight loss in a 150-pound person can make you feel draggy and thus hurt your exercise performance. The minute you go off this diet and eat some carbohydrates, water surges back into your tissues, and you regain the lost water weight.

Clearly, your focus should not be on protein, but on a balance of nutrients. In fact, protein should make up approximately 15 to 20 percent of your total daily calories. In chapter 15, you'll learn how to design your own personal eating plan, one that contains the right amount of protein, carbohydrates, and fat to help you build muscle and stay lean.

Red Meat

Is red meat a good source of protein for strength trainers? Yes. But you may have shied away from red meat in the past because it tends to be very high in fat and dietary cholesterol. Red meat, however, is a good source of protein, as well as iron and zinc.

Iron is necessary for manufacturing hemoglobin, which carries oxygen from the lungs to the tissues, and myoglobin, another transporter of oxygen found only in muscle tissue. The iron in red meat and other animal proteins is known as heme iron. The body absorbs heme iron better than it absorbs iron from plant foods, known as nonheme iron.

Zinc is a busy mineral. As one of the most widely distributed minerals in the body, zinc helps the body absorb vitamins, especially the B-complex vitamins. It is also involved in digestion and metabolism and is essential for growth. Like iron, zinc from animal proteins is absorbed better than zinc from plant foods.

Red meat clearly has some nutritional pluses. The key is to control the amount of fat you get from meat. Here's how to do that.

1. Serving size. Keep the serving size moderate, because about three ounces of lean beef contains just 8.4 grams of total fat and 21 grams of total protein. A three-ounce serving is about the size of a deck of cards or the palm of a woman's hand. To get three ounces of cooked meat, start with four ounces of uncooked, boneless meat.

2. Cut of meat. Certain cuts of meat are leaner than most. Called the "skinniest six," top round, top loin, round tip, tenderloin, sirloin, and eye of round are the leanest cuts you can select. Each three-ounce cooked and trimmed serving contains less than 8.6 grams of total fat, less than 77 milligrams of dietary cholesterol, and less than 180 calories.

Beef is also graded according to fat marbling: prime, choice, and select. Select is the leanest grade. When selecting beef, purchase lean cuts closely trimmed of fat, or trim them yourself at home before you cook.

Pork is also a leaner meat than it used to be. The leanest cuts of pork come from the loin and leg areas, and a three-ounce cooked and trimmed portion of any of these cuts contains less than 9 grams of fat and less than 180 calories. Lamb and veal are also lower in fat content than beef. Follow the same guidelines for selecting lean cuts.

3. Preparation. To keep a lean cut lean and tasty after cooking, it must be handled and prepared properly. Because leaner cuts have less fat in the meat to keep them moist and juicy, the method of preparing the meat is important. More tender cuts, like loin cuts, can be broiled or grilled and served immediately. Avoid overcooking.

Less tender cuts, such as round cuts, should be marinated to tenderize. Because it is the acid in the marinade (vinegar, citrus juice, or wine) that tenderizes the meat, oil can be replaced with water without diminishing the tenderizing effect. To improve the tenderness of roasts, carve into thin slices on the diagonal and across the grain when possible.

Going Meatless, Staying Muscular

Can you be a vegetarian and still build muscle? Absolutely—as long as you plan your diet properly. The key is to mix and match foods so that you get the right balance of amino acids each day.

You can think of amino acids as a construction crew hired to build a house. Each crew member has a specific function, from framing to wiring. If just one crew member calls off, then the construction job doesn't get finished. It's the same with amino acids.

There are 22 amino acids, all of which are combined together to construct proteins required for growth and tissue repair. For your body to build protein, all of these amino acids must be on the job. If just one amino acid is missing or even if the concentration of an amino acid is low, protein construction comes to a halt.

Of the 22 amino acids, eight cannot be made by the body; they must be supplied by the food you eat. These eight amino acids are called the essential amino acids. Seven of the 22 amino acids are termed conditionally essential amino acids. This means that they are made by the body but, under certain conditions, are required in greater amounts. The remaining seven, which can be manufactured by the body, are known as the nonessential amino acids. Your body makes nonessential amino acids from carbohydrates and nitrogen and by chemically re-sorting essential and nonessential amino acids. (The essential, conditionally essential, and nonessential amino acids are listed in table 2.1, on page 26.)

Foods that contain all eight essential amino acids are called complete proteins. Proteins found in dairy products, eggs, meat, poultry, fish, and other animal sources are complete proteins. Various plant foods typically provide incomplete proteins that either completely lack or are low in a particular essential amino acid. The essential amino acid that is missing or in short supply is called the limiting amino acid.

To get enough essential amino acids from a vegetarian diet, select foods that complement one another's limiting amino acid. In other words, mix and match foods during the day so that foods low in an essential amino acid are balanced by one that's higher in the same amino acid. It's not necessary to combine these proteins at one meal, but rather, eat a variety of protein sources throughout the day. For example, grains contain a limited amount of lysine but a higher amount of methionine. Legumes such as navy beans, kidney beans, or black beans are high in lysine but low in methionine. Thus, by combining grains and legumes, you create a complete protein meal. Soybeans are an exception and are considered a complete protein. Other fully nutritious protein combinations include the following:

- Rice and beans
- Corn and beans
- Corn and lima beans
- Corn tortillas and refried beans
- Pasta and bean soup
- Soybeans and seeds

If you are a vegetarian who chooses to eat milk and eggs, you needn't worry about combining complete protein foods. The protein in milk, eggs, cheeses, and other dairy products contains all the essential amino acids you need for tissue growth, repair, and maintenance. A word of caution, though: Dairy products can be high in fat. So be sure to choose nonfat dairy foods such as nonfat milk, cheese, and yogurt. As for eggs, limit yourself to three or four egg yolks a week. Most of the protein in eggs is found in the egg white anyway.

Nutritional Danger Zones for Vegetarian Strength Trainers

Whether to include or exclude meat in your diet is a matter of personal choice. If you decide to go meatless, plan your diet carefully to avoid certain nutritional danger zones—namely, iron, zinc, and B12 deficiencies. These deficiencies can hurt exercise performance. Here are some tips for avoiding deficiencies if you're a vegetarian strength trainer.

Get Enough Protein in Your Diet

A challenge for vegetarian strength trainers is to obtain the 1.6 grams of high-quality protein per kilogram of body weight required daily to support muscle growth. You can do this by including plenty of low-fat dairy products and protein-rich plant sources in your diet. If you are a pure vegan (you eat no animal foods at all), increase your protein intake to 2.0 grams of protein per kilogram of body weight a day.

Include Some Heme Iron Sources in Your Diet

As noted, all types of animal protein contain the more easily absorbed form of iron, heme iron. If you're a semivegetarian—that is, still eating

Power Profiles

I once worked with a professional basketball player, who, for philosophical reasons, was a lactovegetarian. A lactovegetarian eats no animal foods except for eggs and dairy products. Very determined, he wanted to know how he could stick to his vegetarian game plan, both on the road and at home.

Unexpectedly, this player's biggest problem was not protein. He was getting plenty of protein from eating dairy products. But he wasn't getting enough iron, selenium, and zinc—minerals that are plentiful in flesh foods. Also, his diet was very high in fat, because he was eating a lot of cheese-laden vegetable lasagna.

To solve the mineral problem, he began taking a mineral supplement containing the RDA of the minerals he was lacking. After basketball practice, he started drinking one or two meal-replacement beverages, which contain extra nutrients and fit perfectly into a lactovegetarian diet.

With my help, he discovered several new low-fat recipes, like vegetarian chili, that could be packed for road trips and eaten for dinner as long as he had a microwave oven in his hotel room. He took dried fruit on the road, too. An eat-anywhere snack, dried fruit is loaded with energy-packed calories.

At home, he began to vary his diet using vegetarian staples such as beans, tofu, rice, and peanut butter. By varying his diet, he was also packing in plenty of quality calories to fuel both training and competition. Equally important, he learned he could be a strict lactovegetarian, in keeping with his beliefs, and do it successfully.

fish or chicken but no red meat—you're in luck. Chicken and fish contain heme iron.

Watch the Meat-Fish-Poultry Factor

Meat, fish, and poultry (MFP) also contain a special quality called the MFP factor that helps your body absorb more nonheme iron. When meat and vegetables are eaten together at the same meal, more nonheme iron is absorbed from the vegetables than if the vegetables had been eaten alone. If you're a semivegetarian, your body will absorb extra iron from vegetables.

Include Vitamin C Sources

Fruits, vegetables, and other foods that contain vitamin C help the body absorb nonheme iron. For example, if you eat citrus fruits with an iron-fortified cereal, your body will absorb more iron from the cereal than if it had been eaten alone.

Guard Against a B12 Deficiency

Vitamin B12 is one of the most significant nutrients typically missing from the diets of vegans. That's because vitamin B12 is available only from animal products. Fortunately, the body needs only tiny daily amounts of this vitamin (the DRI is 2.4 micrograms for adults), which is used in the manufacture of red blood cells and nerves. Even so, a deficiency is serious, potentially causing irreversible nerve damage.

Fermented food, such as the soybean products miso and tempeh, supplies some vitamin B12 from the bacterial culture that causes fermentation but generally not enough. Vegans should eat B12-fortified foods or take supplements to ensure a healthy diet.

Watch Iron and Zinc Blockers

Some foods contain phytates, oxalates, or other substances that block the absorption of iron and zinc in the intestine. Coffee and tea (regular and decaffeinated), whole grains, bran, legumes, and spinach are a few examples of foods containing blockers. These foods are best eaten with heme iron sources or vitamin C sources to help your body absorb more iron and zinc.

Consider Iron and Zinc Supplements

Our bodies don't absorb the iron that comes from vegetables as easily as the iron that comes from animal foods. Nonmeat eaters, especially active people or menstruating women, must pay attention to their dietary iron needs.

Animal flesh is the major source of zinc in our diets. So all styles of vegetarian eaters may be at greater risk of having marginally low intakes of this mineral.

Although dietary supplements are not good replacements for food, it may be a good idea to supplement if iron and zinc are in short supply in your diet. Daily supplementation of iron and zinc at the level of 100 percent of the DRI is good insurance against harmful deficiencies.

Protein Quality

Protein is rated on its *quality*, or content of *essential amino acids*. To rate the quality of the protein in foods, scientists have developed a number of measurement methods. Here's a rundown of the three most common:

• **The protein digestibility corrected amino acid score, or PDCAAS.** The protein values you read on food labels are calculated using the PDCAAS. It describes the proportion of amino acids in a protein source, as well as its "digestibility"—how well a protein is used by the body. In calculating the PDCAAS, the food is first assigned a score based on its amino acid composition. The score is then adjusted to reflect its digestibility.

Digestibility, which varies from food to food, is important. Generally, more than 90 percent of the protein in animal foods is digested and absorbed, whereas about 80 percent of the protein in legumes is used. Between 60 and 90 percent of the protein in fruits, vegetables, and grains is digested and absorbed.

With the PDCAAS, the highest possible score is 100. For reference, egg whites, ground beef, milk powder, and tuna have scores of 100; soy protein has a score of 94.

• **The protein efficiency rating, or PER.** The PER reflects a particular protein's ability to support weight gain in test animals and thus gives researchers a good indication of which foods best promote growth. The yardstick for comparison is the growth produced by the complete protein found in egg white or milk. Egg protein, in particular, is considered the perfect protein, because it contains all eight essential amino acids in the ideal proportions and is the reservoir of nutrients to build a bird.

• **Biological value, or BV.** This represents the percentage of the protein absorbed from a particular food that your body can use for growth and repair—rather than for energy production. As with the PER, the BV of egg white serves as the yardstick by which other protein sources are compared.

Complete proteins tend to have high biological values, whereas incomplete proteins have lower values. Lower BV foods are used by your body mainly for fuel rather than for growth and repair.

Supplemental Protein Quality

Where supplements such as protein powders and carbohydrate/protein powders are concerned, read the product labels. Many of these supplements are formulated with milk protein, casein (the principal protein of cow's milk), whey protein, or egg white solids—all high-quality proteins. Of interest to vegetarian athletes: Studies have shown that "soy protein isolates" (used in soy-based protein powders) are comparable in quality to that of egg proteins, with a digestibility of 97 percent.

Relevance to Strength Trainers and Athletes

As an exerciser or athlete, you should be concerned about the quality of protein you eat. Bottom line: You need either high-quality protein or a variety of protein sources to ensure adequate intake of all eight essential amino acids—particularly after exercise.

The Bottom Line on Protein

Protein is definitely a key to manufacturing muscle, and the latest research shows that strength trainers who are building muscle, are vegetarians, or do cross-training require slightly elevated amounts of protein. You don't have to go overboard, though, because your body will extract exactly what it needs. By following the recommendations here, you'll get the optimal amount of protein to build muscle and maintain strength.

Sport Nutrition Fact vs. Fiction:

Supplemental Amino Acids Build Muscle

Several years ago, researchers at the Centers for Disease Control and Prevention surveyed 12 popular fitness magazines and found that each contained an average of 26 pitches for muscle-enhancing and/or energy-releasing products. The researchers also counted the number of products (311) advertised in the magazine, noting that 235 unique ingredients were listed under 89 brands. One of every three products listed amino acids as ingredients.

Amino acids, sold as "free-form amino acids" or found in other supplements or powders, are a popular bodybuilding supplement. Because amino acids are endowed with a lot of nitrogen, their use is believed to promote nitrogen retention. Nitrogen retention supposedly enhances the synthesis of proteins by cells, thus leading to muscle growth.

Certain amino acids are being sold as natural "anabolics" or muscle-building supplements. They claim to help increase strength and build muscle.

But what about them? Are their claims valid? Will amino acid supplements work for you? Let's take a look at the evidence.

Amino acid supplements marketed to strength athletes and exercisers can be classified into two groups: those that stimulate growth hormone (GH) release and those that replenish lost protein from muscles, the BCAAs.

Much of the hoopla over amino acids has to do with growth hormone (GH), which occurs naturally in the body. GH regulates growth (including muscle growth) and helps release fat from storage for fuel, among other functions. Sleep, exercise training, and stress are among the factors that stimulate the release of GH in the body.

Over the years, clinical studies have surfaced, reporting that injections of huge amounts of amino acids boost the secretion of GH. Keep in mind, though: Elevated levels of GH in the body don't necessarily lead to increases in muscle mass. Besides, supplemental amino acids are taken orally, not intravenously, and thus don't have the same effect as injections. In one series of experiments, subjects took arginine and ornithine in oral doses of up to 20 grams a day. Less than 10 percent of the subjects experienced any significant effect, and those who were affected had only modest increases in GH, even when supplementation was combined with a strength-training program.

One study did successfully show that an oral dose of 1,200 milligrams of arginine pyroglutamate and 1,200 milligrams of lysine, taken on an empty stomach, did promote GH secretion. However, there was no muscle-building effect.

Another study administered large enough doses of the amino acid ornithine to stimulate GH secretion. But again: no muscle-building effect. Plus, all the participants got sick from the huge doses.

If you're spending a lot of money on arginine and lysine supplements in hope of building more muscle, consider this: A mere three-ounce portion of lean red meat has about 1,700 milligrams of arginine and 2,200 milligrams of lysine. To get the same amount from supplements, you'd have to pop nearly 20 capsules!

In defense of arginine, however, research indicates that it may help initiate recovery. In one study, exercisers consumed either a carbohydrate supplement or a carbohydrate-arginine supplement one, two, and three hours after exercise. The supplements were formulated with either one gram of carbohydrate per kilogram of body weight or one gram of carbohydrate plus 0.08 grams of arginine per kilogram of body weight. During the four-hour recovery period, the increase in muscle glycogen was more rapid in those who had consumed the carbohydrate/arginine formula.

The researchers attributed this response to arginine's ability to increase the availability of glucose for muscle glycogen storage during recovery. There were some untoward side effects associated with the carbohydrate/arginine supplement, however. These included bitter taste and diarrhea.

As for the BCAAs—leucine, isoleucine, and valine—they make up about one third of your muscle protein. They work together to rebuild muscle protein, which is dismantled by exercise, and act as fuel for exercise.

The harder you work out, the more leucine your body will use up. After aerobic exercise, plasma leucine levels drop 11 to 33 percent; after strength-training exercise, 30 percent. Furthermore, high-intensity aerobic exercise drains skeletal muscle stores of leucine.

Of interest to strength trainers: Supplementing with leucine (50 milligrams per kilogram of body weight a day), along with a daily protein intake of 1.26 kilograms of protein per kilogram of body weight, can prevent a decrease in leucine during five weeks of speed and strength training, according to one study.

Other research indicates that consuming BCAAs (30 to 35 percent leucine) before or during endurance training may decrease, even prevent, the rate of protein degradation in the muscle, plus spare muscle glycogen.

So should you supplement with BCAAs? Consider these facts: Your body starts drawing on BCAAs for fuel during exercise only if you're not eating enough or taking in sufficient carbohydrates (carbohydrates keep the body from burning up too much of its BCAA supply). In other words, you should be able to get all the BCAAs you need from food. That's easy to do. Each of the following foods contains all the BCAAs you need daily to prevent protein breakdown during aerobic exercise:

- 3 ounces of water-packed tuna
- 3 ounces of chicken
- 1 cup of nonfat yogurt
- 1 cup of cooked legumes

In addition, a great way to replace BCAAs lost during exercise is to consume dairy products or whey protein after your workout.

The existing scientific research doesn't fully support the muscle-building claims of supplemental amino acids. Nor are the short-term and long-term risks of supplementation known. Taking amino acids could cause physiological imbalances that may interfere with your body's normal functioning. Given the present state of knowledge, I don't support the use of these supplements but would rather see you get your amino acids naturally—from food.

Food is the best protein source for your body. One of the main reasons has to do with absorption. All nutrients are absorbed better when they come from real food. There are substances in foods, which scientists have coined "food factors," that help the body absorb and use nutrients. We don't even know what many of these food factors are, but we do know that they aren't found in food supplements.

As for protein, it is one of the best-absorbed foods, particularly animal protein. Scientific research has found that 95 to 99 percent of animal protein is absorbed and used by the body. Even protein from plant sources is well absorbed: More than 90 percent of the protein from high-protein plants is taken up and put to use by the body.

If you eat a variety of proteins (see table 2.2), you don't need to take protein or amino acid supplements. Just one ounce of chicken contains 7,000 milligrams of amino acids. To get that much, you might pay $20 for an entire bottle of amino acid supplements!

Table 2.2 Good Sources of Protein

Food	Amount	Protein (g)	Calories
Animal foods			
Beef, lean, sirloin, broiled	3 oz.	26	172
Roasted chicken breast (boneless, no skin)	3 oz.	26	140
Sole/flounder, baked or broiled	3 oz.	21	100
Turkey	3 oz.	25	145
Dairy products			
Cheese	1 oz.	8	107
Cottage cheese, 2%	½ c	16	101
Egg, boiled	1 lg.	6	78
Egg white, cooked	1 lg.	4	17

(continued)

Table 2.2 (continued)

Food	Amount	Protein (g)	Calories
Milk, dried nonfat, instant	½ c	12	122
Milk, low-fat, 1%	1 c	8	102
Milk, nonfat	1 c	8	86
Yogurt, low-fat, plain	8 oz.	13	155
Yogurt, low-fat, fruit	8 oz.	11	250
Nuts, seeds, and nut products			
Peanuts, dry roasted	1 oz.	7	166
Peanut butter	2 Tbsp.	8	190
Pumpkin seeds, dry roasted	½ c	6	143
Sunflower seeds, dry roasted, hulled	2 Tbsp.	3	93
Soy products			
Soybeans, cooked	½ c	15	149
Soy milk	1 c	8	79
Tofu	½ c	10	94
Vegetables, high-protein			
Black beans, boiled	½ c	8	114
Chickpeas (garbanzos), boiled	½ c	7	135
Lentils, boiled	½ c	9	115
Pinto beans	½ c	7	117

3 Energizing Workouts

From the oatmeal you eat for breakfast to the baked potato you eat for dinner, carbohydrates are the leading nutrient fuel for your body. During digestion, carbohydrates are broken down into glucose. Glucose circulates in the blood, where it is known as blood sugar, to be used by the brain and nervous system for energy. If your brain cells are deprived of glucose, your mental power will suffer, and because your brain controls your muscles, you might even feel weak and shaky.

Glucose from the breakdown of carbohydrate is also converted to glycogen for storage in either liver or muscle. Two thirds of your body's glycogen is stored in the muscles, and about one third is stored in the liver. When muscles use glycogen, they break it back down into glucose through a series of energy-producing steps.

It is no surprise that pasta, cereal, grains, fruit, vegetables, sport drinks, and other carbohydrates are the foods of choice for endurance athletes, who fill up on carbs by carbohydrate loading to improve their performance in competition. But carbohydrate is just as necessary for strength trainers as it is for endurance athletes. The glycogen it provides is the major source of fuel for working muscles. When carbohydrates are in short supply, your muscles get tired and heavy. Carbohydrate is thus a vital nutrient that keeps your mind and muscles powered up for hard training.

The Force Behind Muscle Building and Fat Burning

Among the nutrients, carbohydrates are the most powerful in affecting your energy levels. But they also affect your muscle-building and fat-burning power. It takes about 2,500 calories to build just one pound of muscle. That's a lot of energy! The best source of that energy is carbohydrate. It provides the cleanest, most immediate source of energy for body cells. In fact, your body prefers to burn carbohydrate over fat or protein. As your body's favored fuel source, carbohydrate spares protein from being used as energy. Protein is thus free to do its main job—build and repair body tissue, including muscle.

Carbohydrate is a must for efficient fat burning, too. Your body burns fat for energy in a series of complex chemical reactions that take place inside cells. Think of fat as a log on a hearth waiting to be ignited. Carbohydrate is the match that ignites fat at the cellular level. Unless enough carbohydrate is available in key stages of the energy-producing process, fat will just smolder—in other words, not burn as well.

Increasing Calories from Carbohydrates to Build Muscle

The single most important nutritional factor affecting muscle gain is calories, specifically calories from carbohydrates. Building muscle requires an intense, rigorous strength-training program. A tremendous amount of energy is required to fuel this type of exercise—energy that is best supplied by carbs. A high-carbohydrate diet allows for the greatest recovery of muscle glycogen stores on a daily basis. This ongoing replenishment lets your muscle work equally hard on successive days. Studies continue to show that high-calorie, high-carbohydrate diets give strength-trained athletes the edge in their workouts. The bottom line: The harder you train, the more muscle you can build.

To build a pound of muscle, add 2,500 calories a week. This means introducing extra calories into your diet. Ideally, you must increase your calories by 500 to 1,000 a day. But do this gradually, so you don't gain too much fat. What I suggest to strength trainers in a building phase is to start by introducing only 300 to 350 calories a day for a while. Then after a week or two, increase to 500 calories a day. As long as you're not gaining fat, start introducing 1,000 extra calories into your diet daily.

Most of these additional calories should come from carbohydrates—in the form of food and liquid carbohydrate supplements. An example of 1,000 calories worth of carbs from food is two cups of pasta, one bagel, and one banana. It just doesn't take that much additional food to up your carbs. You won't be eating these alone, either. Later in the book, I'll show

The single most important nutritional factor affecting muscle gain is calories, specifically calories from carbohydrates.

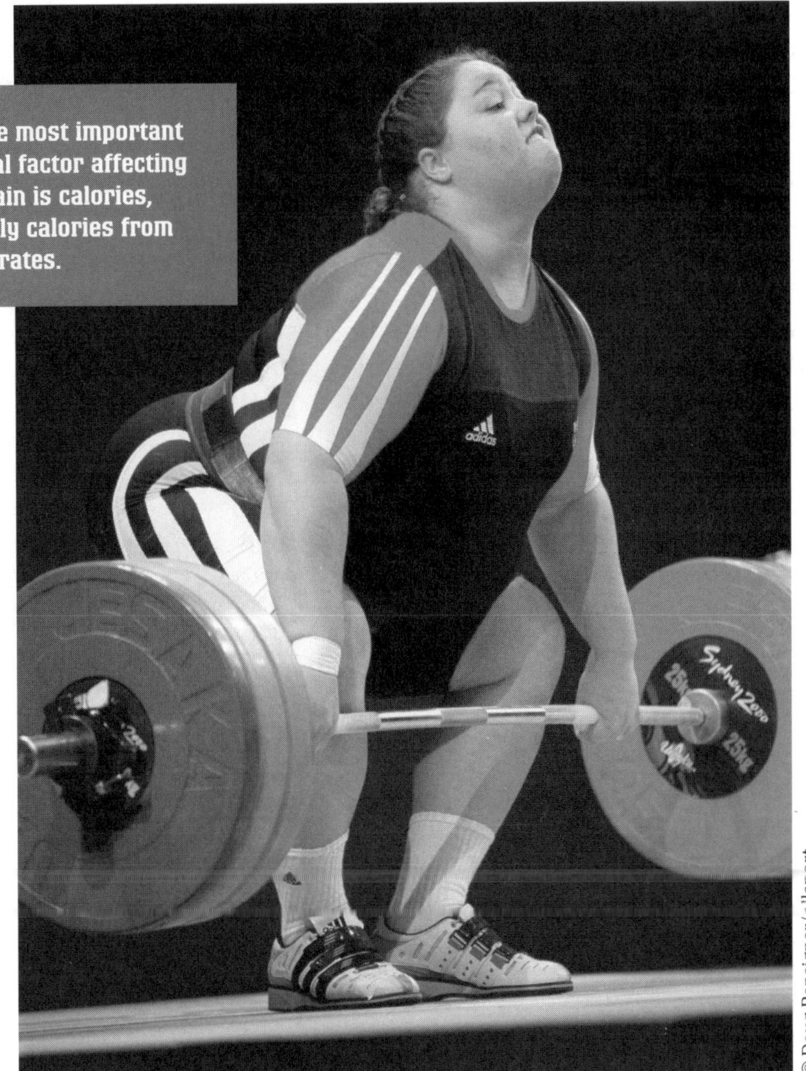

© Doug Pensigner/Allsport

you how to time your carb intake properly, plus combine those carbs with the right foods, to enhance muscle building.

To be really exact, you can match your carb intake to your weight. As a strength trainer who wants to build muscle, you should take in about eight grams of carbohydrate per kilogram of body weight a day. If you're an athlete who cross-trains with strength training and you want to build, figure about nine grams of carb per kilogram of body weight a day.

Supplementing with liquid carbs is an excellent way to increase those calories. Plus, it appears to support muscle growth. Case in point: In a landmark experiment, competitive weightlifters took a liquid high-calorie supplement for 15 weeks. The goal of the study was to see how the supplement affected the athletes' weight gain, body composition, and strength. The weightlifters were divided into three groups: those using the supplement and no anabolic steroids, those using the supplement plus anabolic steroids, and a control group taking no supplements or steroids but participating in exercise. The supplement contained 540 calories and 70.5 grams of carbohydrate, plus other nutrients.

All the participants followed their usual diets. The steroid group and the controls ate most of their calories from fat rather than carbs (45 percent fat, 37 percent carbohydrate). The supplement group ate more carbs and less fat (34 percent fat, 47 percent carbs). What's more, the supplement group ate about 830 more calories a day than the controls and 1,300 more calories a day than the steroid group.

Here's what happened: The weight gain in both supplemented groups was significantly greater than the controls. Those in the supplement-only group gained an average of 7 pounds; in the supplement-plus-steroid group, 10 pounds; in the control group, 3.5 pounds. Lean mass in both the supplement and steroid groups more than doubled, compared with the control group. The supplement group lost 0.91 percent body fat, whereas the steroid group gained 0.50 percent body fat. Both the supplement and steroid groups gained strength—equally.

These results are amazing, really. They prove that ample calories and carbs are essential for a successful strength-training and muscle-building program. Even more astounding is the fact that you can potentially attain the same results with diet alone as you can with drugs. That's powerful news for drug-free strength trainers everywhere. In chapter 12, you'll learn how to plan your own high-calorie, high-carbohydrate diet to support muscle growth.

A High-Energy Diet for Strength Training

You can create a high-carbohydrate diet by using the Food Guide Pyramid, a practical tool for meal planning developed by the United States Department of Agriculture. There are six categories of foods in the pyramid: the bread, cereal, rice, and pasta group; the vegetable group; the fruit group; the meat, poultry, fish, dry beans, eggs, and nuts group; the milk, yogurt, and cheese group; and the fats, oils, and sweets group. The pyramid illustrates the relative importance of various types of foods.

Every group in the pyramid contains carbohydrate foods. However, because the bread, fruit, and vegetable groups are the richest sources of carbohydrates, those foods are emphasized. Your daily carbohydrate

USDA Food Guide Pyramid

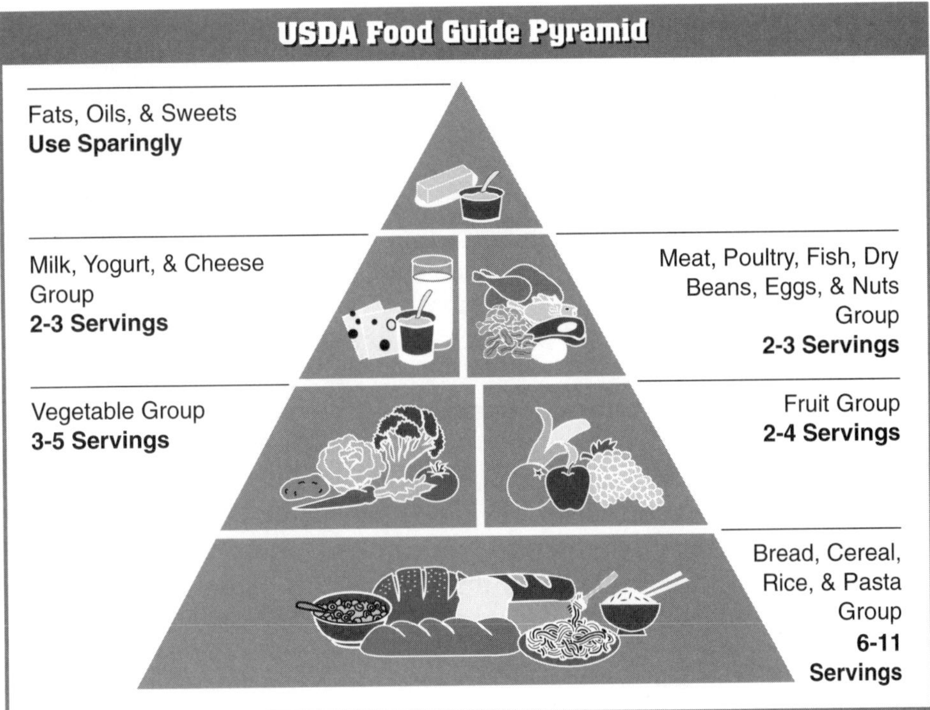

Source: U.S. Department of Agriculture/U.S. Department of Health and Human Services.

selection should include a variety of carbs from these groups. These foods are loaded with fiber, vitamins, minerals, phytochemicals, and other health-giving nutrients. Here's a closer look.

Bread, Cereal, Rice, and Pasta

The base of the Food Guide Pyramid is the bread, cereal, rice, and pasta group—all foods from grains. These are the foods that you need each day to maintain health and prevent disease. But according to most surveys, Americans eat very little of these precious foods (21 percent of total calories), compared with the rest of the world. A healthy diet includes at least 6 to 11 servings of grain-type foods every day. One serving of a grain product is equal to one slice of bread, one ounce of ready-to-eat cereal, or one-half cup of a cooked cereal, rice, or pasta.

Along with many fruits and vegetables, the grain group of foods contains complex carbohydrates, which you know best as starches. Starch is to the plant what glycogen is to your body, a storage form of glucose that supplies energy to help the plant grow. At the molecular level, starch is actually a chain of dozens of glucose units. The links holding the starch chain together are broken apart by enzymes during digestion into single glucose units that are circulated to the body's cells.

Friendly Fibers

Also found in the whole grains of complex carbohydrate foods is cellulose. Like starch, cellulose is a branching chain of glucose units. But unlike starch, these chains can't be broken apart by human digestive enzymes. Cellulose is thus an indigestible remnant of food. It passes through the digestive system largely unchanged.

This characteristic gives cellulose an important place in human nutrition. It is a type of fiber that provides dietary roughage to stimulate the action of the digestive tract muscles. Ample fiber in the diet improves elimination.

Whole-grain foods contain other fibers besides cellulose such as lignins and hemicelluloses, which can be classified by their solubility in water. Cellulose, lignins, and some hemicelluloses are water insoluble. These fibers do not dissolve in water and are bulk formers. They increase stool volume and weight and shorten the transit time of food passage through the intestines. Exposure to cancer-causing agents, in food or the by-products of digestion, is thus reduced greatly. Water-insoluble fiber helps improve intestinal regularity and may be an important safeguard against colon cancer. Good grain sources of water-insoluble fiber include whole grains such as wheat, barley, rice, corn, and oats.

Other fiber is water soluble, including gums, pectins, mucilages, and some hemicelluloses. These fibers can lower cholesterol levels and improve glucose tolerance (the rise and fall of blood sugar). This is also the fiber type that is used in the fiber supplements advertised as diet aids and laxatives. Good sources of water-soluble fibers include oat bran, barley, and soy.

Fiber and Fat Loss

The rich fiber content of the whole-grain complex carbohydrate foods is a factor in weight control, too, for three reasons. First, high-fiber foods take longer to eat, creating a full, satisfied feeling. Second, they lower levels of insulin, a hormone that stimulates appetite. And third, more energy (calories) is used up during the digestion and absorption of high-fiber foods. There are clearly some real benefits to a high-fiber diet if you are trying to control body fat and stay lean.

Refined vs. Whole Grains

Although primitive humans probably gnawed on whole kernels, today we grind or mill grains to ease their preparation and improve their palatability—thus the term "refined grains." Milling subdivides the grain into smaller particles. For example, the whole wheat kernel can be milled to form cracked wheat, fine granular wheat, or even finer whole wheat flour. Refining processes also remove the germ or seed, as well as the bran, a covering that protects the germ and other inner parts of the grain.

When the endosperm, a starch layer that protects the germ, is separated from a corn kernel, you have such products as grits or cornmeal. Another processing technique is known as abrasion, in which the bran of rice or barley is removed, and the remaining portion is polished. The result is white rice or pearled barley.

As parts of the kernel such as the germ or bran are removed so are the nutrients they contain—fiber, unsaturated fat, protein, iron, and several B-complex vitamins. Fortunately, these are replaced in cereal products in a process known as enrichment. Enriched cereals are nearly as nutritious as the original grains, so you should not be afraid to include them in your diet. But they do lack the fiber found in whole grains.

I recommend that most of the starchy foods in your diet be whole grains. First, they are higher in fiber. Second, unlike refined foods, whole grains are less likely to cause insulin resistance—a condition in which elevated blood sugar circulates in the blood because body cells respond abnormally to the action of the hormone insulin. High intakes of refined foods can lead to insulin resistance.

As a strength trainer, you're probably used to eating a lot of oatmeal, rice, and other common grains. For variety, you might experiment with some of the more exotic grains now in supermarkets. For instance, tabbouleh, a Middle Eastern dish, is a delicious cold salad made from bulgur wheat. The Russians traditionally use kasha, roasted buckwheat groats, to make both warm and cold dishes and stuffings. Barley makes a hearty soup, and pearled whole wheat semolina is the traditional variety for making couscous, a Moroccan dish.

Table 3.1 lists fiber-rich foods for strength trainers, bodybuilders, exercisers, and other athletes. Since high-fiber foods can cause bloating, I have carefully selected the least gas-forming high-fiber foods for this list.

Fruits and Vegetables

You've heard it since grade school: Eat your fruits and vegetables, and you'll be healthy. Somewhere between then and now, you may have become skeptical of that advice. It seemed too simplistic. After all, human health and nutrition science must be more complicated than that! But science has put grade school advice to the test and turned up some provocative findings. In a nutshell, the advice you heard as a kid is not only sound, it may be truly life saving.

Thanks to continuing research, there are now more reasons than ever to eat lots of fruits and veggies. In addition to their high vitamin, mineral,

Table 3.1 Recommended High-Fiber Foods
Fresh fruits with skin
Dried fruits
Fruit juices with pulp
Potatoes, sweet potatoes, and yams with skin
Peas
Carrots
Winter squash
Tomatoes
Romaine, leaf, Boston, and Bibb lettuces
Whole grains and cereals

and fiber content, fruits and vegetables are chock-full of other nutritional treasures like the following:

- Antioxidants: Vitamins and minerals such as vitamin A, beta carotene, vitamins C and E, and selenium that fight disease-causing substances in the body known as free radicals. Antioxidants have some real benefits for strength trainers; see chapter 6 for more details.
- Phytochemicals: Plant chemicals that protect against cancer, heart disease, and other illnesses. Table 3.2 lists some of the important phytochemicals found in various carbohydrates.
- Phytoestrogens: Special phytochemicals in tofu and other soy foods that may protect against some cancers, lower dangerous levels of cholesterol, and promote bone building. Phytoestrogens are also listed in table 3.2.

There are lots of reasons why we should be piling more fruits and vegetables on our plates. First, plant foods provide significant protection against many cancers. In fact, people who eat greater amounts of fruits and vegetables have about one half the risk of getting cancer and less risk of dying of cancer.

For example, tomatoes and products containing them may protect against prostate cancer. In a diet study sponsored by the National Cancer Institute, researchers identified the carotenoid, lycopene, as the only one associated with a lower risk of prostate cancer.

Table 3.2 Phytochemicals for Fitness

Phytochemical	Food source	Protective action
Allyl sulfides	Garlic, onions, shallots, leeks, chives	Lower risk of stomach and colon cancers
Sulforafanes, indoles, isothiocyanates	Broccoli, cabbage, Brussels sprouts, cauliflower, kohlrabi, watercress, turnips, Chinese cabbage	Lower risk of breast, stomach, and lung cancers
Carotenes	Carrots, dried apricots and peaches, cantaloupe, green leafy vegetables, sweet potatoes, yams	Lower risk of lung and other cancers
Lycopene, *p*-coumaric acid, chlorogenic acid	Tomatoes	Lower risk of prostate and stomach cancers
Alpha-linolenic acid, vitamin E	Vegetable oils	Lower risk of inflammation and heart disease
Monoterpenes	Cherries, orange peel oil, citrus peel oil, caraway, dill, spearmint, lemongrass	Lower risk of breast, skin, liver, lung, stomach, and pancreatic cancers
Polyphenols	Green tea	Lower risk of skin, lung, and stomach cancers
Phytoestrogens	Soy foods, including tofu, miso, tempeh, soybeans, soy milk, and isolated soy protein	Lower risk of breast and prostate cancers, decrease blood cholesterol, protect against bone loss, decrease symptoms of menopause

Cooked tomato products are concentrated sources of lycopene. Thus, tomato sauce, stewed tomatoes, tomato paste, tomato juice, pizza sauce, and spaghetti sauce are rich in lycopene. Those individuals who consumed greater than 10 servings of these combined foods per week had a significantly decreased risk of prostate cancer developing compared with those who ate less than 1½ servings per week.

Here's more proof of the cancer-fighting power of fruits and vegetables: A study of 2,400 Greek women showed that women with the highest intake of fruit (six servings a day) had a 35 percent lower risk of breast cancer compared with women who had the lowest fruit intake (fewer than two servings a day).

The number of servings of fruits and vegetables in your daily diet makes a difference in cardiovascular health too. Researchers tracked 832 men ages 45 to 65 as part of the famous Framingham Heart Study, which has followed the health of residents of a Boston suburb since 1948. For every increase of three servings of fruits and vegetables that the men ate per day, there was approximately a 20 percent decrease in their risk of stroke. A similar finding was reported previously among women. Those who ate lots of spinach, carrots, and other vegetables and fruits rich in antioxidant nutrients had a 54 percent lower risk of stroke than other women.

There's more: In the United States, men with low vitamin C intakes have significantly higher risk of cardiovascular disease and death compared with men eating the highest levels of vitamin C. Heart disease risks appear to be the lowest in people eating an average of at least 11 pounds of citrus fruit per year.

Want to better control your blood pressure? Eat more fruit. It's loaded with potassium and magnesium—two minerals that have been credited with possible blood pressure–lowering effects. Research shows that people of various ethnic backgrounds generally tend to have lower blood pressure than many Americans. The reason? Ethnic groups eat twice as much fruit and vegetables as Americans do. Other research indicates that high blood pressure can be lowered—without medication—if you eat a diet that's packed with fruits and vegetables.

Fruit, in particular, is important for weight control and weight loss. Case in point: Researchers in Spain wanted to identify the differences between the diets of overweight/obese and the diets of normal-weight elderly people. Amazingly, here's what they learned: There was no difference in calorie intake between the two groups. However, the overweight/obese group ate more of their calories from protein and less as carbohydrate compared with the normal-weight group. In addition, the overweight/obese elderly ate less fruit than the normal-weight subjects did. This goes to show that the composition of your diet can have a huge impact on whether you gain body fat or not.

Can you get the same health benefits from popping supplements? Not exactly. New scientific research has discovered that food factors like antioxidants and phytochemicals work best to fight disease when you get them from food, not when they are isolated as supplements. In other words, a vitamin-mineral supplement, or any other kind of nutritional supplement, can't match the power of eating food.

To get the disease-fighting benefits of fruits and vegetables, you should eat a minimum of three to five servings of vegetables and two to four servings of fruit every day. One serving of a vegetable is equal to one-half cup cooked or chopped raw vegetables; one cup raw, leafy vegetables; one-half cup cooked legumes; or three-fourths cup vegetable juice. One serving of a fruit is equal to one medium piece of raw fruit, one-half grapefruit, one melon wedge, one-half cup berries, one-fourth cup dried fruit, or three-fourths cup of fruit juice.

Table 3.3 includes a list of carbohydrates that are important in a strength-training diet. Now, let's look at how you can plan your meals to include enough carbohydrates to train at peak levels.

Carbohydrates: How Much, How Often?

Clearly, there are plenty of reasons to fill up on carbohydrates, particularly the complex kind. To support the demands of strength training, I strongly recommend that strength trainers eat a diet in which seven to nine grams per kilogram of body weight daily come from carbohydrates. On a diet of 3,600 calories, 2,600 of those calories (eight grams per kilogram of body weight daily) should come from carbs. There's lots of scientific research to back up my recommendation, including the following study.

One group of bodybuilders ate a moderate-protein/high-carbohydrate diet in which 70 percent of the calories were from carbs. A second group followed a high-protein/low-carbohydrate diet in which 50 percent of the calories came from carbs. Before and after each diet, the researchers checked the subjects' muscular endurance (the ability to perform repeated contractions without fatiguing) in their leg muscles. After the diet, the high-carbohydrate group kept going, whereas the low-carb subjects fizzled out early. The message here: A 70 percent high-carb diet gives you the energy to work out hard, with greater intensity. The harder you work out, the more muscle and power you can build.

Often, though, percentages of nutrients don't tell the whole story. Sometimes you have to look at grams of carbohydrate eaten each day. In one study, swimmers were divided into two groups. One group ate a moderate-carbohydrate diet (43 percent of calories from carbs); the other group ate a high-carbohydrate diet (80 percent of calories from carbs). There were no differences in swimming performance between the two groups.

But why not? One explanation may be that all the swimmers were eating high-calorie diets, averaging between 4,000 and 6,075 calories a day. They were all taking in roughly 500 grams of carbohydrate a day. Not only is this ample fuel for strong performance, it's also about as much carbohydrate as muscles will hold. At between 500 and 600 grams of carbohydrate a day, glycogen storage areas in the muscles fill up and won't

Table 3.3 Good Food Sources of Carbohydrates for Strength Trainers

Food	Amount	Carbohydrates (g)	Calories
Fruits			
Apple	1 medium	21	81
Orange	1 medium	15	62
Banana	1 medium	28	109
Raisins	1/4 c	29	109
Apricots, dried	1/4 c	25	107
Vegetables			
Corn, canned	1/2 c	15	66
Winter squash	1/2 c	10	47
Peas	1/2 c	13	67
Carrot	1 medium	7	31
Breads			
Whole wheat	2 slices	26	138
Bagel, plain	1 whole (3.5-in. dia.)	38	195
English muffin	1 whole	26	134
Pita pocket, whole wheat	1 whole (6.5-in.)	35	170
Bran muffin, homemade	1 small	24	164
Matzo	1 sheet	24	112
Granola bar, hard	1 bar	16	115
Granola bar, soft	1 bar	19	126
Low-fat granola bar, Kelloggs	1 bar	29	144

Food	Amount	Carbohydrates (g)	Calories
Grains and cereals			
Grape Nuts	¼ c	22	97
Raisin Bran	½ c	21	86
Granola, low-fat	¼ c	19	91
Oatmeal, plain, instant	1 packet	18	104
Oatmeal, cinnamon spice, instant	1 packet	35	177
Cream of Wheat, cooked	1 c	27	129
Sport drinks			
6% glucose-electrolyte solution	8 oz.	14	50
High-carbohydrate replacer	12 oz.	70	280
Meal replacer	11 oz.	59	360
Pasta and starches			
Baked potato, with skin	1 large	46	201
Baked sweet potato	1 c	49	206
Spaghetti, cooked	1 c	40	197
Brown rice, cooked	1 c	46	218
Ramen noodles, cooked	1 c	29	156
Legumes			
Baked beans, vegetarian, canned	1 c	52	236
Navy beans, canned	1 c	54	296
Black beans	1 c	34	200
Baby lima beans, frozen, cooked	1 c	35	189
Lentils, cooked	1 c	40	230

accept any extra. In other words, there is a ceiling on how much muscle glycogen your body will stock. Think of a gas tank; there are only so many gallons it will hold. Try to fill it with more, and it will only overflow. In fact, once your glycogen stores fill up, the liver turns the overflow into fat, which is stored under the skin and in other areas of the body.

The amount of muscle glycogen you can store depends on your degree of muscle mass. Just as some gas tanks are larger, so are some people's muscles. The more muscular you are, the more glycogen you can potentially store.

To make sure you get the right amount of carbs daily and not too much, figure your carbohydrate intake as follows: To build muscle, consume eight grams of carbs per kilogram of body weight daily. Divide your body weight in pounds by 2.2. This gives you your body weight in kilograms. Then multiply by eight.

Once you up your carbs to the right levels, you should start making additional strength gains. Ample carbs will give you the energy and stamina to push harder and longer for better results in your workout.

Carbohydrates Before and During Your Workout

Preworkout carbs: Are they a good idea? It depends. If you're in a mass-building phase and want to push to the max, fuel yourself with carbohydrate before and during your workout. The best timing recommendations for eating before exercise is to eat a small meal of carbohydrate and protein 1½ to 2 hours before working out. This meal should contain about 50 grams of carbohydrate (200 calories) and 14 grams of protein (56 calories).

And, of course, you should make sure you are always well hydrated. Drink two cups of fluid within two hours of working out and another cup 15 minutes before exercise. Following this pattern will ensure you gain the greatest energy advantage from your pre-exercise meal without feeling full while you exercise.

If you want a little extra boost, try drinking a liquid carbohydrate beverage just before your workout. In a study of strength trainers, one group consumed a carbohydrate drink just before training and between exercise sets. Another group was given a placebo. For exercise, both groups did leg extensions at about 80 percent of their strength capacity, performing repeated sets of 10 repetitions with rest between sets. The researchers found that the carbohydrate-fed group outlasted the placebo group, performing many more sets and repetitions.

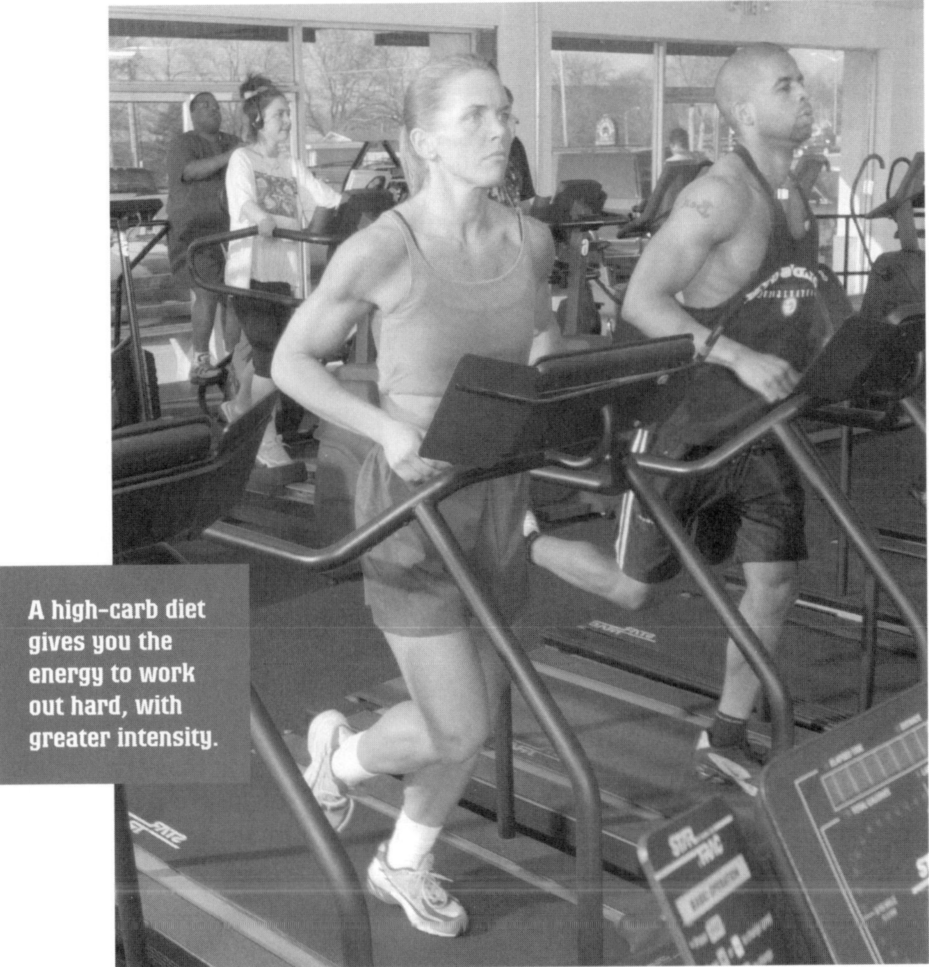

A high-carb diet gives you the energy to work out hard, with greater intensity.

Another study turned up a similar finding. Exercisers drank either a placebo or a 10 percent carbohydrate beverage immediately before and between the fifth, tenth, and fifteenth sets of a strength-training workout. They performed repeated sets of 10 repetitions, with three minutes of rest between each set. When fueled by the carb drink (one gram per kilogram of body weight), they could do more total repetitions (149 vs. 129) and more total sets (17.1 vs. 14.4) than when they drank the placebo. Which all goes to show: Carbs clearly give you an energy edge when consumed before and during a workout. The harder you can work out, the more you can stimulate your muscles to grow.

If you sip a carb drink over the course of a long workout, you can take in too many calories. When counseling clients, I recommend that they alternate between drinking a carb beverage and drinking water during training, especially if their workouts last more than an hour. That way, they don't consume too many calories from the carb drink.

If you're trying to lose body fat, you may want to forgo the preworkout carb drink (but make sure to eat your preworkout carbohydrate-protein snack). Here's why: Although preworkout carbs boost your power and stamina, they may keep your body from dipping into its fat reserves for energy. Your entire workout, including aerobics, may run solely on carb fuel and never significantly tap into fat stores for fuel. By working out in a moderately low-carb state (no preworkout carbs), you can theoretically force your body to start using more fat for fuel.

But there's a tradeoff. You could run low on energy. Although you might choose not to consume any preworkout carbohydrates, make sure your overall daily diet still contains 65 to 70 percent of its total calories from carbs. Research with strength trainers and other power athletes has consistently shown that performance and energy levels suffer when carb intake dips to around 50 percent of total calories. For more information on how to regulate carbohydrates when you're preparing for competition, see chapter 9.

Consider your goals—mass building or fat burning—and listen to your body for signs of fatigue. Adjust your carb intake accordingly, depending on your goals and energy level.

Carb Depletion During Exercise

During strength training, glycogen is pulled from storage to replace ATP, the energy compound inside cells that powers muscular contractions. The ATP is broken down in the cells through a series of chemical reactions. The energy released from this breakdown enables the muscle cells to do their work. As you train, the glycogen in your muscles progressively decreases. In fact, you can deplete as much as 26 percent of your muscle glycogen during high-intensity strength training.

Some people might argue that a 26 percent decrease isn't enough to affect strength-training performance. After all, endurance athletes lose as much as 40 percent or more of their glycogen stores during a competitive event. What's the big deal? Well, research has shown that glycogen depletion is localized to the muscles you work. Let's say you train your legs today. What happens is this. During your workout, glycogen depletion occurs mostly in your leg muscles, but not much in your arms, chest, or elsewhere on your body. If scientists measured your glycogen levels after exercise, they might find a 26 percent depletion overall. But your leg muscles could be totally emptied. Hard, intense training depletes glycogen from the individual muscles worked.

Refueling Your Muscles After a Workout

After working out, you want your muscles to recover. Recovery is essentially the process of replenishing muscle glycogen. The better your recovery, the harder you'll be able to train during your next workout. There are three critical periods in which to "feed" your muscles with carbs. These three periods are explained in the following discussion.

1. Immediately After Your Workout

Your muscles are most receptive to producing new glycogen within the first few hours after your workout. That's when blood flow to muscles is much greater, a condition that makes muscle cells practically sop up glucose like a sponge. Muscle cells are also more sensitive to the effects of insulin during this time, and insulin promotes glycogen synthesis. You should therefore take in some carbs immediately after you work out. The question is this: What's the best type of carb for refueling?

Answer: Carbs with a high-glycemic index. The glycemic index is a scale describing how fast a food is converted to glucose in the blood. Foods on the index are rated numerically, with glucose at 100. The higher the number assigned to a food, the faster it converts to glucose. Table 3.4 ranks foods according to their glycemic effect or rate of conversion. With this table as a guide, you can see that carbs such as sport drinks, raisins, bananas, or potatoes would be good "refueling" foods.

The rate of conversion is unique for each person and depends on how quickly foods are digested. Digestion speed is affected by the makeup of a particular food. For instance, a greater amount of fiber, protein, and fat content in various foods tends to slow digestion. A good example is ice cream. At a low glycemic index rating of 36, it is broken down very slowly, because it contains protein and fat, along with the high-glycemic sucrose (sugar).

Because high-glycemic index foods replenish glycogen best, you should consume at least 50 grams of these carbohydrates as soon as possible after exercise.

Honey, particularly in the form of a carbohydrate gel, is a good postworkout choice. A research study found that combining honey with a protein supplement may boost postworkout recovery and help prevent drops in blood sugar after exercise. In this particular study, honey outperformed maltodextrin—a starch that has been the standard among recovery carbs.

Table 3.4 Glycemic Index of Carbohydrate Foods (Glucose = 100)*

High glycemic	Moderate glycemic	Low glycemic
Beverages	**Bread and grain products**	**Fruits**
Gatorade—91	Pasta—41	Apple—36
Carbonated soft drink—68	Rice, white—56	Apricots, dried—31
Bread and grain products	Rice, brown—55	Bananas, underripe—30
Bagel—72	Pumpernickel bread—41	Grapefruit—25
Bread, white—70	Bran muffin—60	Pear—36
Bread, whole wheat—69	Popcorn—55	Fructose—23**
Corn flakes—84	**Fruits**	**Legumes**
Oatmeal—61	Orange juice—57	Lima beans—32
Graham crackers—74	Bananas, overripe—52	Chickpeas—33
Grape Nuts—67	Orange—43	Green beans—30
Fruits	Apple juice, unsweetened—41	Kidney beans—27
Watermelon—72	**Vegetables**	Lentils—29
Raisins—64	Corn—55	Split peas, yellow—32
Honey—73**	Peas—48	**Dairy products**
Vegetables	Sweet potato—54	Chocolate milk—34
Potato, baked—85	**Legumes**	Skim milk—32
Potato, microwaved—82	Baked beans—48	Whole milk—27
	Lentil soup—44	Yogurt, low-fat, fruit—33
		Bread and grain products
		Barley—25
		Power bar—30-35
		PR bar—33

*Index based on 50 g of carbohydrate per serving.

**Not nutritionally the equivalent of fruit.

If you're not hungry for food at this time (most of us aren't), polishing off a sports drink is a convenient alternative. It's a great way to refuel with carb calories, as well as rehydrate your body.

A sport drink containing glucose, sucrose, or a glucose polymer (all high on the glycemic index) is a rapid and efficient restorer of glycogen. Some of these drinks may also contain fructose, which isn't as fast at replenishing muscle glycogen as either glucose or sucrose. That being so, try to avoid fructose, including fruit, as the sole source of carbohydrate in the period immediately after your workout. Stick to high-glycemic index choices containing glucose and sucrose.

Consuming carbs with protein after a workout has some additional benefits. Be sure to read chapter 7 for more details.

2. Every Two Hours After Your Workout

Continue to take in high-glycemic carbs every two hours after your workout until you have consumed at least 100 grams within four hours after exercise and a total of 600 grams within 24 hours after your workout. That equates to roughly 40 to 60 grams of carbohydrate an hour during the 24-hour recovery period.

A word of caution: There is a drawback to high-glycemic index foods. They may produce a fast, undesirable surge of blood sugar. When this happens, the pancreas responds by oversecreting insulin to remove sugar from the blood. Blood sugar then drops to a too-low level, and you can feel weak or dizzy.

Low-glycemic index foods, on the other hand, provide a more constant release of energy and are unlikely to lead to these reactions. By mixing and matching low- and high-glycemic foods in your diet, you can keep your blood-sugar levels stable from meal to meal. The watchword here is moderation. Don't overdose on high-glycemic index foods or beverages.

3. Throughout the Week

To keep carbohydrate replenishment on track, stay on a high-carbohydrate diet from week to week. An excellent study of hockey players, whose sport requires both muscular strength and aerobic endurance, found that during a three-day period between games, a high-carb diet caused a 45 percent higher glycogen refill than a diet lower in carbs. By consistently fueling yourself with carbs, you can keep your muscles well stocked with glycogen.

You can also supercharge your energy levels. In another study, athletes filled up on carbs for three straight days. They then pedaled at a super-high level of intensity—104 percent of their $\dot{V}O_2$max, which describes the ability of the body to take in, transport, and use oxygen. The athletes were able to perform this ride for 6.6 minutes straight, compared with only 3.3 minutes after eating a very low-carbohydrate diet (2.6 percent carbs). So you see, carbs are pure gas for high-intensity exercise.

Should You Practice Carbohydrate Loading?

Endurance athletes practice a type of nutritional jump start known as carbohydrate loading. Basically, it involves increasing the amount of glycogen stored in the muscle just before an endurance competition. With more glycogen available, the athlete can run, cycle, or swim longer before fatigue sets in and thus gain a competitive edge. When done properly, carbohydrate loading works wonders for endurance athletes.

Among strength athletes, bodybuilders have experimented the most with carbohydrate loading. Their goal is not endurance, but bigger muscles. This is generally how they do it. About seven days before the contest, the bodybuilder cuts back on carbs, the depletion stage. Then, a few days before the contest, the bodybuilder starts increasing carb intake, the loading stage. The depletion stage theoretically prepares the muscles to hold more glycogen once more carbs are eaten just before competition. With more glycogen, the muscles supposedly look fuller.

But does this actually happen? Not really, says one study. Researchers put nine men, all bodybuilders, on a carbohydrate-loading diet. The diet involved three days of heavy weight training (designed to deplete muscle glycogen) and a low-carb diet (10 percent of the calories were from carbs, 57 percent from fat, and 33 percent from protein). This was followed by three days of lighter weight training (to minimize glycogen loss) and a diet of 80 percent carbohydrate, 5 percent fat, and 15 percent protein. A control group followed the same strength-training program but ate a standard diet. At the end of the study, the researchers measured the muscle girth of all the participants. The results? Carbohydrate loading did not increase muscle girth in any of the bodybuilders.

Of course, this is just one study. Its results should be interpreted cautiously. More information needs to be uncovered about what role, if any, carbohydrate loading plays in preparing for bodybuilding contests. If you're a competitive bodybuilder, you have to be careful with carbohydrate loading, because an excess of carbs in the precompetition diet can cause water retention.

Your diet should be high in carbohydrate on a daily basis, but this is not carbohydrate loading. Keep in mind, too, that carbohydrate depletion can actually result in the loss of hard-earned muscle.

Power Profiles

Suppose you want to splurge on treats every so often. Can you do it and not jeopardize your physique goals? Absolutely. A good example is a 38-year-old modern dancer and dance instructor who, like many competitive bodybuilders, needs to stay in reasonably good shape all year round. She indulges herself in occasional splurges such as pizza and desserts, which is perfectly all right, as long as she adjusts for her splurge calories. She does this by eating a low-fat, high-carbohydrate lunch whenever she plans to eat a high-fat dinner. That way, fat calories don't dominate her meals for the day.

She also likes desserts, so she plans her diet accordingly. Most days during the week, she eats fruit for dessert. While fulfilling her desire for something sweet after dinner, this plan solves a couple of other nutritional problems. First, it boosts her fiber intake. At the time we met, she was eating a mere 4.5 grams of fiber a day (25 to 35 grams are recommended). Plus, the plan ups her carb intake, which had been too low (52 percent of total calories) for her activity level and occupation.

Mental Muscle

The amount of carbohydrate in your diet can affect your mental performance. Not only are carbs fuel for muscles, they're also fuel for your brain. On a very low-carb diet, you can feel quite out of sorts—anxious, easily upset, irritable, or depressed. These are all signs of hypoglycemia, too little glucose in the blood.

At Auburn University, researchers put seven female cyclists on three different diets: a low-carb diet (13 percent of calories from carbohydrates); a moderate-carb diet (54 percent of calories from carbohydrates); and a high-carb diet (72 percent of calories from carbohydrates). The cyclists followed each of the three diets for one week at a time. While on the low-carb diet, the cyclists felt tired, tense, depressed, and more likely to get angry.

Mounds of research have shown that carbs do have a positive effect on state of mind. So in a very real sense, sufficient carbs are a natural mood elevator.

Go for the Carbs

The most important dietary factor that will influence your strength-training performance is the amount of carbohydrate in your daily diet. Giving careful thought to what you eat—and making sure you get plenty of carbohydrates—will provide a solid foundation for optimizing both your performance and your health.

Sport Nutrition Fact vs. Fiction: Do Carbs Make You Fat?

Recently, several books hit the bookstores claiming that high-carbohydrate diets make you fat and are therefore bad. The authors based this theory on the fact that some people (only about 10 to 25 percent of the population) are insulin-resistant, a condition in which the pancreas oversecretes insulin to maintain normal blood levels of glucose after a high-carbohydrate meal. This oversecretion theoretically causes the carbs to be converted to stored body fat.

There's just no proof that high insulin levels in the blood will make you fat. In fact, to bodybuilders, insulin is an anabolic hormone that helps build muscle mass by fueling the muscles.

As someone who's active, you're already keeping your insulin levels in line. Though the exact mechanism isn't clear, exercise makes muscle cells more "sensitive" to insulin. For glucose to enter muscle cells, it has to have help from insulin. Once insulin gets to the outer surface of the cell, it acts like a key and unlocks tiny receptors surrounding the cell. The cell opens up and lets glucose in for use as fuel. Maintaining muscle tissue through strength training helps normalize the flow of glucose from the blood into muscle cells where it can be properly used for energy.

Should you be worried about eating pasta and bread? No!

You should be eating a variety of complex carbs like beans and whole grains, in addition to breads and pasta. Even in the unlikely event you are insulin-resistant, the variety minimizes the effects. Also, staying active helps control body weight—and builds muscle tissue, which helps regulate the body's use of glucose.

Insulin and carbohydrates are not the "bad guys" when it comes to fat—calories are. You gain body fat when you eat more calories than you burn. It's just that simple.

4 Eating and Burning Fat

After about an hour of hard, intense exercise, your glycogen supply can dwindle down to nothing. But not so with your fat stores—another energy source for muscles. In contrast to your limited but ready-to-use glycogen stores, fat stores are practically unlimited. In fact, it's been estimated that the average adult man carries enough fat (about a gallon) to ride a bike from Chicago to Los Angeles, a distance of roughly 2,000 miles.

So if fat stores are nearly inexhaustible, why worry about carb intake and glycogen replenishment? And why not supplement with fat as an extra source of energy?

True, there is certainly a large enough tank of fat on your body to fuel plenty of exercise, and for a long time. (That's one reason there's no need to supplement with extra fat.) But the problem is that fat can be broken down only as long as oxygen is available. Oxygen must be present for your body to burn fat for energy, but not to burn glycogen. In the initial stages of exercise, oxygen is not yet available. It can take from 20 to 40 minutes of exercise before fat is maximally available to the muscles as fuel. The glucose in your blood and glycogen in your muscles are pressed into service first.

That's not to say fat is hard to burn. It isn't. But how efficiently your body burns fat depends on your level of conditioning. One of the advantages of strength training and aerobic exercise is that your body becomes better accustomed to burn fat as fuel in two major ways.

First, exercise (particularly aerobic exercise) enhances the development of capillaries to the muscles, thus improving blood flow where it's needed. In addition, exercise increases the amount of myoglobin, a protein found in muscles that transports oxygen from the blood into the cells. With better blood flow and greater oxygen to the muscles, your body becomes more efficient at burning fat, which is why you should not neglect the aerobic portion of your training.

Second, exercise stimulates the activity of an enzyme known as hormone-sensitive lipase, which promotes the breakdown of fat for energy. The more fat you can break down and burn, the more defined you will look.

Fat is most definitely an exercise fuel, but a second-string source of energy nonetheless. During strength training, your body still prefers to burn carbohydrate for energy, from glucose in the blood or glycogen in the muscles. In fact, one of the main reasons our bodies store fat is not to supply energy for exercise, but rather to help us survive in the event of a long famine or debilitating illness.

Fat is certainly one of the more controversial issues in nutrition. There is so much confusing information in the media about different kinds of fat and their pros and cons. Let us try to clear up the confusion, once and for all.

A Fat Fighter's Primer

There are three major types of fatty material in the body: triglycerides, cholesterol, and phospholipids. Triglycerides, true fats, are the form stored in fat tissue and in muscle. A small percentage of fatty material is found in the blood, circulating as free fatty acids, which have been chemically released from the triglycerides. Of the three types of fatty material, triglycerides are the most involved in energy production. In fact, research with bodybuilders has found that triglycerides do serve as a significant energy source during intense strength training. So not only will strength training help you build muscle, but it will also help you burn body fat.

Cholesterol is a waxy, light-colored solid that comes in two distinctly different forms. You might call the first kind "the cholesterol in the blood," and the second, "the cholesterol in food." Required for good health, blood cholesterol is a constituent of cell membranes and is involved in the formation of hormones, vitamin D, and bile, which is a substance necessary for the digestion of fats. Because your body can make cholesterol from fats, carbohydrates, or proteins, you don't need to supply any cholesterol from food.

When you eat a food that contains cholesterol, that cholesterol is broken into smaller components that are used to make various fats, proteins, and other substances that your body requires. The cholesterol you eat doesn't become the cholesterol in your blood. Although it is important to reduce your intake of high-cholesterol foods, it is even more critical to lower your intake of saturated fat (the kind found mostly in animal foods). That's because the liver manufactures blood cholesterol from saturated fat. The more saturated fat you eat, the more cholesterol your liver makes.

If your liver produces large amounts of cholesterol, the excess circulating in the bloodstream can collect on the inner walls of the arteries. This accumulation is called plaque. Trouble starts when plaque builds up in an artery, narrowing the passageway and choking blood flow. A heart attack can occur when blood flow to the heart muscle is cut off for a long period of time, and part of the heart muscle begins to die. High blood cholesterol is therefore a major risk factor for heart disease, but one that can be controlled with exercise and a low-fat diet.

Cholesterol may be present in blood as a constituent of low-density lipoprotein (LDL) or of high-density lipoprotein (HDL). LDL and HDL affect heart disease risk differently. LDL contains the greater amount of cholesterol and may be responsible for depositing cholesterol on the artery walls. LDL is known as bad cholesterol; the lower your blood value, the better.

HDL contains the smaller amount of cholesterol; its job is to remove cholesterol from the cells in the artery wall and transport it back to the liver for reprocessing or excretion from the body as waste. HDL is the good cholesterol; the higher the amount in your blood, the better.

A total cholesterol reading of greater than 200 may be a danger sign. But what really counts is your ratio of the good HDL cholesterol to the bad LDL cholesterol. Generally, your HDL should be greater than 35, whereas your LDL should be less than 130.

The third type of fatty material, phospholipids, is involved primarily in the regulation of blood clotting. Along with cholesterol, phospholipids form part of the structure of cell membranes.

Food Fats

Want to get rid of that extra fat on your body? Then cut down on the fat in your diet. There's no question that the fat you eat turns into body fat more easily than carbohydrates and proteins do. The more fat you eat, the more fat you wear. It's just that easy.

What hasn't been so easy, though, is figuring out how much fat and what kind of fat to eat to stay healthy. Here's a closer look.

Fatty acids from food, the tiny building blocks of fat, are chemically classified into three groups according to their hydrogen content: saturated, polyunsaturated, and monounsaturated. Saturated fatty acids are usually solid at room temperature and, with the exception of tropical oils, come from animal sources. Beef fat and butter fat are high in saturated fatty acids. Butter fat is found in milk, cheeses, cream, ice cream, and other products made from milk or cream. Low-fat or skimmed milk products are much lower in saturated fat. Tropical oils high in saturated fat include coconut oil, palm kernel oil, and palm oil, and the cocoa fat found in chocolate. They are generally found in commercial baked goods and other processed foods.

Polyunsaturated and monounsaturated fats are usually liquid at room temperature and come from nut, vegetable, or seed sources. Polyunsaturated fats like vegetable shortening and margarines are solid because they have been "hydrogenated"—a process that changes the chemical makeup of the fat to harden it up. The resulting fat is composed of substances known as "trans-fatty acids," which have been found in recent studies to raise blood cholesterol. However, you can safely consume hydrogenated fats in margarine and other fats if the product contains liquid vegetable oil as the first ingredient and no more than two grams of saturated fat per tablespoon, according to the American Heart Association (AHA). Read the label of margarines and spreads to determine their fatty acid content.

Monounsaturated fatty acids are found in large amounts in olive oil, canola oil, and peanut oil, and in fish from cold waters, such as salmon, mackerel, halibut, swordfish, black cod, and rainbow trout, and in shellfish. Monounsaturated fats appear to have a protective effect on blood cholesterol levels. They help lower the bad cholesterol (LDL cholesterol), but maintain the higher levels of good cholesterol (HDL cholesterol).

Essential Fats

Of all dietary fats, only two polyunsaturated fats—linoleic acid and linolenic acid—are considered "essential." In other words, your body can't make these fats; you have to get them from food. They are required for normal growth, the maintenance of cell membranes, and healthy arteries and nerves. As well, essential fats keep your skin smooth and lubricated and protect your joints. They also assist in the breakdown and metabolism of cholesterol. Vegetable fats such as corn, soybean, safflower, and walnut oils are all high in essential fats. So are nuts, seeds, and green vegetables like broccoli.

The Healing Power of Omega-3 Fatty Acids

Omega-3 fatty acids are a special kind of polyunsaturated fat found mostly in fish. The designation "3" refers to the chemical structure of these fatty acids. Omega-3 fatty acids, including alpha linoleic acid, eicosapentaenoic acid, and docosahexaenoic acid, are now considered essential fats that must be included in your diet. The same is true for omega-6 fatty acids, which are found mostly in vegetable oils.

Here's why: Omega-3 fatty acids, in particular, have far-reaching benefits on health and the management of chronic disease. Current research shows that they lower blood levels of triglycerides and a heart-damaging form of cholesterol called very low-density lipoproteins (VLDL). In addition, omega-3 fats lower blood pressure in people with high blood pressure and may reduce the risk for sudden cardiac death. There is emerging evidence, too, that omega-3 fats may bolster the immune system.

Based on these health benefits, the AHA now recommends that you eat two to three fish meals a week. The best fish sources of omega-3 fatty acids are mackerel, salmon, sardines, and herring. (Refer to Table 4.1 for nutritional information on seafood.) Omega-3 fats are also found in green leafy vegetables, nuts, canola oil, and tofu.

If fish is such a good source of omega-3 fats, wouldn't it be just as wise to take fish oil supplements? Not really. There isn't enough research to justify their use—except by patients with severely high triglycerides who haven't responded well to treatment or in patients at risk of pancreatitis (inflammation of the pancreas).

With the exception of those situations, the AHA does not recommend the use of fish oil supplements, and neither do I. You can get the same protection by eating two to three fish or shellfish meals each week. An excess of these oils can be harmful and cause internal or external bleeding. Being a fat, they're high in calories, and that can promote weight gain. Unregulated, fish oil supplements are rarely pure and often contain concentrations of highly toxic elements.

How Much Essential Fat Is Enough?

If you slash fat to miniscule levels, or cut it out altogether, you risk an essential fat deficiency. This is not a widespread problem, because Americans get their fill of fat. Even so, I have seen many athletes, bodybuilders in particular, go to extremes in cutting fat. When this happens, the body has trouble absorbing the fat-soluble vitamins A, D, E, and K. Furthermore, the health of cell membranes is jeopardized because low-fat diets are low in vitamin E. Vitamin E is an antioxidant that prevents disease-causing free radicals from puncturing cell membranes. Plus, it helps in the muscle repair process that takes place after exercise.

Table 4.1 Nutritional Content of Seafood

Salmon 3.5 oz.	Calories	Protein (g)	Fat (g)	Saturated fat (g)	Sodium (mg)	Cholesterol (mg)	Omega-3 (g)*
King (Chinook)	231	25.7	13.3	3.2	60	85	1.737
Sockeye (red)	216	27.3	10.9	1.9	66	87	1.230
Coho (silver)	184	27.3	7.5	1.5	53	57	1.374
Keta (chum)	154	25.8	4.8	1.0	64	95	0.804
Pink	149	25.5	4.4	0.71	86	67	1.288
Whitefish 3.5 oz.							
Halibut	140	26.6	2.9	0.41	69	41	0.465
Cod	105	22.9	0.81	0.1	91	47	0.276
Rockfish	121	24.0	2.0	0.47	77	44	0.443
Flounder	117	24.1	1.5	0.36	105	68	0.501
Sablefish	250	17.2	19.6	4.0	72	63	1.787
Shellfish 3.5 oz.							
King crab	97	19.3	1.5	0.13	1072	53	0.413
Snow crab	90	18.4	1.3	0.16	100-900	60	0.44
Dungeness crab	110	22.3	1.2	0.16	378	76	0.394
Oysters	90	11.1	2.2	0.49	106	47	0.71
Shrimp	99	20.9	1.0	0.28	224	195	0.315
Canned salmon 3.5 oz.							
Sockeye (red)	153	20.4	7.3	1.6	538	44	1.156
Pink	139	19.7	6.0	1.5	554	55	1.651

Source: Alaska Seafood Marketing Institute, 311 North Franklin Street, Suite 200, Juneau, Alaska 99801; (800) 478-2903

*Omega-3 values represent the sum of EPA and DHA.

You can go overboard on fat, too. Too much fat in your diet causes weight gain and gradually leads to obesity and related health problems. Excessive saturated fat in the diet can also elevate cholesterol, particularly the dangerous type (LDL cholesterol). On the other hand, polyunsaturated and monounsaturated fats have been shown to cut cholesterol levels. However, polyunsaturates may also lower the protective type of cholesterol known as HDL cholesterol. Very high intakes of polyunsaturated fats have been linked to higher risks of cancer.

So where's the happy medium—between too much fat and too little? Exactly how much fat should you eat daily for good health?

According to the AHA, the maximum amount of fat considered healthy in your daily diet is 30 percent or less, based on the number of calories you eat over several days, such as a week. Saturated fat and trans-fatty acids combined should be 7 to 10 percent or less of total daily calories; polyunsaturated fats should also be at 10 percent or less; and monounsaturated fats should make up to 15 percent of total calories. Dietary cholesterol should be kept to a daily maximum of 300 milligrams or less.

Fat Recommendations for Active People

If you're an exerciser, bodybuilder, or strength trainer trying to stay lean, you should lower your total fat intake to 20 percent of calories each day. Your low-fat diet should contain much more unsaturated than saturated fat: 5 percent saturated, 8 percent monounsaturated, and 7 percent polyunsaturated.

One way to monitor your fat intake is by counting the grams of fat in your diet each day. You can calculate your own suggested daily fat intake by using the following formulas:

Total fat:

Total calories × 20% = daily calories from fat/9 = ___ grams total fat

(example: 2,000 calories × .20 = 400/9 = 45 grams total fat)

Saturated fatty acids (SFA):

Total calories × 5% = daily calories from SFA/9 = ___ grams SFA

(example: 2,000 calories × .05 = 100/9 = 11 grams SFA)

Following the Power Eating plan, first determine your protein and carbohydrate needs. All of your leftover calories are fat calories—most of which should be monounsaturated and polyunsaturated fats.

Be sure to read food labels for the fat content per serving of the foods you buy in the supermarket. The grams of fat are listed under Nutrition Facts Per Serving on any food package that provides a nutrition label.

Another way to monitor your fat intake is by limiting most foods in your diet to those that have only 20 percent or less of their calories from fat. By using the fat calories per serving information on the nutrition label, you can easily determine whether a food meets this criterion. Use the following formula to find percentage of calories from fat:

$$(\text{Total fat calories per serving divided by total calories per serving}) \times 100 = \%\ \text{calories from fat}$$

Here's an example of how this formula works:

$$(\text{54 fat calories divided by 220 calories}) \times 100 = 24\%\ \text{of calories from fat}$$

Fat Substitutes and Fat Replacers

These fake fats are concocted by food technologists who alter the properties of everyday ingredients to make them feel and taste like fat in foods. Fake fats are made from carbohydrates, proteins, and fats.

Carbohydrate-based fats are formulated from starches and fibers. An example is polydextrose, a partially absorbable starch that supplies about one calorie per gram (versus nine calories per gram from fat). Polydextrose is used in frozen desserts, puddings, and cake frostings. A similar product is maltodextrin, a starch made from corn used to replace fat in margarines and salad dressings.

Cellulose and gum are two types of fibers used to manufacture fat replacers. When ground into tiny particles, cellulose has a consistency that feels like fat when eaten. Cellulose replaces some or all of the fat in certain dairy-type products, sauces, frozen desserts, and salad dressings. Gums such as xanthan gum, guar gum, pectin, and carrageenan are used to thicken foods and give them a creamy texture. Added to salad dressings, desserts, and processed meats, gums cut the fat content considerably.

Protein-based fat replacers are formulated from milk or eggs, heated or blended into mistlike particles that feel creamy on the tongue. These

Fat-Fighting Tips

When there is no nutrition information available about a particular food, remember these helpful hints about the sources of fat and cholesterol in foods.

1. The major sources of saturated fats are meats and whole milk dairy products. Choose lean cuts of select meat like round, sirloin, and flank, and eat portions that are no larger than the palm of your hand. Chicken, turkey, and fish are always leaner meat choices.
2. When preparing and eating meats, make sure to trim all visible fat and skin, and use cooking racks to bake, broil, grill, steam, or microwave to avoid melting the fat back into the meat.
3. When eating lunch meats, select low-fat or fat-free chicken or turkey breast, rather than high-fat bologna or salami.
4. Dairy foods are very important in your diet. To cut the fats, choose low-fat or nonfat products rather than whole milk, and include them two to three times each day.
5. Cholesterol is found only in animal products, and egg yolk is a concentrated source. Substitute three egg whites and one yolk for two whole eggs, or use egg substitutes. Because meats and dairy also contain cholesterol, limit egg yolks to four a week to maintain a low-cholesterol diet.
6. Processed and prepared foods, especially snack foods, can be very concentrated sources of fat. Hydrogenated vegetable fats contain trans-fatty acids that promote heart disease, so pay most attention to the types and total amounts of fat in the food. Read labels carefully, even if they are called "lite" products, to determine whether they really are lower in fat.

fat replacers are found in ice cream, yogurt, sour cream, dips, cheese spreads, salad dressings, mayonnaise, margarine, and butter spreads.

A fat-based fat substitute now on the market is Olestra from Procter & Gamble. Technically, Olestra is a sucrose polyester, meaning a combination of sugar and fatty acids. Your body can't digest Olestra, so it's virtually calorie free. But because of its makeup, some people eating it may get a laxative effect, ranging from mild to severe, depending on how much is consumed. Reports that Olestra may block the absorption of fat-soluble vitamins, beta-carotene, and other carotenes forced the Food and Drug

Administration to require that all Olestra-containing products be fortified with vitamins A, D, E, and K.

We don't yet know what effect artificial fats have on health. There's a concern among nutritionists and other health advocates that consumers may get so carried away with eating fat-free foods, that they'll eat fewer nutrient-dense food such as fruits, vegetables, and grains.

If you enjoy the new fat-free products, do so in moderation. Current research supports the notion that fat replacers and fat substitutes may help slash total fat in the diet. But the safety of some of the products is still in question—a fact you should consider before using them.

In addition, continue to read the nutrition labels and determine the fat content and caloric content for yourself. Don't rely on advertising hype on the front of the label. Just because a product is low in fat doesn't mean it contains fewer calories. In fact, some lower fat products are higher in calories than their regular fat counterparts are.

Burning Fat

Why do you want to lose body fat? To compete in a lower weight class? Get ready for a bodybuilding contest? Improve your performance? Look better in your clothes?

All are admirable goals for fat loss, and there are umpteen ways to reach them. Two of the most widely used, though I don't recommend them, are crash dieting and fad dieting. Crash dieting involves a drastic reduction in calories, usually to about 800 calories or fewer a day, with equally drastic consequences, such as the following:

- Muscle and fluid losses, along with fat loss. If you lost 20 pounds in 20 days, the first 6 to 10 pounds would be fluid; the rest, fat and muscle. So you are not gaining anything by dropping a lot of weight in a short period of time.
- Loss of aerobic power. Your body's capacity to take in and process oxygen, or $\dot{V}O_2max$, will decline significantly. As a result, less oxygen will be available to help your muscle cells combust fat for fuel.
- Loss of strength. That is a major handicap if you need strength and power for competition—or to get through a workout without fizzling out.
- Metabolic slowdown. Crash dieting slows your metabolic rate down to a crawl. Metabolic rate refers to the speed at which your body processes the food you eat into energy and bodily structures. It is made up of two interrelated factors: basal metabolic rate (BMR)

> and resting metabolic rate (RMR). Your BMR represents the energy it takes just to exist. Or put another way, your BMR is the energy required to keep your heart beating, your lungs breathing, and your other vital internal functions going strong. Basal metabolic needs must be met. If you're a woman, for example, you spend as many as 1,200 to 1,400 calories a day just to maintain the basic work of your body's cells. Imagine the harm you are doing to life processes by subsisting on an 800-calorie-a-day diet!

Your RMR includes the BMR, plus additional energy expenditures required for activity. Your RMR accounts for about 60 percent of the energy you expend daily. The higher this rate, the more efficient your body is at burning fat.

Specifically, it is your RMR that slows down when you restrict calories. In a one-year study of overweight men, those who cut calories to lose weight (as opposed to those who exercised) experienced a significant drop in their

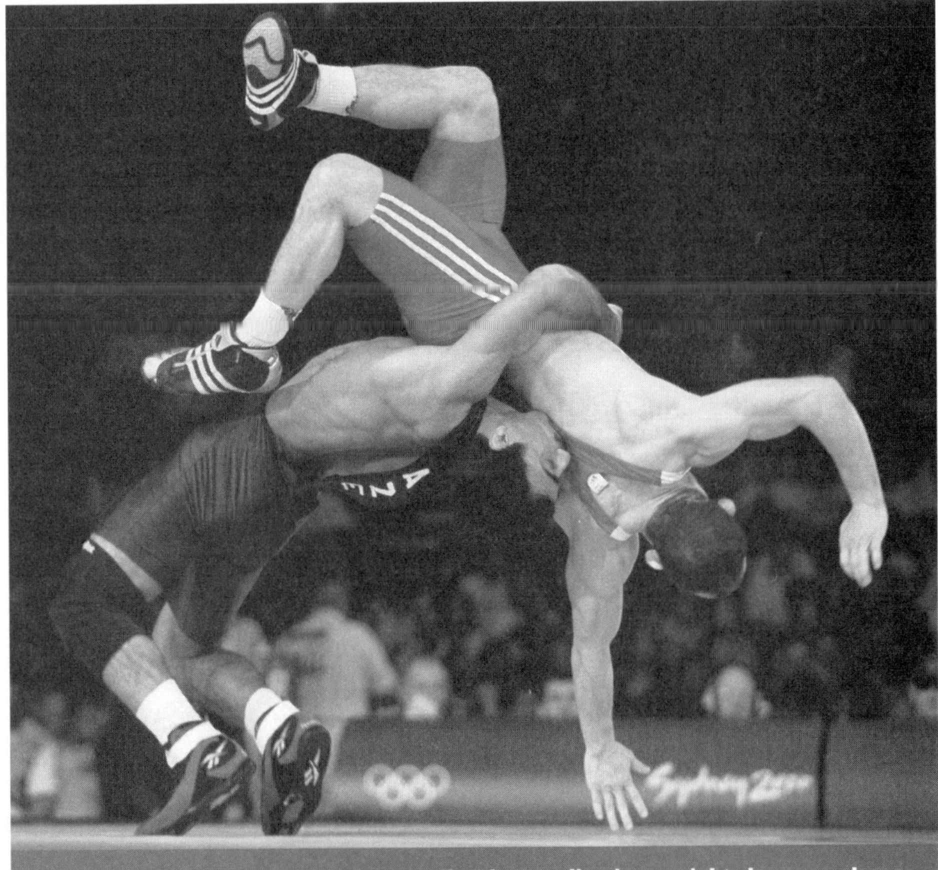

© Jamie Squire/Allsport

Wrestlers who want to burn fat to maintain standing in a weight class can choose from many ways to do it.

RMR. One reason was that they lost muscle tissue, and RMR is closely linked to how much muscle you have. The moral of the story here is that restrictive diets, if followed for an extended period, will decelerate your RMR and kiss good-bye the muscle you worked so hard to build.

Crash dieting is a losing proposition all the way around. There is nothing to be gained—except more weight! About 95 to 99 percent of all people who go on such diets are likely to regain their weight, with interest, within a year.

Fad diets—eating plans that eliminate certain foods and emphasize others—are just as bad. A major problem with fad diets is that they are nutritionally unbalanced, and you could be missing out on some of the key nutrients you need for good health. In fact, an analysis of 11 popular diets revealed deficiencies in one or more essential nutrients, and for several of the B-complex vitamins, calcium, iron, or zinc. One diet derived 70 percent of its calories from fat. Such dangerously high levels of fat can lead to heart disease.

But there are other problems, too. Take the high-protein diet, one of the most popular fad diets among strength trainers. And no wonder it is popular! At first, it works great. You get on the scale, see a huge weight loss, and feel wonderful—until you go off the diet. The weight comes back as fast as it left. That is because high-protein diets are very dehydrating; they flush water right out of your system to help the body get rid of excess nitrogen. Dehydration is dangerous, too, potentially causing fatigue, lack of coordination, heat illnesses such as heat stress and heatstroke, and in extreme cases (a loss of 6 percent or more of body fluid), death. Even with a mere 2 percent drop in body weight as fluid, your performance will diminish. That is the equivalent of three pounds of water loss in a 150-pound person.

Enough said about what doesn't work. There are anti-fat exercise and diet strategies that do work, namely a fat-burning training program and an individualized, nutritionally balanced eating plan that emphasizes carbohydrates and de-emphasizes fat. Before beginning, set some physique goals.

Go for Your Goal

Whether you realize it or not, you already know what your goal is. Just ask yourself: At what weight, or body fat percentage, do I look, feel, or perform the best? The answer to that question is your goal. The first step is to figure out how close to, or far from, the mark you are.

There are lots of ways to figure this out, including height and weight charts, body mass index (BMI) calculations, and the bathroom scales.

But the problem with most of these is that they are not very accurate for people who strength train. None of these methods takes into account the amount of muscle you have on your body. In fact, they might indicate that you are overweight!

Bathroom scales tempt you to step on them every morning. That can be a downer, because your weight goes up and down daily as a result of normal fluid fluctuations. You can get obsessed with the numbers you see on your scales.

A better measurement technique is body-composition testing, which determines how much of your weight is muscle or fat. Several methods are in use. One is underwater weighing, considered the "gold standard" and very accurate if done properly with the right equipment. But it is not convenient—I certainly don't have a water tank in my office—and it can be rather expensive.

Another method that is rapidly improving in reliability and validity is bioelectrical impedance analysis (BIA), which involves passing a painless electrical current through the body by means of electrodes placed on the hands and feet. Fat tissue won't conduct the current, but fat-free tissue (namely water found in muscle) will. Thus, the faster the current passes through the body, the less body fat there is. Readings obtained from the test are plugged into special formulas adjusted for height, gender, and age to calculate body fat and fat-free mass percentages. The problem with BIA is that your level of hydration dramatically affects the outcome. If you are dehydrated even a little, as most people are, you just won't get an accurate reading. So if you use this method, make sure to follow the directions for physical preparation closely. In addition, request that the equations used are based on a muscular, athletic population. When done well, this method is reliable.

Among the most accurate of the indirect methods is the skinfold technique, which measures fat just under the skin and uses those measurements to calculate body composition, including body fat percentage. One of the keys to getting accurate and reliable measurements with the skinfold method is to use the same technician, time after time, month after month. That way, you don't get as much variability in the measurements.

I use another strategy with strength trainers and athletes, one that can be a real motivator and reinforcement as you progress toward your goal. Simply use the skinfold caliper device to measure the skinfolds at selected points on your upper arm, chest, waist, hips, thighs, and calves. Do not plug these readings into the equation; instead, record them.

Do this every four to six weeks, being careful to position the calipers at the same site each time you measure a body part. You can even plot your measurements over time as evidence of the positive changes strength training, combined with the right diet, makes in your body.

Your Optimal Body Fat Percentage

Exactly what is optimal in terms of body fat? Healthy ranges of body fat are 22 to 25 percent for women and 15 to 20 percent for men. But if you are a strength trainer or bodybuilder, it is desirable to have even lower percentages: 18 to 10 percent for women and 15 to 7 percent for men.

A lot of elite female athletes, however, have less than 10 percent body fat. Female competitive runners, for example, may have as little as 5 or 6 percent body fat, according to some studies. A low percentage of body fat may be perfectly normal for some female athletes and desirable, because it enhances sports performance. As long as you don't consciously restrict calories while training for a sport, there is nothing unhealthy about having a naturally lean figure. However, calorie restriction, combined with overexercising, depletes body fat stores to unhealthy levels. This depletion can lead to an estrogen deficiency similar to what occurs during menopause, and your periods cease. This condition is called amenorrhea. There are some risky side effects to amenorrhea, including premature osteoporosis, heart disease, and the inability to become pregnant.

For women who are not elite athletes, a body fat percentage less than 14 can be risky. Hormone levels start to change, and this can lead to the same health problems.

Men are naturally leaner than women are. Even when men and women follow the same exercise and diet program, the men will typically lose more body fat. Women usually carry more body fat, because fat provides much of the energy for pregnancy and lactation. A woman's body thus tends to hang onto its fat, which partially explains why it is so hard to get body fat to budge.

If a man's body fat stores dip too low, there could be trouble, too. Strong evidence for this comes from a study of army rangers, who were put through an eight-week training course involving strenuous exercise and drills. Their food intake was reduced drastically, often to just one meal a day. By the end of the experiment, the soldiers had lost as much as 16 percent of their body weight and had reduced their body fat to 4 to 6 percent. At these low levels, their bodies were starting to feed on muscle tissue for energy. Clearly, the message for men is to not go below 6 percent body fat or you could sacrifice precious muscle mass. Even the leanest athletes I have worked with have never reduced their body fat to less than 4 percent.

How Much Fat Do You Want to Lose?

Once you have determined your body composition through an appropriate method, you can figure out how many pounds you need to lose to reach a lower body fat percentage with the following formula:

1. Present body weight × present body fat % = fat weight
2. Present body weight – fat weight = fat-free weight
3. Fat-free weight/desired % of fat-free mass = goal weight
4. Present body weight – goal weight = weight-loss goal

As an illustration, let's say you weigh 140 pounds, with a present body fat percentage of 12 percent. Your goal is to achieve 7 percent body fat. Your goal weight will be composed of 7 percent fat and 93 percent fat-free mass. How many pounds do you need to lose? Here's the calculation:

1. 140 lb × .12 = 16.8 lb fat weight
2. 140 lb – 16.8 lb = 123.2 lb fat-free weight
3. 123.2 lbs/.93 = 132.5 lb
4. 140 lb – 132.5 lb = 7.5 lb

So, to arrive at 7 percent body fat, you need to lose seven and a half pounds. Naturally, you want those seven plus pounds to be fat pounds. Here's a look at how to maximize your fat loss and minimize your muscle loss.

Antifat Exercise Strategies

Your objective is to lose body fat without losing muscle mass. You don't want to lose strength or endurance, either, and you don't want your performance to suffer. So how can you keep on the "losing" track? Forget about diet for a moment; the real key is exercise.

Exercise and Fat Loss

When it comes to burning fat, exercise is your best friend—in three ways:

1. The more exercise you do, the less you have to worry about calories. One pound of body fat equals 3,500 calories. By burning 250 to 500 calories a day through exercise, you could lose up to a pound of fat a week (7 days × 500 calories per day = 3,500 calories)—without restricting food. If you need to lose extra body fat, either for competition, health, appearance, or performance, the solution may be as simple as increasing your activity. During an intense strength-training program, for example, you can expend as many as 500 calories an hour; walking at a brisk pace burns 300 calories an hour; bicycling, 600 calories an hour; or aerobic dancing, up to 500 calories an hour.

2. Exercise hikes your RMR. After you exercise, your RMR stays elevated for several hours, and you burn extra calories even at rest. And if you strength train, you get even more of a metabolic boost: The muscle you develop is calorie-burning, metabolically active tissue. Having more of muscle tissue cranks your metabolic rate up even higher.

At Colorado State University, researchers recruited 10 men, ages 22 to 35, to see what effect, if any, strength training had on metabolism. At various times in the study, the men participated in strength training, aerobic exercise, or a control condition of quiet sitting. During the experiment, the subjects were fed controlled diets with a composition of 65 percent carbohydrate, 15 percent protein, and 20 percent fat.

In the strength-training portion of the experiment, the men performed a fairly standard, yet strenuous, routine: five sets of 10 different upper and lower body exercises for a total of 50 sets. They worked out for about 100 minutes. For aerobic exercise, the men cycled at moderate intensities for about an hour.

The researchers reported these findings: Strength training produced a higher rate of oxygen use than either aerobic exercise or quiet sitting, meaning that it was a better elevator of RMR. In fact, the men's RMR stayed elevated for about 15 hours after working out. Clearly, strength training stood out as a metabolic booster and a calorie burner. With strength training, it is easy to keep fat off and control your weight.

3. Exercise preserves muscle. If you lose 10 pounds of body weight, you may be lighter, but if five of those pounds are muscle, you sure won't be stronger, and your performance can really suffer. Appearance-wise, you can still look flabby when muscle tissue is lost. Exercise is one of the best ways to make sure you are shedding weight from fat stores, rather than from muscle stores.

Researchers have put this principle to the test. In a study of 10 overweight women, half of the women were placed in a diet-plus-exercise group and half of the women in an exercise-only group. The women in the diet-plus-exercise group followed a diet that reduced their calories by 50 percent of what it took to maintain their weight. They worked out aerobically six times a week. The exercise-only group followed the same aerobic exercise program but followed a diet designed to stabilize their weight.

After 14 weeks, it was time to check the results. Here is what happened: Both groups lost weight. But the composition of that loss was vastly different between the groups. In the diet-plus-exercise group, the weight lost was 67 percent fat and 33 percent lean mass. In the exercise-only group, the women lost much more fat—86 percent fat and only 14 percent lean mass! Not only that, RMR declined by 9 percent among the dieters, whereas it was maintained in the exercisers.

What does all this tell us? Sure, you can lose weight by low-calorie dieting. But you risk losing muscle. Not only that, your metabolic rate can plummet, sabotaging your attempts at successful weight control. With exercise and a nonrestrictive diet, you preserve calorie-burning muscle and keep your metabolism in gear.

Exercise Intensity Counts

"Intensity" has several different meanings, depending on the type of exercise you do, but it basically describes how hard you work out. With aerobic exercise, intensity can be measured by heart rate, which indicates the amount of work your heart does to keep up with the demands of various activities, including exercise.

For optimum fat burning, you should exercise at a level hard enough to raise your heart rate to 70 to 85 percent of your maximum heart rate, which is expressed as 220 minus your age. At low-intensity exercise—20 minutes or longer at around 50 percent of your maximum heart rate—fat supplies as much as 90 percent of your fuel requirements.

Higher intensity aerobic exercise at roughly 75 percent of your maximum heart rate burns a smaller percentage of fat (around 60 percent), but results in more total calories burned overall, including more fat calories.

To illustrate this concept, here's a comparison based on studies of aerobic intensity. At 50 percent of your maximum heart rate, you burn 7 calories a minute, 90 percent of which come from fat. At 75 percent of your maximum heart rate, you burn 14 calories a minute, 60 percent from fat. So at 50 percent intensity, where 90 percent of the calories are from fat, you are burning only 6.30 fat calories per minute (0.90×7 calories/minute), but at 75 percent intensity, where only 60 percent of the calories are from fat, you are burning as much as 8.40 fat calories per minute (0.60×14 calories/minute). In short, you burn more total fat calories at higher intensities.

If it is difficult for you to exercise at a high intensity, try increasing your duration—how long you exercise. You can burn just as much fat at a lower intensity by working out longer as you can by exercising at a higher intensity for a shorter duration.

To increase your rate of fat loss, gradually increase your aerobic exercise sessions from 30 to 60 minutes or strive for longer distances. For example, jogging a mile expends about 100 calories. Jog five miles, and you will burn 500 calories. If you are jogging only a mile a day, it would take a month to lose a pound of fat compared with about a week if you jog five miles a day.

The Competitive Strategy of a Professional Bodybuilder

Several years ago, a group of researchers at Arizona State University studied the diet and exercise strategies of Mike Ashley, known in bodybuilding circles as "Natural Wonder," because he does not use anabolic steroids. During an eight-week precontest period, Mike did the following:

- Consumed roughly 5,000 calories daily—3,674 calories from food, plus a carbohydrate-rich sport drink, and an amino acid supplement.
- Supplemented with an additional 1,278 calories a day from supplemental MCT oil. (This meant that 25.5 percent of his calories came from a fat source, not including food intake. However, MCTs are not metabolized like conventional fats; the body uses them immediately for energy, rather than storing them as fat. Although MCTs represent a more compact source of energy—nine calories per gram versus four calories per gram for carbs—this approach is not recommended for everyone. The nutrition plan outlined in chapter 12 has wider application and will work for more people.)
- Trained on a stair-climbing machine for a full hour, six days a week.
- Weight trained six days a week, dividing his routine into two or three workouts a day. In total, Mike worked out five to six hours a day at a very high level of intensity.

With these strategies—lots of quality calories and lots of intense exercise—Mike was able to reduce his body fat from 9 percent to a contest-sharp 6.9 percent, without sacrificing muscle.

You don't have to start working out five hours a day (unless perhaps you are a professional bodybuilder training for a contest). But there is a connection between exercise and diet to burn body fat. You don't necessarily have to cut calories. In fact, you can keep them high. Exercising at moderate to high levels of intensity will take care of the fat.

Another option related to duration is frequency—working out more times a week to obtain a greater caloric expenditure. Perhaps you could add bicycling or aerobic dance to your aerobics program for some variety, as well as for some extra calorie burning.

Intensity in strength training refers to how much weight you lift. For your muscles to respond—that is, get stronger and better developed—you have to challenge them to handle heavier poundages. That means continually putting more demands on them than they're used to; in other words, progressively increasing your poundages from workout to workout. The more muscle you can develop, the more efficient your body becomes at fat burning, because muscle is the most metabolically active tissue in the body.

© UPI Photo Service/Bill Greenblatt

For your muscles to get stronger and better developed, you have to challenge them to handle heavier poundages.

Anti-Fat Diet Strategies

Here's how to eat to give yourself the best chances at losing fat and saving muscle.

1. Don't fast. Because you strength train and probably do aerobics as well, you actually need more food, not less. Researchers at Tufts University found that when older men and women began a strength-training program, they needed 15 percent more calories just to maintain their body weight. This finding is not so surprising, really. With strength training, the exercisers began to expend more calories. Plus, their RMR increased because they had built more muscle.

You can figure out exactly how many calories you personally need to lose fat. Based on my research with competitive bodybuilders, I have concluded that an intake of 35 to 38 calories per kilogram of body weight a day is reasonable for fat loss and muscle preservation. The minimum is 30 to 33 calories per kilogram for a rapid cut. Anything less than that is too restrictive, and you won't be well nourished.

Let's say you weigh 180 pounds (82 kilograms). Here's how to figure your calorie requirements to lose fat: 82 kilograms × 35 calories/kilogram = 2,870 calories. For maintaining body weight, you should eat up to 44 calories per kilogram of body weight a day, or 3,608 calories a day. If you increase your exercise intensity, duration, or frequency, go even higher—to 54 calories per kilogram of body weight, or 4,428 calories a day.

If you still need a calorie deficit to continue losing fat or to break a plateau, get that deficit by increasing your activity level and modifying your calories slightly. For example, restrict your calories by about 500 a day and increase aerobic exercise—maybe by 500 calories a day. That way, you would have an energy deficit of 1,000 calories.

2. Slash the fat. Fat calories are more likely to be deposited as body fat. The reason has to do with the thermic effect of food, which describes the energy spent to metabolize food. Very little energy is expended to metabolize fat compared with carbohydrates. The energy cost of metabolizing carbs and converting them to glycogen for storage is rated at 25 percent, in contrast to just 4 percent to store fat. In other words, your body works harder at breaking down carbs and using them for energy. This is not so with fat. The body recognizes fat as fat and prefers to hang on to it rather than break it down for energy. As noted previously, your fat intake should be 20 percent or less of your total daily calories.

3. Preserve muscle with protein. To lose mostly fat, with muscle mass preserved, you must have adequate protein in your diet. If you go on a

diet that is too low in calories, there is a good chance that your dietary protein would not be used to build tissue but instead might be broken down and used for energy much like carbs and fat are.

So how much protein do you need to maximize muscle mass while minimizing body fat? Those of us who work with strength-training athletes favor eating 1.6 to 2.0 grams of protein per kilogram of body weight depending on your calorie reduction. In a study of 19 drug-free bodybuilders, researchers at Virginia Tech divided the athletes into three groups: a high-protein/moderate-carbohydrate group, a moderate-protein/high-carbohydrate group, and a control group. The high-protein/moderate-carb group consumed twice the recommended daily allowances (RDA) for protein, or 1.6 grams per kilogram of body weight, whereas the moderate-protein/high-carbohydrate group consumed the RDA (0.8 grams per kilogram of body weight).

With the high-protein/moderate-carbohydrate diet, more body protein was retained than with the other diet, which meant that the extra protein was being used to synthesize and repair new tissue. One drawback of the higher protein diet, however, was that it compromised muscular endurance, the ability to repeat contractions over and over without fatiguing. Even so, the overall results of this study suggest that if you are trying to lose body fat, you should eat more than the RDA of protein to protect your muscle mass. But keep your carbs up too, so you can maintain high levels of exercise intensity.

1. Concentrate on carbs. Regardless of what you hear or read, carbohydrates are critical to fat loss for reasons that bear repeating. First, carbohydrates are required in the cellular reactions involved in burning fat.

Second, they spare protein from being used as fuel. Your body prefers to burn carbohydrates for energy over protein. Protein is thus spared so that it can be used to do its main job of repairing tissue and building lean muscle.

Third, carbohydrates restock the body with glycogen, which helps power the muscles during exercise. The more glycogen in the muscles, the harder you can train. Hard training burns body fat and builds metabolically active muscle.

Fourth, when your body is digesting carbohydrates, your metabolic rate goes up higher than it does when metabolizing fat. This is due to the thermic effect of food—the energy cost of assimilating food.

Finally, carbohydrates (namely, complex carbs) are loaded with fiber, which has its own set of fat-burning benefits. More energy (calories) is spent digesting and absorbing high-fiber foods than most foods. Fiber keeps your appetite in check by stimulating the release of appetite-suppressing hormones. In addition, fiber accelerates the time it takes for food to move through your body, meaning fewer calories are left to be stored as fat. So you see: Carbs are key for fat burning.

If you are strength training and doing aerobics as part of your fat-loss program, you need to eat 5 to 6 grams of carbohydrate per kilogram of body weight daily. That amount will keep you well fueled for high-intensity exercise while still allowing enough room for your extra protein needs.

5. Cut down on sugary foods. One type of carb to go easy on is sugar, and foods that contain a lot of it. Sugar-laced foods have a fattening effect on the body. The reason is that many sugary foods, particularly dessert-type foods, such as ice cream, cakes, and pies, contain a lot of fat. Overindulging in these foods increases your risk of gaining body fat.

Researchers at Indiana University in Bloomington, Indiana, analyzed the diets of four groups of people: lean men (average body fat was 15 percent), lean women (average body fat was 20 percent), obese men (average body fat was 25 percent), and obese women (average body fat was 35 percent).

The obese men and women ate more of their calories from fat (as high as 36 percent of total calories) and refined sugars, such as candy, doughnuts, and ice cream, which are also high in fat, than the lean men and women. In other words, there was a link between high-fat, high-sugar diets and obesity.

The lesson here is: Change the composition of your diet to keep the fat off. This means cutting down on high-fat sugary foods. The easiest way to do this is by increasing the complex carbs in your diet. Remember, when you are dieting to lose fat, 60 percent of your total daily calories should come from carbs.

If you have a sweet tooth, you may want to choose sweets that are primarily carbohydrate and not fat. Even so, don't overindulge on these either, because they are not as nutrient dense as complex carbs.

There may also be a link between high-fructose corn syrup-sweetened beverages and overeating. Researchers have linked these beverages to the incidence of obesity in adolescents, and they theorize that our bodies may not recognize that we've consumed the calories. Even though they contribute to our caloric totals, we are still hungry and eat more than we need. So watch out for all bottled soft drinks and sweetened beverages that contain high-fructose corn syrup.

You may have thought about using artificially sweetened foods. But proceed with caution. See the sidebar article for an update on the current controversy over artificial sweeteners.

6. Don't skip breakfast. Skipping breakfast is not a good way to lose body fat. In fact, it could fatten you up! Most people who skip breakfast make up those calories, with interest, throughout the day. In Madrid, Spain,

Do Artificial Sweeteners Have a Place in a Fat Loss Program?

Artificial sweeteners are swirling in controversy. As a strength trainer, be aware of the controversies because you most likely eat a lot of food—some of which you may sweeten with these products.

The oldest artificial sweetener on the market is saccharin. A zero-calorie sweetener, saccharin was originally developed in 1900 to help diabetic individuals and improve the taste of other medically supervised diets. One hundred years later, the use of artificial sweeteners has become enormously popular, and there are several new products to choose from (see table 4.2).

Cyclamate, also a noncalorie sweetener, was introduced in the 1950s. It tasted better than saccharin and soon surpassed it in popularity. But by the 1970s, the FDA banned its use in foods after studies showed that it increased the risk of cancer in animals. Then in 1977, because of research suggesting that saccharin caused blad-

Table 4.2 Fake Sugars

Brand name	Calories/ serving	Advantages/ disadvantages
Saccharin	4	Bitter aftertaste; has been found to cause cancer in lab rats.
Aspartame	4	Good taste; destroyed during cooking; may cause reactions in vulnerable populations.
Acesulfame-K	0	As sweet as aspartame but more stable and less expensive; consumer safety groups concerned about safety.
Cyclamate	0	Lacks FDA approval; has been linked to cancer in lab rats.
Sucralose	0	May be the most “natural” of all the fake sugars.

der tumors in rats, the FDA required a warning label on all saccharin-containing foods.

In 1981, the FDA approved the use of a new artificial sweetener, aspartame. Commercially available as EQUAL, aspartame is an artificially synthesized compound of two natural ingredients, the amino acids phenylalanine and aspartic acid. Aspartame is virtually calorie free and 200 times sweeter than sugar.

Aspartame's natural ingredients and superior taste catapulted it to popularity. But no sooner had the FDA approved the use of aspartame than its apparent safety came into question.

It was already well known that eating aspartame could be dangerous for people with phenylketonuria (PKU), an inability to metabolize phenylalanine. All products containing aspartame must be labeled with a warning for people who have PKU. But the specter of other risks to normal, healthy people began to rise among the scientific community.

According to researchers, there may be populations other than those with PKU that are sensitive to aspartame. Mood disorder patients are one example. A study conducted at Northeastern Ohio University's College of Medicine had to be halted because a group of patients with clinical depression had severe reactions to aspartame.

The question of whether aspartame could cause brain tumors in rats was a focus of research reviews and discussions conducted by the FDA before approving the sweetener. Now some researchers are claiming that there were flaws in the FDA's research and review process regarding the risk of brain tumors.

To date, the FDA stands by its approval. However, Dr. John Olney, a neuroscientist at the Washington University School of Medicine, disagrees with the decision. After studying aspartame's effects on the brain for more than 20 years, Dr. Olney believes that there may be a link between the rising rates of brain tumors in the United States and the nearly 17 years of aspartame use in foods. According to Dr. Olney, "... about three to five years after aspartame was approved, there's been a striking increase in the incidence of malignant brain tumors."

Dr. Olney is not calling for a ban on aspartame. In an interview, he stated: "I'm not saying that aspartame has been proven to cause brain tumors. I'm saying that there is enough basis to suspect aspartame, that it needs to be reassessed."

In 1988, another sweetener was approved—acesulfame-K. It is 200 times sweeter than sugar, yet has a bitter taste. The "K" in its name stands for potassium. Acesulfame-K is not metabolized by the body. You can cook and bake with it. Marketed under the name Sunette and Sweet One, this sweetener has been tested for more than 15 years, with no apparent side effects.

Acesulfame-K has its critics, however. Some consumer groups contend that the sweetener causes cancer in animals.

The newest artificial sweetener to be approved by the FDA is sucralose. It is 600 times sweeter than table sugar, and remarkably, it is made from a process that begins with regular sugar. Marketed under the name Splenda, sucralose has been approved for use in many products, including baked goods, baking mixes, nonalcoholic beverages, chewing gum, desserts, fruit juices, confections, toppings, syrups, among many others. You can cook with sucralose and add it directly to foods. The FDA reviewed more than 100 animal and human studies and concluded that sucralose was safe.

Because the safety of many of these products remains in question, I recommend that you use them in moderation, if at all.

researchers found that overweight and obese people spent less time eating breakfast and ate smaller quantities and less varied types of food at breakfast compared with normal-weight people.

Eating breakfast stokes your metabolic fires for the day. By contrast, going hungry in the morning is just another form of fasting, which slows down your metabolism. Plus, your physical and mental performance will suffer when you are running on empty.

If you are like me, you're rushed in the morning, with barely enough time to shower and dress, let alone eat breakfast. If that is the case, eat what you can. Something is better than nothing. A study done in England found that because ready-to-eat cereals are high in vitamins and minerals and low in fat, they make a great choice for breakfast.

The best breakfasts include a combination of carbohydrate, protein, and fat. They should meet about one quarter to one third of your daily caloric requirements. If you live an on-the-go lifestyle, you need some nutritious breakfasts that take minutes to fix. There are several breakfast recipes in chapter 16 to help you. Some of these can even go on the road with you—so there is no excuse to skip breakfast again!

Individualize Your Diet

Making dietary changes doesn't mean giving up your favorite foods or altering your lifestyle. Simply moderate how much of your favorite foods you eat by having them less often, and then learn how to make healthier substitutions.

Take the case of Doug, a 17-year-old defensive lineman. His dream was to play quarterback. But he just didn't have the speed and was always exhausted by the fourth quarter. After Doug had his body composition tested, his coaches decided that he needed to lose fat.

I analyzed his diet to see where substitutions could be made so that Doug could shed body fat. His breakfast was usually a Danish and orange juice. He replaced the Danish with a more nutritious English muffin.

Doug's typical lunch was a Quarter Pounder with cheese, french fries, and apple pie. So instead of going to his favorite fast-food restaurant, he began eating lunch at the deli next door, where he could order a lower fat meal like chicken on rye and pretzels.

Snacks usually consisted of a cola and a candy bar, high-fat, high-sugar foods that made him feel full and sluggish. Doug switched to a banana as a snack.

After practice, Doug would have a home-cooked meal for dinner. Here, he substituted a baked potato for mashed potatoes, used a lower-fat salad dressing on his salad, and ate low-fat ice milk instead of ice cream for dessert.

These minor alterations resulted in some major changes. Doug's carb intake went up, while his fat intake went down. He was able to trim down without sacrificing muscle. Equally important, his performance improved on the field. You can achieve the same success by taking a similar approach to dietary planning. Are you game? Then be sure to check out my sample diets in chapter 13 for examples of how to eat to lose fat.

Sports Nutrition Fact vs Fiction:

Diet Pills: A Shortcut to Cutting Up?

Should you use diet pills to lose fat and make weight? Unequivocally, "no."

In recent years, a flood of prescription diet pills has hit the market. Among the most widely prescribed have been the appetite suppressants fenfluramine, phentermine, and dexfenfluramine (Redux). They affect chemicals in the brain that short circuit the desire to eat. But the FDA withdrew fenfluramine and Redux from the market in September 1997 after studies found that 30 percent of 290 patients who took them showed signs of heart-valve abnormalities.

Dexfenfluramine has a rare but potentially fatal side effect—primary pulmonary hypertension, in which the blood vessels supplying the lungs become scarred and thickened. The disease is progressive, eventually ending in death within a few years.

Phentermine can still be prescribed. Its side effects include dry mouth, nervousness, constipation, and insomnia.

These drugs have been prescribed primarily for people who are considered obese, defined as being at least 20 percent over ideal weight. No ethical physician should have recommended or prescribed them for anyone 10 pounds or less over a healthy weight.

A newer diet drug is sibutramine (Meridia). It is designed to treat serious obesity, especially those cases accompanied by other health problems such as diabetes.

Sibutramine works differently than other prescription weight loss drugs. It prevents appetite-promoting brain chemicals from being reabsorbed, creating a sensation of fullness. The drug also helps stimulate the metabolism. When taking sibutramine, you still have to follow a diet and engage in regular exercise to encourage weight loss.

Inconvenient side effects include dry mouth, headache, constipation, and insomnia. More serious side effects include increases in blood pressure and pulse rate—both of which could be life threatening if you have hypertension or certain heart conditions.

Another new diet drug is orlistat (Xenical), which works in the intestines to partially block fat from being absorbed. A side effect of orlistat is that it may interfere with the absorption of fat-soluble vitamins, namely vitamins A, D, E, and K.

What about over-the-counter diet pills? These pills are classified as appetite suppressants too. They all contain an amphetamine-derivative called phenylpropanolamine (PPA). A mild stimulant, this drug causes various untoward reactions, including nervousness, anxiety, and increased blood pressure. More troubling is that some people, especially teenagers, can suffer stroke if they exceed the recommended dosage. The FDA has recommended that all over-the-counter products remove PPA from their ingredients due to its potential health dangers.

Forget diet pills. As an exerciser and strength trainer, you have the best weapons available to fight body fat: high-energy eating habits and exercise that builds calorie-burning muscle and stokes your metabolic fires.

Sport Nutrition Fact vs. Fiction:

The Truth About High-Fat Diets

Many bodybuilders, strength trainers, and exercisers have been experimenting with high-fat diets to lose body fat. Basically, these diets call for a high protein intake (around 25 to 30 percent of total daily calories), low carbs (around 40 percent of total daily calories), and lots of fat (anywhere from 30 to 70 percent of total daily calories). The diets theoretically reduce insulin levels in the body. Insulin is a hormone that, among other functions, promotes fat storage. With low insulin levels, the body supposedly burns more stored fat for energy. As noted in previous chapters, insulin doesn't make you fat. Overeating and underexercising do. Besides, regular exercise and weight control automatically keep insulin levels in line.

High-fat diets are self-defeating for strength trainers. First, they are too low in carbs. When carbs are in short supply in the muscle, the body has no other source of energy it can use to build muscle. Fat cannot be used as fuel for strength-training exercise. Workouts are not as intense, and you can actually lose muscle as a result. Muscle loss compromises your ability to burn fat.

Second, these diets are too high in protein. As noted previously, you don't need an excess of protein to build muscle. And third, high-fat diets tend to be too low in calories. On a diet that supplies an insufficient number of calories, you would lose some fat, but you would also lose hard-earned muscle.

A few more points: You may have heard that a high-fat diet is a good energy booster. This claim is based partly in fact. Research with cyclists has shown that a high-fat diet can extend endurance. But here's the catch. The cyclists didn't have the power to pedal uphill during their daily training rides. So although they had the endurance, they didn't have the oomph. Strength trainers and other athletes need both.

The explanation behind this has to do with muscle fibers. The muscle fibers used in endurance activity are technically known as slow-twitch, or type I. They contract very slowly but can sustain their contractions for long periods without fatiguing. Slow-twitch fibers get most of their energy from burning fat, a process that requires oxygen. The cyclists had good endurance because their slow-twitch muscle fibers had adapted to using fat for fuel.

Medium-Chain Triglyceride Oil

Processed mainly from coconut oil, medium-chain triglyceride oil (MCT oil) is a special type of dietary fat that was first formulated in the 1950s by the pharmaceutical industry for patients who had trouble digesting regular fats. Still used in medical settings, MCT oil is also a popular fitness supplement, marketed as a fat burner, muscle builder, and energy source.

At the molecular level, MCT oil is structured quite differently from conventional fats such as butter, margarine, and vegetable oil. Conventional fats are made up of long carbon chains, with 16 or more carbon atoms strung together, and are thus known as long-chain triglycerides (LCTs). Body fat is also an LCT. MCT oil, on the other hand, has a much shorter carbon chain of only 6 to 12 carbon atoms, which is why it is described as a medium-chain triglyceride.

As a result of this molecular difference, MCTs are digested, transported, and metabolized much more quickly than fatty acids from regular oils or fats, and thus have some interesting properties. To begin with, MCTs are burned in the body like carbohydrates. Unlike conventional fats, MCTs are not stored as body fat but are shuttled directly into the cells to be burned for energy. In fact, MCT oil is burned so quickly that its calories are turned into body heat—a process known as thermogenesis, which boosts the metabolic rate. The higher your metabolism, the more calories your body burns.

Does that mean if you take MCT oil you can rev up your metabolism and therefore burn more fat? Researchers at the University of Rochester looked into this possibility. In an experiment involving seven healthy men at the University of Rochester, they tested whether a single meal of MCTs would increase the metabolic rate more than an LCT meal would. The men ate test meals containing 48 grams of MCT oil or 45 grams of corn oil, given in random order on separate days. In the study, metabolic rate increased 12 percent over six hours after the men ate the MCT meals but increased only 4 percent after LCTs were consumed. What's more, concentrations of triglycerides in plasma (the liquid portion of blood) were elevated 68 percent after the LCT meal, but did not change after the MCT meal. These findings led the researchers to speculate that replacing LCTs with MCTs over a long period of time might be beneficial in weight loss.

Other researchers aren't so sure. In a study at Calgary University in Alberta, Canada, healthy adults were placed on a low-carbohydrate diet supplemented with MCT oil. The researchers found that the diet had no real effect on elevating the metabolism. The calories burned over a 24-hour period were less than 1 percent of total caloric intake. However, there was a decrease in muscle protein burned for energy. Although MCT might not be a fat burner per se, it may help preserve lean mass by inhibiting its breakdown.

In most studies on MCT oil and fat burning, volunteers ingest huge amounts of the fat—usually 30 grams or more—to bring on metabolic-boosting results. Such amounts are just not tolerable for most people, because too much MCT oil produces intestinal discomfort and diarrhea. In my opinion, taking such huge doses of MCT oil to spur fat burning just isn't practical.

There's another problem with using MCT oil to try to burn fat. The recommended way to take MCT oil is with carbohydrates, a practice that prevents ketosis. In ketosis, by-products of fat metabolism called ketones build up if carbs aren't available to assist in the final stages of fat breakdown. But when MCTs are taken with carbs, there is no effect on fat burning whatsoever. Here's why. Carbs trigger the release of insulin, which inhibits the mobilization of fat for energy. Thus, there's simply no benefit to the use of MCT oil as a fat-burner. You have to do it the old-fashioned way, by exercising and watching your diet.

Another claim attached to MCT oil is that it helps you put on muscle. But there are no controlled studies to prove this. Using some MCT oil to sneak in extra calories for harder workouts makes some sense, though. Go easy at first by taking one-half tablespoon to one tablespoon a day. Its fast absorption can cause cramping and diarrhea if you eat too much. Before experimenting with MCT oil, get your doctor's okay.

As for power and strength, that's another story altogether. The muscle fibers used to sprint, lift weights, or power an uphill ride are called fast-twitch, or type II fibers. They contract rapidly but fatigue more easily. Their energy comes from burning glycogen, not fat. They simply can't adapt to using fat for energy. The bottom line: A high-fat diet will sap your strength.

Remember, too, that dietary fat is easily stored as body fat because the fats are chemically similar. Calorie for calorie, fat in the diet turns into fat on the body more easily than carbohydrate. As I've already stated: Eat fat, wear fat.

What's more, following a high-fat diet is playing Russian roulette with your health. Excessive dietary fat is linked to all sorts of life-shortening illnesses, including heart disease and cancer. Steer clear of these fad approaches to dieting and stick to high-carbohydrate fare instead.

5 Hydrating for Heavy-Duty Workouts

Quick: What's the most critical nutrient for growth, development, and health? If you guessed "water," congratulations!

People frequently overlook the importance of water in the diet, and most people don't even consider water an essential nutrient. Without enough water and other fluids, you'll die within a week.

Although water does not provide energy in the same way carbs and fat do, it plays an essential role in energy formation. As the most abundant nutrient in your body, water is the medium in which all energy reactions take place. Thus, you need ample fluids for fuel and stamina. You get those fluids from a variety of sources—the foods you eat, the beverages you consume, and the plain, pure water you drink. Here's a closer look at the importance of water and other fluids in the diet.

An Essential Nutrient

The fluids in your body form a heavily trafficked river through your arteries, veins, and capillaries that carries nutrients to your cells and waste products out of the body. Fluids fill virtually every space in your cells and between each cell. Water molecules not only fill space, but they also help form the structures of macromolecules such as proteins and glycogen.

The chemical reactions that keep you alive occur in water, and water is an active participant in those reactions.

It's hard to say enough good things about water. It makes up about 60 percent of the body weight in adults. As the primary fluid in your body, water serves as a solvent for minerals, vitamins, amino acids, glucose, and many other nutrients. Without water, you can't even digest these essential nutrients, let alone absorb, transport, and use them.

In addition to carrying nutrients throughout the body, water transports waste products out of the body. It is a part of the lubricant fluid in your joints to keep them moving. And when your body's temperature begins to rise, water acts as the coolant in your radiator. Enough said! You can see why water is so vital to health.

The Temperature Regulator

Your body produces energy for exercise, but only 25 percent of that energy is actually used for mechanical work. The other 75 percent is released as heat. The extra warmth produced during exercise causes your body to heat up, raising your core temperature. To get rid of that extra heat, you sweat. As sweat evaporates, your blood and body cool. If you couldn't cool off, you would quickly succumb to heat stress caused by the increase in your body's core temperature. Thank goodness for water!

Water and Fat-Burning

Drinking more water can actually help you stay lean, indirectly. Your kidneys depend on water to do their job of filtering waste products from the body. In a water shortage, the kidneys need backup, so they turn to the liver for help. One of the liver's many functions is mobilizing stored fat for energy. By taking on extra assignments from the kidneys, the liver can't do its fat-burning job as well. Fat loss is compromised as a result.

In addition, water can help take the edge off hunger so that you eat less, and it has no calories. If you are on a high-protein diet, water is required to detoxify ammonia, a by-product of protein energy metabolism. And, as you mobilize your stored fatty acids to burn off as energy, you release any fat-soluble toxins that have been benignly stored in your fat cells. The more fluid you drink, the more dilute the toxins in your bloodstream, and the more rapidly they exit from your body.

Water and Your Muscles

Ever wonder why some days you're so pooped you can't pump iron? One reason may be dehydration. To move your muscles, you need water. Of all the places in your body, water is found in highest concentration in metabolically active tissues such as muscle, and in lowest concentrations in relatively inactive tissues such as fat, skin, and some parts of bone. Muscles are controlled by nerves. The electrical stimulation of nerves and contraction of muscles occurs as a result of the exchange of electrolyte minerals dissolved in water (sodium, potassium, calcium, chloride, and magnesium) across the nerve and muscle cell membranes.

If you're low on water or electrolytes, muscle strength and control are weakened. In fact, a water deficit of just 2 to 4 percent of your body weight

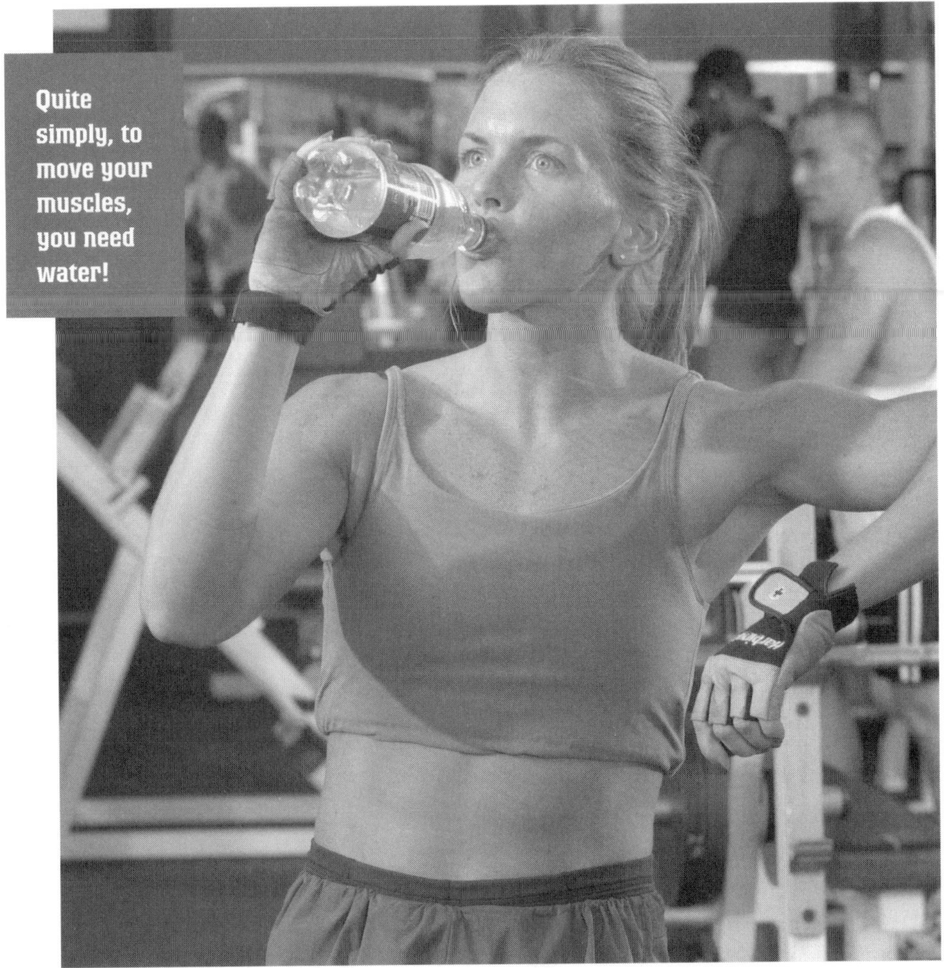

Quite simply, to move your muscles, you need water!

can cut your strength training workout by as much as 21 percent if you're dehydrated—and your aerobic power by a whopping 48 percent. Your body's thirst mechanism kicks in when you've lost 2 percent of your body weight in water. But by that time, you're already dehydrated. To prevent dehydration, you must get yourself on a scheduled plan to drink often throughout the day. (See the drinking schedule that follows on page 98.)

If gaining muscle is your goal, you should care about cell volumization, or the hydration state of your muscle cells. In a well-hydrated muscle cell, protein synthesis is stimulated and protein breakdown is decreased. On the other hand, muscle-cell dehydration promotes protein breakdown and inhibits protein synthesis. Cell volume has also been shown to influence genetic expression, enzyme and hormone activity, and metabolism.

Joint Lubrication

Water also forms the makeup of synovial fluid, the lubricating fluid between your joints; and cerebrospinal fluid, the shock-absorbing fluid between vertebrae and around the brain. Both fluids are essential for healthy joint and spine maintenance. If your diet is water deficient, even for a brief period, less fluid is available to protect these areas. Strength training places tremendous demands on joints and spines, and the presence of adequate protective fluid is essential for optimum performance and long-term health.

Water and Your Brain

When it comes to peak mental capacity, whether at the office or in competition, your hydration state will affect your performance. In a study of subjects' abilities to perform mental exercises after heat-stress–induced dehydration, a fluid loss of only 2 percent of body weight caused reductions in arithmetic ability, short-term memory, and the ability to visually track an object by 20 percent compared with their well-hydrated state. Thus, to think, we need to drink plenty of water!

Water and Your Health

Probably the most surprising fact about water is the effect that chronic, mild dehydration has on health and disease. It was a practice of

Hippocrates to recommend large intakes of water to increase urine production and decrease the recurrence of urinary tract stones. Today, approximately 12 to 15 percent of the general population will form a kidney stone at some time. Many factors can modify the risk factors for developing stones. Of these, diet—especially fluid intake—is the only one that can be easily changed and that has a marked effect on all aspects of urinary health.

A little-known fact is that low water intake is a risk factor for certain types of cancers. One study found that patients with urinary tract cancer (bladder, prostate, kidney, and testicle) drank significantly smaller quantities of fluid compared with healthy controls.

In another study, researchers discovered that women who drank more than five glasses of water a day had a 45 percent lower risk of colon cancer, compared with those who consumed two or fewer glasses a day. For men, the risk was cut by 32 percent when they drank more than four glasses a day versus one or fewer glasses a day.

Why does adequate water intake appear to have such an anticancer effect? One theory holds that the more fluid you drink, the faster you flush the toxins and carcinogenic substances out of the body, and the less chance for them to be resorbed into the body or be concentrated long enough at the site to cause tissue change.

Even more fascinating: A pilot study reported that the odds of developing breast cancer were reduced by 79 percent, on average, among water drinkers. In this case, possibly maintaining a dilute solution within the cells reduces the potency of estrogen and its ability to cause hormone-related cancers, according to the theory proposed by the authors of this research.

Mild dehydration can also be a factor in the occurrence of mitral valve prolapse, a defect of a heart valve that controls the flow of blood between chambers of the heart. Mitral valve prolapse is a relatively harmless condition, but in a small percentage of cases, it may cause rapid heartbeat, chest pain, and other cardiac symptoms. In a study of 14 healthy women with normal heart function, mitral valve prolapse was induced by mild dehydration and resolved with rehydration.

How Much Do You Need?

Nearly all the foods you eat contain water, which is absorbed during digestion. Most fruits and vegetables are 75 to 90 percent water. Meats contain roughly 50 to 70 percent water. And beverages such as juice, milk, and glucose-electrolyte solutions are more than 85 percent water. On average, you may consume about four cups of water daily from food alone, but this is true only if you're eating an abundance of fruits and vegetables, which are the major food sources of water. Most of us don't do this, so we can't count these foods as sources of fluids.

Most people are walking around in a moderately dehydrated state. You need a bare minimum of 8 to 12 cups of fluids daily—even more to replace the fluid you lose during exercise. Of these 8 to 12 cups, make sure at least five of them are pure water.

You lose about a quart (four cups) of water per hour of exercise, depending on your size and perspiration rate. When you're working out moderately in a mild climate, you are probably losing one to two quarts (two to four pounds) of fluid per hour through perspiration. That means that a 150-pound person can easily lose 2 percent of their body weight in fluid (three pounds) within an hour. If exercise is more intense, or the environment is more extreme, fluid losses will be greater. Thus, you can see how easily you become dehydrated.

If you don't replenish your fluid losses during exercise, you will fatigue early, and your performance will be diminished. If you don't replenish fluid after exercise, your performance on successive days will decay, and your long-term health may be at risk.

Moreover, according to the National Athletic Trainers' Association (NATA), dehydration

- will impair your physical performance in less than an hour of exercise—or sooner if you start working out in a dehydrated state;
- can cut your performance by as much as 48 percent; and
- increases your risk of developing symptoms of heat illness, such as heat cramps, heat exhaustion, and heat stroke.

In addition to exercise, many other factors increase water requirements, including high heat, low humidity, high altitude, a high-fiber diet, illness, travel, and pregnancy.

What about you? Are you dehydrated? Table 5.1 lists the early and severe warning signs of dehydration and heat stress.

How to Monitor

It's easy to monitor yourself for early signs of dehydration:

- Check your urine. It should be relatively odorless and no darker in color than straw. If it's a golden color or deep color with a strong odor, you're dehydrated and need to consume more water.

Table 5.1 Symptoms of Dehydration and Heat Stress

Early signs	Severe signs
Fatigue	Difficulty swallowing
Loss of appetite	Stumbling
Flushed skin	Clumsiness
Heat intolerance	Shriveled skin
Light-headedness	Sunken eyes and dim vision
Dark urine with a strong odor	Painful urination
Dry cough	Numb skin
Burning in stomach	Muscle spasm
Headache	Delirium
Dry mouth	

- Weigh yourself without clothing before and after exercise. For every pound lost during exercise, you've lost about two to three cups of fluid. Any weight lost during exercise is fluid loss and should be replaced by fluids as soon after exercise as possible.
- Dehydration is cumulative. Your body can't rehydrate itself. If you fail to rehydrate on consecutive occasions, you'll become increasingly dehydrated and begin to have the early symptoms of dehydration.
- Sore throat, dry cough, and a hoarse voice are all signs of dehydration.
- A burning sensation in your stomach can signal dehydration.
- Be aware of muscle cramps. No one knows for sure what causes muscle cramps, but a shortfall of water may be an important factor. Muscle cramps are more apt to occur if you're doing hard, physical work in the heat and don't drink enough fluids. You can usually alleviate the cramps by moving to a cool place, drinking fluids, and replacing electrolytes with a glucose-electrolyte solution.

A Drinking Schedule for Strength Trainers

You usually can't rely on thirst to tell you when to drink fluids. The body's drive to drink is not nearly as powerful as its drive to eat, and the thirst mechanism is even less powerful. By the time your thirst mechanism kicks in during exercise, you've already lost about 1 to 2 percent of your body weight as sweat. You need to drink water at regular intervals, thirsty or not. And you need to do so every day. Remember, if you fail to drink enough fluids one day, your body can't automatically rehydrate itself the next. You'll be doubly dehydrated and possibly begin to show some signs of dehydration.

For some additional guidelines, read the Position Stand on Exercise and Fluid Replacement issued by the American College of Sports Medicine. This appears in the sidebar article on page 99.

For workouts, here's a schedule that will keep you well hydrated.

Before Exercise

Drink at least 16 ounces (2 cups) of fluid two to three hours before exercise. Then, drink 8 ounces (1 cup) of fluid immediately before exercise to make sure the body is well hydrated. In very hot or cold weather, you need even more water: 12 to 20 ounces (1½ to 2½ cups) of fluid 10 to 20 minutes before exercise. Exercising during cold weather elevates your body temperature, and you still lose water through perspiration and respiration.

During Exercise

Drink 7 to 10 ounces every 10 to 20 minutes during exercise (8 ounces = 1 cup), and more in extreme temperatures. Although this might seem tough at first, once you schedule it into your regular training routine, you'll quickly adapt to the feeling of fluid in your stomach. In fact, the fuller your stomach, the faster it will empty. Dehydration slows the rate that your stomach will empty. Make regular water breaks part of your training now.

After Exercise

This is the time to replace any fluid you've lost. Weigh yourself before and after exercise; then drink two to three cups of fluid within two hours

American College of Sports Medicine Position Stand on Exercise and Fluid Replacement

It is the position of the American College of Sports Medicine that adequate fluid replacement helps maintain hydration and, therefore, promotes the health, safety, and optimal physical performance of individuals participating in regular physical activity. This position statement is based on a comprehensive review *and* interpretation of scientific literature concerning the influence of fluid replacement on exercise performance and the risk of thermal injury associated with dehydration and hypothermia. Based on available evidence, the American College of Sports Medicine makes the following general recommendations on the amount and composition of fluid that should be ingested in preparation for, during, and after exercise or athletic competition.

1. It is recommended that individuals consume a nutritionally balanced diet and drink adequate fluids during the 24-hour period before an event, especially during the period that includes the meal before exercise, to promote proper hydration before exercise or competition.

2. It is recommended that individuals drink about 500 milliliters (about 17 ounces) of fluid two hours before exercise to promote adequate hydration and allow time for excretion of excess ingested water.

3. During exercise, athletes should start drinking water early and at regular intervals in an attempt to consume fluids at a rate sufficient to replace all the water lost through sweating (i.e., body weight loss) or consume the maximal amount that can be tolerated.

4. It is recommended that ingested fluids be cooler than ambient temperature (between 15 degrees and 22 degrees C (59 degrees and 72 degrees F) and flavored to enhance palatability and promote fluid replacement. Fluids should be readily available and served in containers that allow adequate volumes to be ingested with ease and minimal interruption of exercise.

5. Addition of proper amounts of carbohydrates and/or electrolytes to a fluid-replacement solution is recommended for exercise

events of duration greater than one hour, because it does not significantly impair water delivery to the body and may enhance performance. During exercise lasting less than one hour, there is little evidence of physiological or physical performance differences between consuming a glucose-electrolyte drink and plain water.

6. During intense exercise lasting longer than one hour, it is recommended that carbohydrate be ingested at a rate of 30 to 60 grams per hour to maintain oxidation of carbohydrates and delay fatigue. This rate of carbohydrate intake can be achieved without compromising fluid delivery by drinking 600 to 1200 milliliters per hour of solutions containing 4 percent to 8 percent carbohydrates (grams per 100 milliliters). The carbohydrates can be sugars (glucose or sucrose) or starch (e.g., maltodextrin).

7. Inclusion of sodium (0.5 to 0.7 grams per liter of water) in the rehydration solution ingested during exercise lasting longer than one hour is recommended, because it may be advantageous in enhancing palatability, promoting fluid retention, and possibly preventing hyponatremia in certain individuals who drink excessive quantities of fluid. There is little physiological basis for the presence of sodium in an oral rehydration solution for enhancing intestinal water absorption as long as sodium is sufficiently available from the previous meal.

This pronouncement was written for the American College of Sports Medicine by Victor A. Convertino, PhD, FACSM (chair); Lawrence E. Armstrong, PhD, FACSM; Edward F. Coyle, PhD, FACSM; Gary W. Mack, PhD; Michael N. Sawka, PhD, FACSM; Leo C. Senay, Jr., PhD, FACSM; and W. Michael Sherman, PhD, FACSM.

after exercise for every pound body weight you've lost. Continue to drink an additional 25 to 50 percent more fluid for the next four hours.

What Not to Drink During Your Workout

Certain types of beverages should be shunned during exercise, according to the National Athletic Trainers' Association (NATA) in its recent position paper on fluid replacement for athletes. These beverages include fruit juices, carbohydrate gels, sodas, and glucose-electrolyte solutions with carbohydrate levels greater than 8 percent. These beverages slow fluid absorption and may cause gastrointestinal problems. NATA also discourages the consumption of beverages containing caffeine, alcohol, and carbonation, because they stimulate excess urine production and thus dehydrate your body. For more on juices, alcohol, and soda, see the information later in this chapter.

Best Sources of Water

The easiest way to get water is right from your faucet. But reports of contaminated tap water are of concern to many people—and with good reason. The water supply in some areas contains contaminants such as lead, pesticides, and chlorine by-products that exceed federal limits. A good move is to buy a water purifier, which filters lead and other contaminants from tap water. Some filters attach right to the tap; others can be installed as part of the entire water system. One of the most convenient and economic filtering methods is the pour-through filter you can place in a special pitcher and put right in your refrigerator. If you use a filtration product that removes fluoride from your water, discuss this issue with your dentist, because the mineral fluoride can support good dental health.

Another option is to purchase bottled water, and there are hundreds of brands. The most popular brands are "spring water" and "mineral water." Spring water is taken from underground freshwater springs that form pools on the surface of the earth. Mineral water comes from reservoirs located under rock formations. It contains a higher concentration of minerals than most other sources.

Another type of bottled water is well water, which is tapped from an aquifer. Well, mineral, and spring waters still may contain some contaminants. For this reason, federal regulations are tightening on the bottled water industry.

Distilled water is another type of bottled water. It has been purified through vaporization and is then condensed. A drawback of distilled water is that it does not usually contain any minerals. And fluoride is missing from many bottled waters.

Some people like seltzer water. This is a sparkling water that is bubbly because of the addition of pressurized carbon dioxide. Many of these products are flavored and contain sucrose or fructose.

Regardless of what type of water you drink, be sure to drink the 8 to 12 cups or more of fluids you need daily to stay well hydrated. Remember: Make at least five of these cups pure water.

Designer Waters

Water now comes in more varieties than ever before. Today, there's fortified water, fitness water, herbal water, oxygen-enriched water, electrolyzed water—the list goes on. Welcome to the world of "designer" waters.

Fortified Water

Featuring a splash of flavor and sweetness, these waters are fortified with predissolved vitamins and minerals. Some are formulated for people who want to drink their supplements; others, for active people who drink water during workouts and want a little more flavor than plain water provides.

Fortified waters are not to be confused with sports drinks or glucose-electrolyte solutions, which are packed with more carbohydrate energy and higher amounts of electrolytes than specialty waters contain.

Fitness Water

This is a category of designer waters owned by Propel, made by Gatorade. This product is flavored water with some vitamins, but with only 10 calories per serving. It is meant to be used when you want some flavor in your water but don't need a glucose-electrolyte solution or extra calories.

Herbal Water

Fairly new on the water front are herb-enhanced waters. You can now swill water containing such popular herbs as echinacea, ginkgo biloba, Siberian ginseng, ginger, or St. John's Wort. These beverages are a good option if you want the benefits of medicinal herbs without popping pills or capsules. Generally, herb-enhanced waters have a hint of flavor without sugar, calories, or carbonation.

Be aware of how many servings you consume of herbal or fortified waters, along with other sources of the same herbs, vitamins, and minerals. You might easily take in too much of these substances. And because the herbal part of the food industry is yet to be regulated, there's no guarantee that you're getting the ingredients listed on the label.

Oxygen-Enriched Water

These beverages are said to be enhanced with up to 40 times the normal oxygen concentration found naturally in water. Available as flavored or unflavored, they claim to boost energy by increasing oxygen saturation in the red blood cells. To date, though, there's no published medical evidence to validate such claims. There appears to be no value in them, other than as another good source of water.

Electrolyzed Water

This category describes water that has been separated into alkaline and acid fractions. The alkaline fraction is bottled for drinking with a pH of about 9.5, compared with other bottled waters, in which pH ranges from 6 to 8.

The process removes contaminants and most of the total dissolved solids but leaves in electrolytes such as calcium, magnesium, potassium, sodium, and bicarbonates. Claims for electrolyzed water include smoother taste, healthier water, improved hydration ability, electrolyte availability, and antioxidant properties. Aside from smoother-tasting water, the scientific research into most of these claims is in its infancy. Keep your eye on this research.

Are Sport Drinks Superior to Water?

In some cases, yes. For general types of exercise lasting less than one hour, water is still the best sport drink around. The nutrient you most need to replace during and after these types of workouts is water.

Glucose-electrolyte solution drinks (also known as sport drinks) do have their place—mostly for high-intensity intermittent exercise, for exercise lasting more than 45 minutes, and especially for use by endurance and ultraendurance athletes. These products are a mixture of water, carbohydrate, and electrolytes. Electrolytes are dissolved minerals that form a salty soup in and around cells. They conduct electrical charges that let them react with other minerals to relay nerve impulses, make muscles contract or relax, and regulate the fluid balance inside and outside cells. In hard workouts or athletic competitions lasting 45 minutes or longer, electrolytes can be lost through sweat. For a comparison of the various ingredients in these products, see table 5.2.

Table 5.2 Fluid Replacement Beverage Comparison Chart (per 8 oz. serving)

Beverage	Carb (%)	Sodium (mg)	Potassium (mg)	Other minerals	Calories
1st Ade	7	55	25	Phosphorus	60
10-K	6.3	55	30	Chloride, phosphorus, vitamin C	60
Allsport	8	55	55	Chloride, phosphorus, calcium	70
Cytomax	5	53	100	Chloride, magnesium	66
Endura	6.2	46	80	Chloride, calcium, magnesium, chromium	60
Exceed	7.2	50	45	Chloride, magnesium, calcium	70
Gatorade	6	110	30	Chloride, phosphorus	50
Hydra Fuel	7	25	50	Chloride, phosphorus, magnesium, vitamin C, chromium	66
PowerAde	8	55	30	Chloride	70
Quickick	7	100	23	Chloride, phosphorus, calcium	67

Where glucose-electrolyte solutions may have an edge over water is in their flavor. A lot of people just don't drink much water because it doesn't taste good. Soldiers participating in a study at the U.S. Army Research Institute of Environmental Medicine were given the choice of drinking plain chlorinated water, flavored water, or lemon-lime glucose-electrolyte solution drinks. Most soldiers chose the glucose-electrolyte solutions or flavored water over plain water. If you don't need to benefit from the extra carbs and electrolytes, one way to sneak more water in and still get the flavor is to dilute your glucose-electrolyte solution or use one of the new flavored fitness waters. But remember, you will not get the performance-enhancement effect for exercise over one hour if you do this.

If you're an avid water drinker and really like water, you'll benefit just as much from water as you will from using a glucose-electrolyte solution—unless you're exercising an hour or more. But if you don't like water, or

Table 5.3 Fluid Replacement for Athletes—A Summary of Practical Applications from the NATA Position Statement

Fluid Guidelines		
Before exercise	**During exercise**	**After exercise**
2–3 h before, drink 17–20 oz. of water or a sport drink	• Athletes benefit from drinking fluid with carbohydrate in many situations. • If exercise lasts more than 45 min or is intense, fluid with carbohydrate (sport drink) should be provided during the session. • A 6%–8% carbohydrate solution maintains optimal carbohydrate metabolism. • During events when a high rate of fluid intake is necessary to sustain hydration, carbohydrate composition should be kept low (less than 7%) to optimize fluid delivery. • Fluids with salt (sodium chloride) are beneficial to increasing thirst and voluntary fluid intake, as well as offsetting losses. • Cool beverages at temperatures of 10°–15° C (50°–59° F) are recommended.	Within 2 h, drink enough to replace any weight loss from exercise: approximately 20 oz. of water or sport drink per pound of weight loss.
10–20 min before, drink 7–10 oz. of water or a sport drink.	Every 10–20 min, drink 7–10 oz. of water or a sport drink. Athletes should be encouraged to drink beyond their thirst.	Within 6 h, drink an additional 25%–50% more than weight loss from exercise.

tend to avoid it during exercise, try a filtered water or electrolyzed water, which have a better taste. Or try a glucose-electrolyte solution that contains less than 8 percent carbohydrate and some sodium. Another idea is to put some powdered sport drink mix into your water, although the powdered mixes sometimes don't taste as good as their premixed counterparts. At the least, if a glucose-electrolyte solution encourages you to drink more, it has done its job.

Is Juice a Good Sport Drink?

Juices are a source of fluids. Orange juice, for example, is nearly 90 percent water and full of vitamins and minerals. Although juices count as part of your fluid requirement, you'll feel at your best if you base your fluid plan on at least 5 cups of water daily and use juice to help you attain your minimum 8 to 12 cups of total fluids daily.

There are some cautions to consider regarding juice as a fluid in your training diet. In recent years, there has been a lot of hype surrounding the health benefits of drinking fruit and vegetable juices. The makers of commercial juicing machines claim fresh juices are a panacea for all kinds of ills, from digestive upsets to cancer. But is it better to drink your five servings of fruits and veggies every day than eat them? No way!

In most juices, the pulp has been removed from the fruit or vegetables to make the juice. That means all-important fiber has been subtracted too, because the pulp is where you find the fiber.

Granted, some juice machines boast that their process keeps the pulp in the juice to retain the important fibers and concentrate the nutrients. But these products usually make a juice so thick that it must be diluted before you drink it, as with any concentrated fruit juice. Once you water it down, it's nutritionally the same as the other types of extracted juices, but with a little more fiber.

Freshly squeezed juice is often touted as a better source of nutrients than commercial juices. But commercially prepared juices that are frozen and refrigerated properly are only slightly lower in nutrients than fresh juice. In fact, if you don't buy fresh produce, don't store it properly at home, and don't drink your freshly squeezed juice immediately, your homemade juice could be lower in nutrients than a well-done commercially frozen or refrigerated brand.

Whether they are cooked, squeezed, dried, or raw, fruits and vegetables need to be a big part of your diet. If using a juice machine is one way of getting more fruits and vegetables and is enjoyable for you, go for it. But remember the drawbacks, and don't use juice as your only source of fruits and veggies.

If you want to drink juice to rehydrate your body, dilute it with water by at least twofold. A cup of orange or apple juice plus a cup of water will provide a 6 to 8 percent carb solution, similar to a sport drink formulation. Don't use this combination during exercise, however, because of its fructose content. The body doesn't use fructose as well as the combination of sugars in a regular sport drink. In addition, some people are fructose sensitive and may experience intestinal cramping after drinking juice. As I noted earlier, juice may interfere with fluid absorption if consumed during exercise.

Instead, drink your juice/water drink as part of your fluids an hour or more after exercise. The addition of water will speed the emptying of the fluid from your stomach and thus rehydrate your body more rapidly. And the carbohydrate will help replenish glycogen.

Alcohol: A Danger Zone for Strength Trainers

It has been a long time since any client has asked me whether drinking beer is a good way to replenish fluids and carbs. But clients frequently ask whether alcohol will hurt their exercise performance. And even more frequently, they want to know whether drinking a little bit of alcohol may actually be heart healthy. Thanks to an ever-growing body of scientific research and knowledge, here are some answers to those questions, and more.

What's in Alcohol?

Alcohol is a carbohydrate, but it's not first converted to glucose as other carbohydrates are. Instead, it is converted into fatty acids and thus more likely to be stored as body fat. So if you drink and train, alcohol puts fat metabolism on hold. It's not your friend if you're trying to stay lean.

Pure alcohol supplies 7 calories per gram and nothing else. In practical terms, a shot (1.5 ounces) of 90-proof gin contains 110 calories, and 100-proof gin contains 124 calories. Beer has a little more to offer, but not much. On the average, a 12-ounce can of beer contains 146 calories, 13 grams of carbohydrate, traces of several B-complex vitamins, and, depending on the brand, varying amounts of minerals. Light beer and nonalcoholic beer are lower in calories and sometimes carbohydrates. All table wines have similar caloric content. A 3½-ounce serving of table wine contains about 72 calories, 1 gram of carbohydrate, and very small amounts of several vitamins and minerals. Sweet or dessert wines are higher in calories, containing 90 calories per 2-ounce serving.

What Are Alcohol's Side Effects?

Today, alcohol is the most abused drug in the United States. Ten percent of users are addicted, and 10 to 20 percent are abusers or problem drinkers. Alcohol is a central nervous system depressant. Compared with any other commonly used substance, alcohol has one of the lowest effective dose/lethal dose ratios. In other words, there's a very small difference in the amount of alcohol that will get you drunk and the amount that will kill you. But the reason that more people don't die from alcohol intoxication is that the stomach is very alcohol sensitive and rejects it by vomiting.

Acute alcohol intoxication results in tremor, anxiety and irritability, nausea and vomiting, decreased mental function, vertigo, coma, and death. In large amounts, alcohol causes the loss of many nutrients from the body, including thiamin, vitamin B6, and calcium. Furthermore, chronic alcohol abuse has negative side effects on every organ in the body, particularly the liver, heart, brain, and muscle and can thus lead to cancer and diseases of the liver, pancreas, and nervous system.

Also, don't drink alcohol in any form if you're pregnant. It can cause birth defects.

Drinking alcohol in large amounts can also lead to accidents, as well as social, psychological, and emotional problems.

How Does Alcohol Affect Exercise Performance?

Because alcohol depresses the central nervous system, it impairs balance and coordination and decreases exercise performance. Strength and power, muscle endurance, and aerobic endurance are all zapped with alcohol use. Alcohol also dehydrates the body considerably.

Is Alcohol Really Heart Healthy?

Research has found that daily consumption of one drink per day can do your heart good by positively affecting the levels of good cholesterol (HDL) in your blood. The higher your HDL levels, the lower your risk of heart disease.

However, excessive alcohol intake increases your chance of developing heart disease. More than two drinks a day can raise your blood pressure and contribute to high triglycerides, a risk factor for heart disease. Drinking large amounts of alcohol on a habitual basis can also cause heart failure and lead to stroke.

Alcohol consumption contributes to obesity, another major risk factor in the development of heart disease. Extra pounds are hard on your heart. The higher your weight climbs, the greater your risk. Being overweight also raises blood pressure and cholesterol, which are risk factors themselves.

Is a Drink a Day Good Prevention?

The risks of alcohol outweigh its positives. If you drink alcoholic beverages, do so in moderation, with meals, and when consumption does not put you or others in harm's way. Moderation is defined as no more than one drink per day for women and no more than two drinks per day for men. One drink is 12 ounces of regular beer, 5 ounces of wine, and 1.5 ounces of 80-proof distilled liquor.

Remember: Exercising, quitting smoking, and lowering your blood cholesterol through a healthy diet are better ways to prevent heart disease without any added risks.

Sport Nutrition Fact vs. Fiction: Soft Drinks Will Rehydrate the Body

If given the option, many people would choose a soft drink over water to rehydrate themselves following workouts. And who can blame them? Soft drinks taste good, seem to quench thirst, and are generally refreshing.

But soft drinks are among the worst choices for rehydration. Soft drinks are laced with huge amounts of sugar—roughly the equivalent of 10 teaspoons per can. Because of their sugar content, soft drinks are absorbed less rapidly than pure water. The sugar in them keeps the fluid in your stomach longer, so less water is available to your body. Rather than rehydrating your system, soft drinks can make you feel even thirstier. Also, the sugar can trigger a sharp spike in insulin, followed by fast drop in blood sugar. This reaction can leave you feeling tired and weak. Also, the sugar in soft drinks is high-fructose corn syrup, which does not replenish glycogen as rapidly as other forms of carbohydrate. Fructose can cause cramps in people who are sensitive to it.

What about no-sugar soft drinks? These beverages contain artificial sweeteners, which remain controversial. All soft drinks are, of course, carbonated, and carbonation produces gas. Who wants a gassy stomach, especially during a workout?

Diluting a soft drink isn't a good option either. Even in a diluted concentration, a soft drink has nothing beneficial to offer. As far as rehydration is concerned, no fluids—including artificially sweetened soft drinks—have yet been proven to do a better job than plain old water or a good glucose-electrolyte solution.

Part II

Supplements

Now that you've built your nutrition foundation and have your diet down to a science, it's time to consider supplements. Of course, supplements are just that—extras that you can add to your well-designed food plan. In addition, supplements play an important role as convenience tools in our very busy lives. For example:

- Perhaps there are critical foods that you can't eat or don't like. Supplements can fill in the nutritional gaps left by excluding such foods.
- Or, perhaps your schedule is so busy that you don't have time to prepare food immediately after exercise when your body really needs it for muscle growth. Supplements to the rescue.
- And maybe you want to gain just a little competitive edge. There are a few supplements that work powerfully to give you that edge.

This section reviews the most popular supplements used by strength training athletes. I evaluate the usefulness of these supplements, based on the most current scientific research, as well as the potential that they may have for being harmful. Use my rating system to decide for yourself what's worth it, what's wasting your time, or what is potentially harmful.

6 Vitamins and Minerals for Strength Trainers

Want to get ripped, shredded, striated, and vascular? Every supplement company says they've got the product for you. You have probably stood in the supplement aisle for hours, reading ingredients and wondering which ones really work. Ads for supplements certainly promise dramatic results.

Scientists have only begun to research the nutritional requirements of muscle building. The research is promising, but the whole story on what works and what doesn't is not in yet.

Among the many pills and potions on store shelves are vitamins and minerals. Quite possibly, you may need extra amounts of both. Research shows that most Americans fall short of the requirements for many key nutrients, including vitamins C, E, B12, folic acid, zinc, and magnesium, which is why a growing number of Americans are turning to supplements. A survey by the Centers for Disease Control and Prevention shows that more than 60 percent of the general population takes supplements daily.

Hard workouts do increase your nutritional needs, as does dieting. That's why you may want to add certain vitamins and minerals to your nutritional arsenal. Keep in mind, though, vitamin and mineral supplements should not replace food. Your body can get almost all the nutrients it needs from a balanced diet. What's more, your body absorbs nutrients best from food.

However, if you would like the insurance, a good move is to take a daily antioxidant multiple containing 100 percent of the daily values for vitamins and minerals. These formulations help you "cover your nutritional bases" and contain nutrients that have special value to strength trainers.

The Daily Reference Intake and What It Means

A new way of rating the amounts of the nutrients we need for good health is termed the daily reference intake, or DRI. It expands on and includes the familiar "RDA." Whereas the RDAs target nutrient deficiencies, the DRIs aim to prevent chronic diseases.

Applied to vitamins, minerals, and proteins taken by men and women in specific age groups, the DRI contains three different rating sets appropriate for discussion here: the RDAs; a set of values that help us maintain our health; a set of values called tolerable upper intake levels, which establish ceilings to help us avoid taking too much of a nutrient; and adequate intakes, or AIs, an estimate of average intake that seems healthy and won't harm health. For the purposes of this book, I will place all nutrient recommendations under the heading of DRIs.

The Antioxidants

There's a lot of excitement in strength sports about antioxidants—beta-carotene, vitamin C, vitamin E, and the minerals selenium, copper, zinc, and manganese. Antioxidants help fight "free radicals," chemicals produced naturally by the body that cause irreversible damage (oxidation) to cells. Free radical damage can leave your body vulnerable to advanced aging, cancer, cardiovascular disease, and degenerative diseases such as arthritis.

Certain environmental factors such as cigarette smoke, exhaust fumes, radiation, excessive sunlight, certain drugs, and stress can increase free radicals. And, ironically, so can the healthy habit of exercise.

No one knows for sure how or why exercise does this, but there are some theories. One has to do with respiration. During respiration, cells pick off electrons from sugars and add them to oxygen to generate energy. As these reactions take place, electrons sometimes get off course and collide with other molecules, creating free radicals. Exercise increases respiration, and this produces more free radicals.

Body temperature, which tends to rise during exercise, may also be a factor in generating free radicals. A third possibility is the increase in "catecholamine" production during exercise. Catecholamines are hormones released in response to muscular effort. They increase heart rate, let more blood get to muscles, and provide the muscles with fuel, among other functions.

Another source of free radical production is the damage done to the muscle cell membrane after intense exercise, especially "eccentric" exercise, such as putting down a heavy weight or running downhill. In a domino-like series of chemical reactions, free radicals hook up with fatty acids in cell membranes to form substances called "peroxides." Peroxides attack cell membranes, setting off a chain reaction that creates many more free radicals. Technically, this process is known as "lipid peroxidation" and can lead to muscle soreness. The point is, several complex reactions occur with exercise, and each one may accelerate free radical production.

Beta-Carotene

Beta-carotene is a member of a group of substances known as carotenoids. There are hundreds of carotenoids in nature, found mostly in orange and yellow fruits and vegetables and dark green vegetables.

Once ingested, beta-carotene is converted to vitamin A in the body on an as-needed basis. As an antioxidant, beta-carotene can destroy free radicals after they're formed. In fact, it has been shown to reduce muscle soreness by minimizing exercise-induced lipid peroxidation. With less soreness, you may be able to work out more times a week.

Vitamin C

Also known as ascorbic acid, vitamin C is a nutrient that can be synthesized by many animals, but not by humans. It's an essential component of our diets and functions primarily in the formation of connective tissues such as collagen. Vitamin C is also involved in immunity, wound healing, and allergic responses. As an antioxidant, vitamin C keeps free radicals from destroying the outermost layers of cells.

If you work out regularly or train for athletic competition, you know that a cold or respiratory infection can sideline you pretty fast. Vitamin C to the rescue. Researchers have found that supplementing with 500 milligrams daily of vitamin C appears to cut the risk of upper respiratory tract infections. This benefit may be due to vitamin C's antioxidant effect or to its overall immune-boosting capability.

Vitamin E and Exercise

By far the most promising studies on antioxidants and exercise have centered on vitamin E. Vitamin E resides in muscle cell membranes. Part of its job is to scavenge the free radicals produced by exercise, saving the tissues from damage. Researchers have put vitamin E's power to the test and discovered that it does work.

In a study conducted by Dr. William Evans of Penn State, subjects age 55 and older were given either a daily 800-milligram vitamin E supplement or a placebo. For exercise, they walked or ran downhill. The clues to whether vitamin E protected their muscles against damage were found in the production of two key substances—neutrophils (a special type of white blood cell) and creatine kinase (an enzyme involved in energizing muscle cells). When production of these substances is down, little muscle repair takes place. Free radicals multiply, inflicting their damage for several days after exercise. Conversely, when production is up, muscles are on the mend, and free radicals are kept in check.

Here's what happened: The vitamin E-supplemented group showed much higher production of neutrophils and creatine kinase than the placebo group did. What this indicates is that vitamin E protected against muscle damage and its aftermath of free radical production.

The study also tested subjects who were 30 years old or younger. They responded similarly, regardless of whether they were given the vitamin E supplement or placebo. Dr. Evans concluded that as people age, their vitamin E levels decrease—but their need for them increases—and that supplements can help. Although the study used 800 International Units of vitamin E a day, Dr. Evans believes that 400 International Units per day would result in similar benefits.

There's more good news about vitamin E: It appears to prevent the destruction of oxygen-carrying red blood cells. That means your muscles benefit from improved or sustained oxygen delivery during exercise. What's more, vitamin E may improve exercise performance at high altitudes.

If you supplement with vitamin E, choose a natural form of the nutrient over a synthetic version. Labeled as d-alpha tocopherol, natural vitamin E is isolated from soybean, sunflower, corn, peanut, grapeseed, and cottonseed oils. Synthetic vitamin E, or dl-alpha tocopherol, is processed from substances found in petrochemicals. A recent review of 30 published studies on vitamin E concluded that the natural version is absorbed better by the body than the synthetic form.

Other Antioxidants and Exercise

An antioxidant cocktail may help too, especially in preventing oxidative stress, a condition in which free radicals outnumber antioxidants, according to a study from the Washington University School of Medicine in St. Louis. For one month, unexercised medical students took high doses of antioxidants daily: 1,000 International Units of vitamin E, 1,250 milligrams of vitamin C, and 37.5 milligrams of beta-carotene. The doses were divided into five capsules a day. Some of the group took placebos.

Before supplementation, the students ran at a moderate pace on a treadmill for about 40 minutes, followed by 5 minutes of high-intensity running to exhaustion. The same exercise bout was repeated after supplementation.

The researchers discovered that oxidative stress caused by exercise was high before supplementation. In other words, there was a lot of tissue damage going on. With antioxidants, there was still some oxidative stress caused by exercise, but it wasn't as great. The researchers concluded that taking antioxidants offered protection against tissue damage.

Most of the research in antioxidant supplementation has been done with endurance athletes. But what about strength trainers? If you work out consistently, you are tearing down a lot of tissue. Not only that, muscles generate free radicals during and after exercise. For these reasons, there may be some benefit for strength trainers to take antioxidant supplements. They can help you protect yourself from the potential onslaught of free radicals.

Most of the people I have worked with eat diets that are deficient in vitamin E and other antioxidants. One of the reasons is that active, health-conscious people typically go on diets that are low in fat, but dietary fat from vegetable oils, nuts, and seeds is one of the best sources of vitamin E. What's more, some active people, particularly strength trainers, are known to limit their intake of fruit. Misinformed, they think the fructose it contains will turn up as body fat on their physiques. But by cutting out fruits, they cut out foods that are loaded with the antioxidants beta-carotene and vitamin C.

Antioxidant Supplements and Performance

If you take antioxidants, will you be able to work out longer and harder? Whether antioxidant supplementation really improves performance hasn't been adequately nailed down by research. But if you are undernourished—that is, you have a vitamin deficiency—you will definitely feel better and perform better by correcting that deficiency. But if your diet is already high in antioxidants, supplementing with extra antioxidants may not make much of a difference in your performance.

How Much?

The amounts of vitamin C and beta-carotene that seem to be protective are easily obtained from food. To get enough of these two vitamins, follow the U.S. Department of Agriculture's Food Guide Pyramid recommendations. Strive to eat at least three to five servings of vegetables and two to four servings of fruits every day.

As for vitamin E, a supplement of 200 to 400 International Units per day is adequate. To boost your intake of the other antioxidants, be sure your daily vitamin-mineral supplement contains antioxidants.

The functions of the key antioxidants are summarized in table 6.1.

The B-Complex Vitamins

In this family of nutrients, there are eight major B-complex vitamins—thiamin, riboflavin, niacin, vitamin B12, folic acid, pyridoxine, pantothenic acid, and biotin—that work in accord to ensure proper digestion, muscle contraction, and energy production. Although these nutrients do not enhance performance, training and diet do alter the body's requirement for some of them.

Thiamin

Thiamin helps release energy from carbohydrates. The amount of carbs and calories in your diet determines your dietary requirement for this vitamin. By eating a well-balanced, high-carbohydrate diet, you generally get all the thiamin you need. The best food sources of thiamin are unrefined cereals, brewer's yeast, legumes, seeds, and nuts.

There is one possible exception, however. Are you supplementing with a carbohydrate supplement to increase calories? If so, you may need extra thiamin, particularly if your carb formula contains no thiamin. For every 1,000 calories of carbs you consume from a formula, you need to add 0.5 milligrams of thiamin to your diet.

Table 6.1 Key Antioxidants

VITAMINS	
Beta-Carotene	
Exercise-related function	May reduce free radical production as a result of exercise and protect against exercise-induced tissue damage; complements the antioxidant function of vitamin E.
Best food sources	Carrots, sweet potatoes, spinach, cantaloupe, broccoli, any dark green leafy vegetable, and orange vegetables and fruits.
Side effects and toxicity	None known because the body carefully controls its conversion to vitamin A. Daily intakes of 20,000 IU from either food or supplements over several months may cause skin yellowing. This disappears when the dosage is reduced.
DRIs for adults	No established limits. 2,500 IU daily from supplements is safe. You can get the same amount from a large carrot.
Vitamin C	
Exercise-related function	Maintains normal connective tissue; enhances iron absorption; may reduce free radical damage as a result of exercise and protect against exercise-induced tissue damage.
Best food sources	Citrus fruits and juices, green peppers, raw cabbage, kiwi fruit, cantaloupe, and green leafy vegetables.
Side effects and toxicity	The body adapts to high dosages. Dosages higher than 250 mg daily may harm immunity. Dosages between 5,000 mg and 15,000 mg daily may cause burning urination or diarrhea.
DRIs for adults	Women, 75 mg; pregnant women, 85 mg; lactating women, 120 mg; men, 90 mg. Also, 110 milligrams for female smokers; and 130 milligrams for male smokers.
***UL for adults**	2,000 mg.
Vitamin E	
Exercise-related function	Involved in cellular respiration, assists in the formation of red blood cells, scavenges free radicals, protects against exercise-induced tissue damage.

(continued)

Table 6.1 Continued

VITAMINS (continued)	
Vitamin E (continued)	
Best food sources	Nuts, seeds, raw wheat germ, polyunsaturated vegetable oils, and fish liver oils.
Side effects and toxicity	None known.
DRIs for adults	15 mg; lactating women, 19 mg.
UL for adults	1,000 mg.
MINERALS	
Selenium	
Exercise-related function	Interacts with vitamin E in normal growth and metabolism; preserves the elasticity of the skin; produces glutathione peroxidase, an important protective enzyme.
Best food sources	Cereal bran, Brazil nuts, whole grain cereals, egg yolk, milk, chicken, seafood, broccoli, garlic, and onions.
Side effects and toxicity	5 mg a day from food has resulted in hair loss and fingernail changes. Higher daily dosages are linked to intestinal problems, fatigue, and irritability.
DRIs for adults	Women, 55 mcg; pregnant women, 60 mcg; lactating women, 70 mcg; men, 55 mcg.
UL for adults	400 mcg.
Copper	
Exercise-related function	Assists in the formation of hemoglobin and red blood cells by aiding in iron absorption; required for energy metabolism; involved with superoxide dismutase, a key protective antioxidant enzyme.
Best food sources	Whole grains, shellfish, eggs, almonds, green leafy vegetables, and beans.
Side effects and toxicity	Toxicity is rare.
DRIs for adults	Women and men, 900 mcg; pregnant women, 1,000 mcg; lactating women, 1,300 mcg.

Copper *(continued)*	
UL for adults	10,000 mcg.
Zinc	
Exercise-related function	Involved in energy metabolism and immunity.
Best food sources	Animal proteins, oysters, mushrooms, whole grains, and brewer's yeast.
Side effects and toxicity	Dosages higher than 20 mg a day may interfere with copper absorption, reduce HDL cholesterol, and impair the immune system.
DRIs for adults	Women, 8 mg; men, 11 mg; pregnant women, 11 mg; lactating women, 12 mg.
UL for adults	40 mg.
Manganese	
Exercise-related function	Involved in metabolism; involved with superoxide dismutase, a key protective antioxidant enzyme.
Best food sources	Whole grains, egg yolks, dried peas and beans, and green leafy vegetables.
Side effects and toxicity	Large dosages can cause vomiting and intestinal problems.
DRIs for adults	Women, 1.8 mg; pregnant women, 2.0 mg; lactating women, 2.6 mg; men, 2.3 mg.
UL for adults	11 mg.

*UL refers to tolerable upper intake levels, which have been established for vitamins and minerals. These levels represent the maximum intake of a nutrient that is likely to pose no health risks.

Dieting and erratic eating patterns can leave some nutritional gaps, too. To be on the safe side, be sure to take a daily multiple vitamin that contains 100 percent of the DRI for thiamin or up to 1.2 milligrams of the nutrient.

Riboflavin

Riboflavin also helps release energy from foods. As with thiamin, your dietary requirement of riboflavin is linked to your caloric intake. As a strength trainer, you need to consume at least 0.6 milligrams of riboflavin for every 1,000 calories of carbs in your diet.

Some athletes may need even more. Riboflavin is easily lost from the body, particularly in sweat. In a study of older women (ages 50 to 67), researchers at Cornell University discovered that exercise increases the body's requirement for riboflavin. But increasing riboflavin intake did not improve performance. An earlier study at Cornell found that very active women required about 1.2 milligrams of riboflavin a day.

Foods rich in riboflavin include dairy products, poultry, fish, grains, and enriched and fortified cereals. A daily multiple containing 100 percent of the DRI or up to 1.3 milligrams of riboflavin will help prevent a shortfall.

Niacin

Like the previously mentioned B-complex vitamins, niacin is involved in releasing energy from foods. The amount you need each day is linked to your caloric intake. For every 1,000 calories you eat daily, you need 6.6 milligrams of niacin, or 13 milligrams for every 2,000 calories. If you are using a carb formula that contains no niacin, make sure you take 6.6 milligrams of niacin for every 1,000 calories that you supplement. The best food sources of niacin are lean meats, poultry, fish, and wheat germ. Taking your multiple vitamin every day will help you guard against deficiencies.

Vitamin B12

Vital to healthy blood and a normal nervous system, vitamin B12 is the only vitamin found primarily in animal products. It works in partnership with folic acid to form red blood cells in the bone marrow.

If you are a vegetarian who eats no animal foods, be sure to get enough vitamin B12. Fermented and cultured foods such as tempeh and miso contain some B12, as do vegetarian foods fortified with the nutrient. The safest approach is to supplement with a multiple vitamin containing 3 to 10 micrograms of vitamin B12.

If you are over 50 years old, your ability to absorb vitamin B12 from food may be limited. The Institute of Medicine recommends that you consume foods fortified with B12 or take a vitamin B12 supplement.

Folic Acid

Folic acid is the vitamin that, with B12, helps produce red blood cells in the bone marrow. Found in green leafy vegetables, legumes, and whole grains, it also helps reproducing cells synthesize proteins and nucleic acids.

Folic acid first attracted attention for its role in pregnancy. During pregnancy, folic acid helps create red blood cells for the increased blood volume required by the mother, fetus, and placenta. Because of folic acid's role in the production of genetic material and red blood cells, a deficiency can have far-reaching consequences for fetal development. If the fetus is deprived of folic acid, birth defects can result. So important is folic acid intake to women in their childbearing years that foods are now being fortified with it.

There is renewed excitement over folic acid because of its protective role against heart disease and cancer. The vitamin reduces homocysteine, a proteinlike substance, in the tissues and blood. High homocysteine levels have been linked to heart disease. Scientists predict that as many as 50,000 premature deaths a year from heart disease can be prevented if we eat more folic acid.

Recent scientific experiments have revealed that folic acid deficiencies cause DNA damage resembling the DNA damage in cancer cells. This finding has led scientists to suggest that cancer could be initiated by DNA damage caused by a deficiency in this B-complex vitamin. Other studies show that folic acid suppresses cell growth in colorectal cancer. It also prevents the formation of precancerous lesions that could lead to cervical cancer, a discovery that may explain why women who don't eat many vegetables and fruits (good sources of folic acid) have high rates of this form of cancer.

Stress, disease, and alcohol consumption all increase your need for folic acid. You should make sure that you're getting 400 micrograms a day of this vitamin, a level that is found in most multiple vitamins.

Pyridoxine

Pyridoxine, also known as vitamin B6, is required for the metabolism of protein. It's also vital in the formation of red blood cells and the healthy functioning of the brain. The best food sources of pyridoxine are protein foods such as chicken, fish, and eggs. Other good sources are brown rice, soybeans, oats, and whole wheat.

Researchers in Finland found that exercise alters pyridoxine requirements somewhat. They learned this by testing the blood levels of various nutrients in a group of young female university students who followed a 24-week exercise program.

Ever feel anxious before an athletic competition? If so, try supplementing with a cocktail of pyridoxine, thiamin, and vitamin B12. By increasing levels of serotonin—a mood-elevating chemical in the brain—this trio has been found to reduce anxiety and thus improve competitive performance.

The DRI for pyridoxine in women aged 19 to 50 is 1.3 milligrams; for women aged 51 and older, 1.5 milligrams; for pregnant women, 1.9 milligrams; for lactating women, 2.0 milligrams; for men aged 19 to 50, 1.3 milligrams; and for men aged 51 and older, 1.7 milligrams.

If you're wondering whether your own requirement for pyridoxine falls within safe bounds, rest assured that it probably does. A training diet that contains moderate amounts of protein will give you all the pyridoxine you need. In other words, there's no need to supplement. Besides, large doses (in excess of 50 milligrams a day) can cause nerve damage.

Pantothenic Acid

Pantothenic acid participates in the release of energy from carbohydrates, fats, and protein. Because this vitamin is so widely distributed in foods (particularly meats, whole grains, and legumes), it is rare to find a deficiency without a drop in other B-complex vitamins. They all work as a team.

The safe range of intake for pantothenic acid is 4 to 7 milligrams a day. Exercise does affect pantothenic acid metabolism, but only to a very slight degree. By following my strength-training nutrition plan, you'll take in plenty of this vitamin to cover any extra needs you might have from exercise.

Biotin

Biotin is involved in fat and carbohydrate metabolism. Without it, the body can't burn fat. Biotin is also a component of various enzymes that carry out essential biochemical reactions in the body. Some good sources of biotin are egg yolks, soy flour, and cereals. Even if you don't get the 30 to 100 micrograms you need daily from food, your body can synthesize biotin from intestinal bacteria. So there's no reason to supplement with extra biotin.

Together with choline and inositol, two other B-complex vitamins, biotin is often found in lipotropic supplement formulations promoted as fat burners. But there is no credible evidence that biotin or any other supplemental nutrient burns fat.

Some research shows that biotin levels are low in active people. No one is sure why, but one explanation may have to do with exercise. Exercise causes the waste product lactic acid to build up in working muscles. Biotin is involved in the process that breaks down lactic acid. The more lactic acid that accumulates in muscles, the more biotin that is needed to break it down. But don't rush out to buy a bottle of biotin. There is no need to supplement with this vitamin, because your body can make up for any marginal deficiencies on its own.

Some strength trainers are in the habit of concocting raw egg milkshakes. Raw egg white contains the protein avidin. Avidin binds with biotin in the intestine and prevents its absorption. Eating raw eggs on a consistent basis can thus lead to a biotin deficiency. But once eggs are cooked, the avidin is destroyed, and there is no danger of blocking biotin absorption.

Choline

Present in all living cells, choline is another B-complex vitamin. It is synthesized from two amino acids, methionine and serine, with help from vitamin B12 and folic acid. Choline works together with another lipotropic, inositol, to prevent fat from building up in the liver and to shuttle fat into cells to be burned for energy.

Choline is a constituent of acetylcholine in the body. Acetylcholine is a "neurotransmitter." Neurotransmitters are chemicals that send messages from nerves to nerves and nerves to muscles. When muscles reach a fatigue point during exercise, this transmission system gets blocked. No messages are sent, and muscular work slows down or ceases temporarily.

Researchers at MIT studied runners before and after the Boston Marathon and found a 40 percent drop in their plasma choline concentrations. They don't know why this happened; however, they speculated that choline is used up during exercise to produce the neurotransmitter acetylcholine. Once choline is depleted, there's a corresponding drop in acetylcholine production. When production falls off, the ability to do muscular work falls off too. Or so the theory goes.

Some research suggests that choline supplementation (1.5 to 2 grams daily) may improve performance in athletes who do not get enough of this vitamin in their diets. Normally though, your body can easily manufacture enough choline for good health as long as you eat a balanced, nutrient-rich diet. Choline is found in egg yolks, nuts, soybeans, wheat germ, cauliflower, and spinach.

Other Vitamins

The fat-soluble vitamins A, D, and K are rarely promoted as exercise aids, most likely because they're toxic in large doses. Vitamin A, or retinol, is found primarily in animal sources such as liver, fish, liver oils, margarine, milk, butter, and eggs. Vitamin A is involved in the growth and repair of tissues, maintenance of proper vision, and resistance to infection. It also helps maintain the health of the skin and mucous membranes. Massive doses in excess of the DRI can cause nausea, vomiting, diarrhea, skin problems, and bone fragility, among other serious problems.

Vitamin D is rather unique; it is also a hormone your body can manufacture on its own when your skin is exposed to sunlight. Vitamin D also promotes strong bones and teeth and is necessary for the absorption of calcium. Milk fortified with vitamin D is one of the best dietary sources of this important nutrient. If you do not get out into the sunshine and you avoid dairy products, you might need to supplement with 100 percent of the DRI for vitamin D. Do not take high doses because megadoses can be toxic.

Vitamin K's primary function is to assist in the process of normal blood clotting. It is also required for the formation of other body proteins found in the blood, bone, and kidneys.

However, research has revealed a side to vitamin K that most people have never seen: It is vital for building healthy bones—which is why a number of calcium supplements are now being formulated with vitamin K. With a shortfall of vitamin K, bone can become weakened because of insufficient levels of osteocalcin, an important material involved in bone hardening. In one study with female athletes, vitamin K (10 milligrams daily) decreased the process of bone breakdown and increased bone formation. These improvements were measured by looking at the amount of osteocalcin (a indicator of bone formation), as well as by-products of bone breakdown, in the bloodstream and urine.

A vitamin K deficiency is extremely rare, and there's usually no need for supplementation unless recommended by your physician. The best food sources are dairy products, meats, eggs, cereals, fruits, and vegetables.

The functions of vitamins and their possible roles in exercise performance are summarized in table 6.2.

Electrolytes

The tissues in your body contain fluids both inside cells (intracellular fluid) and in the spaces between cells (extracellular fluid). Dissolved in both fluids are electrolytes, which are electrically charged minerals or ions. The electrolytes work in concert, regulating water balance on either side of the cell membranes. Electrolytes also help make muscles contract by promoting the transmission of messages across nerve cell membranes.

The two chief electrolytes are sodium and potassium. Sodium regulates fluid balance outside cells, whereas potassium regulates fluids inside cells.

Table 6.2 Vitamins

VITAMIN B-COMPLEX	
Thiamin (B1)	
Exercise-related function	Carbohydrate metabolism; maintenance of a healthy nervous system, growth, and muscle tone.
Best food sources	Brewer's yeast, wheat germ, bran, whole grains, and organ meats.
Side effects and toxicity	None known.
DRIs for adults	Women, 1.1 mg; pregnant women, 1.4 mg; lactating women, 1.4 mg; men, 1.2 mg.
Riboflavin (B2)	
Exercise-related function	Metabolism of carbohydrate, protein, and fat; cellular respiration.
Best food sources	Milk, eggs, lean meats, and broccoli.
Side effects and toxicity	None known.
DRIs for adults	Women, 1.1 mg; pregnant women, 1.4 mg; lactating women, 1.6 mg; men, 1.3 mg.
Pyridoxine (B6)	
Exercise-related function	Protein metabolism, formation of oxygen-carrying red blood cells.
Best food sources	Whole grains and meats.
Side effects and toxicity	Liver and nerve damage.
DRIs for adults	Women, ages 19–30, 1.3 mg; women, ages 31–70, 1.5 mg; pregnant women, 1.9 mg; lactating women, 2.0 mg; men, ages 19–30, 1.3 mg; men, ages 31–70, 1.7 mg.
UL for adults	100 mg.
B12	
Exercise-related function	Metabolism of carbohydrate, protein, and fat; formation of red blood cells.
Best food sources	Meats, dairy products, eggs, liver, and fish.

(continued)

Table 6.2 *(Continued)*

VITAMIN B-COMPLEX *(continued)*	
B12 *(continued)*	
Side effects and toxicity	Liver damage, allergic reactions.
DRIs for adults	Women, 2.4 mg; pregnant women, 2.6 mg; lactating women, 2.8 mg; men, 2.4 mg.
Niacin	
Exercise-related function	Cellular energy production; metabolism of carbohydrates, protein, and fat.
Best food sources	Lean meats, liver, poultry, fish, peanuts, and wheat germ.
Side effects and toxicity	Liver damage, jaundice, skin flushing and itching, nausea.
DRIs for adults	Women, 14 mg; pregnant women, 18 mg; lactating women, 17 mg; men, 16 mg.
UL for adults	35 mg.
Folic Acid	
Exercise-related function	Regulation of growth; breakdown of proteins; formation of red blood cells.
Best food sources	Green leafy vegetables and liver.
Side effects and toxicity	Gastric problems; can mask certain anemias.
DRIs for adults	Women, 400 mcg; pregnant women, 600 mcg; lactating women, 500 mcg; men, 400 mcg.
UL for adults	1,000 mcg.
Biotin	
Exercise-related function	Breakdown of fats.
Best food sources	Egg yolks and liver.
Side effects and toxicity	None known.
DRIs for adults	Women, 30 mcg; pregnant women, 30 mcg; lactating women, 35 mcg; men, 30 mcg.

Choline	
Exercise-related function	May improve fatigue and performance in aerobic sports.
Best food sources	Egg yolks, nuts, soybeans, wheat germ, cauliflower, and spinach.
Side effects and toxicity	None known.
DRIs for adults	Women, 425 mg; pregnant women, 450 mg; lactating women, 550 mg; men, 550 mg.
UL for adults	3,500 mg.
Pantothenic Acid	
Exercise-related function	Cellular energy production; fatty acid oxidation.
Best food sources	Found widely in foods.
Side effects and toxicity	None known.
DRIs for adults	Women, 5 mg; pregnant women, 6 mg; lactating women, 7 mg; men, 5 mg.
OTHER VITAMINS	
Vitamin A	
Exercise-related function	Growth and repair; building of body structures.
Best food sources	Liver, egg yolks, and whole milk; orange and yellow vegetables.
Side effects and toxicity	Digestive system upset; damage to bones and certain organs.
DRIs for adults	Women, 700 mcg; pregnant women, 770 mcg; lactating women, 1,300 mcg; men, 900 mcg.
Vitamin D	
Exercise-related function	Normal bone growth and development.

(continued)

Table 6.2 (Continued)

OTHER VITAMINS (continued)	
Vitamin D (continued)	
Best food sources	Sunlight, fortified dairy products, and fish oils.
Side effects and toxicity	Nausea, vomiting, hardening of soft tissues, kidney damage.
DRIs for adults	Women, ages 19–50, 5 mcg; women, ages 51–70, 10 mcg; women, 70+, 15 mcg; pregnant women, 5 mcg; lactating women, 5 mcg; men, ages 19–50, 5 mcg; men, ages 51–70, 10 mcg; men, 70+, 15 mcg.
UL for adults	50 mcg.
Vitamin K	
Exercise-related function	Involved in glycogen formation, blood clotting, and bone formation.
Best food sources	Vegetables, milk, and yogurt.
Side effects and toxicity	Allergic reactions, breakdown of red blood cells.
DRIs for adults	Women, 90 mcg; men, 120 mcg.

Sodium in the diet is obtained mostly from salt and processed foods. On average, Americans eat two to three teaspoons of salt every day—far too much for good health. A healthier sodium target is 500 milligrams (the minimum requirement) to 2,400 milligrams per day, or no more than one and one-quarter teaspoons of table salt each day.

Although some sodium can be lost from sweat during exercise, you don't have to worry about replacing it with supplementation. Your usual diet contains enough sodium to replace what was lost. What's more, the body does a good job of conserving sodium on its own.

Severe sodium depletion, however, can occur during ultraendurance events such as triathlons that last more than four hours. Consuming one half to three quarters of a cup of a sport drink every 10 to 20 minutes, along with adding salty foods to the diet, is enough to replenish an endurance athlete's need for sodium. Salt tablets, on the other hand, should never be a consideration. They tend to draw water out of your cells and into your gut, making the situation worse, not better.

Potassium works inside cells to regulate fluid balance. Potassium is also involved in maintaining a regular heartbeat, helping muscles contract, regulating blood pressure, and transferring nutrients to cells.

In contrast to sodium, potassium is not as well conserved by the body. That being the case, be sure to eat plenty of potassium-rich foods, such as bananas, oranges, and potatoes. You need between 1,600 and 2,000 milligrams of potassium a day, which can be easily obtained from a diet plentiful in fruits and vegetables.

To get cut, some competitive bodybuilders use diuretics, drugs that increase the formation and excretion of urine in the body. This is a dangerous practice, because diuretics can flush potassium and other electrolytes from the body. Life-threatening mineral imbalances can occur, and some professional bodybuilders have died during competition as a result of diuretic abuse. I can see no rational reason for taking diuretics for competitive purposes. The potential damage just isn't worth it.

The sodium lost through sweat during a workout is easily replaced in the diet.

Food First

Always count on food first. Food is your body's best source of nutrients. Take the time to plan a healthy, well-balanced diet full of fruits, vegetables, grains, beans, lean meats, and nonfat dairy foods, and use the diet-planning guidelines in chapter 10. Along with dedicated training, a good diet is your best ticket to building a better body.

Soda Loading

A type of sodium—sodium bicarbonate (better known as baking soda)—is used by athletes to delay muscular fatigue. The practice is called "soda loading," and it neutralizes levels of lactic acid in the blood. Lactic acid accumulation makes muscles "burn" and eventually brings them to a point of fatigue. The ability of soda loading to neutralize lactic acid reduces muscle pain and can potentially prolong your workouts. The recommended dose is 300 milligrams per kilogram of body weight, taken with several glasses of water, about one to two hours before exercise. Generally, soda loading is safe but may cause nausea, bloating, and stomach cramps.

Phosphate Loading

For a long time, athletes have experimented with phosphate loading as a way to extend performance. Phosphate is a type of salt made from phosphorus, the second most abundant mineral in the body. The supplement is usually taken in large doses several times daily a few days before competition. By some indications, phosphate loading increases the oxygen-carrying capacity of the blood and makes more glucose available to the working muscles—two pluses if you're a competitive athlete. The recommended dosage is four grams a day.

But be forewarned: Phosphate loading can cause vomiting, upset the body's electrolyte balance, and lead to other untoward reactions.

Phosphates are constituents of some natural weight-loss supplements too. A Polish study found that phosphate supplementation may increase RMR in women on a 1,000-calorie-a-day diet.

Other Vital Minerals

Several other minerals could be low in your diet, particularly if you're a competitor. These vital minerals are discussed in the following, and their functions are summarized in table 6.3.

Calcium

Ninety-nine percent of the calcium in your body is stored in your skeleton and teeth. The other one percent is found in blood and soft tissues.

Although calcium does not have any effect on exercise performance, it is absolutely essential for good health. Calcium is responsible for building healthy bones, conducting nerve impulses, helping muscles contract, and moving nutrients into and out of cells. Exercise helps your body better absorb calcium.

The chief sources of calcium in the diet are milk and other dairy products. But almost every strength trainer and bodybuilder I have ever counseled has avoided all dairy products like the plague during precompetition dieting. These athletes believe that these foods are high in sodium. I say, nonsense. One cup of nonfat milk contains 126 milligrams of sodium and 302 milligrams of calcium. Two egg whites, a popular food in the diet of strength trainers and bodybuilders, contain 212 milligrams of sodium and only 12 milligrams of calcium. Sodium hardly seems to be a problem here, and there is no better low-fat source of calcium than nonfat milk.

So are milk and dairy products really your enemy?

No. You absolutely need these foods in your diet to maintain good health. With plenty of high-calcium foods, your diet provides the calcium needed to maintain healthy blood calcium levels. If you don't have enough in your diet, your body will draw calcium from bones to maintain blood calcium levels. As more and more calcium is removed from bones, they become brittle and break. The most susceptible areas are the spine, the hip, and the wrist. An exit of calcium from the bones can lead to the bone-weakening disease of osteoporosis.

Female bodybuilders are at particular risk of losing bone calcium. In a study I conducted at the 1990 National Physique Committee (NPC) USA Championships in Raleigh, North Carolina, female bodybuilders recorded their diets, were weighed and fat measured, and answered questions about their training, nutrition, and health.

None of the women ate or drank any milk products for at least three months before competition, and most of them never used dairy products at all. Nor did any of these women take calcium supplements.

Table 6.3 Major Minerals and Trace Minerals

MAJOR	
Calcium	
Exercise-related function	A constituent of body structures; plays a part in muscle growth, muscle contraction, and nerve transmission.
Best food sources	Dairy products and green leafy vegetables.
Side effects and toxicity	Excessive calcification of some tissues; constipation; mineral absorption problems.
DRIs for adults	Women, ages 19–50, 1,000 mg; women, ages 51–70+, 1,200 mg; pregnant women, 1,000 mg; lactating women, 1,000 mg; men, ages 19–50, 1,000 mg; men, ages 51–70+, 1,200 mg.
UL for adults	2,500 mg.
Phosphorus	
Exercise-related function	Metabolism of carbohydrate, protein, and fat; growth, repair, and maintenance of cells; energy production; and stimulation of muscular contractions.
Best food sources	Meats, fish, poultry, eggs, whole grains, seeds, and nuts.
Side effects and toxicity	None known.
DRIs for adults	Women, 700 mg; pregnant women, 700 mg; lactating women, 700 mg; men, 700 mg.
UL for adults	Women and men, ages 19-70, 4,000 mg; ages 70+, 3,000 mg.
Potassium	
Exercise-related function	Maintenance of normal fluid balance on either side of cell walls; normal growth; stimulation of nerve impulses for muscular contractions; assists in the conversion of glucose to glycogen; synthesis of muscle protein from amino acids.
Best food sources	Potatoes, bananas, fruits, and vegetables.

Potassium *(continued)*	
Side effects and toxicity	Heart disturbances.
DRIs for adults	No DRI; but a minimum requirement of 1,600–2,000 mg and 3,500 for active adults.
Sodium	
Exercise-related function	Maintenance of normal fluid balance on either side of cell walls; muscular contraction and nerve transmission; keeps other blood minerals soluble.
Best food sources	Found in virtually all foods.
Side effects and toxicity	Water retention and high blood pressure.
DRIs for adults	No DRI; a recommended safe minimum intake is 2,400 mg daily.
Chloride	
Exercise-related function	Helps regulate the pressure that causes fluids to flow in and out of cell membranes.
Best food sources	Table salt (sodium chloride), kelp, and rye flour.
Side effects and toxicity	None known.
DRIs for adults	No DRI; a recommended safe minimum intake is 500 mg daily.
Magnesium	
Exercise-related function	Metabolism of carbohydrates and proteins; assists in neuromuscular contractions.
Best food sources	Green vegetables, legumes, whole grains, and seafood.
Side effects and toxicity	Large amounts are toxic.
DRIs for adults	Women, ages 19–30, 310 mg; women, ages 31–70+, 320 mg; pregnant women, ages 19–30, 350 mg; pregnant women, age 31+, 360 mg; lactating women, ages 19–30, 310 mg; lactating women, age 31+, 320 mg; men, ages 19–30, 400 mg; men age 31+, 420 mg.
UL for adults	350 mg from supplements alone.

(continued)

Table 6.3 (Continued)

TRACE	
Iron	
Exercise-related function	Oxygen transport to cells for energy; formation of oxygen-carrying red blood cells.
Best food sources	Liver, oysters, lean meats, and green leafy vegetables.
Side effects and toxicity	Large amounts are toxic.
DRIs for adults	Women, ages 19-50, 18 mg; women, ages 51-70+, 8 mg; pregnant women, 27 mg; lactating women, 9 mg; men, 8 mg.
UL for adults	45 mg.
Iodine	
Exercise-related function	Energy production; growth and development; and metabolism.
Best food sources	Iodized salt, seafood, and mushrooms.
Side effects and toxicity	Thyroid enlargement.
DRIs for adults	150 mcg.
UL for adults	1,000 mcg.
Chromium	
Exercise-related function	Normal blood sugar; fat metabolism.
Best food sources	Corn oil, brewer's yeast, whole grains, and meats.
Side effects and toxicity	Liver and kidney damage.
DRIs for adults	Women, ages 19-50, 25 mcg; women, ages 51+, 20 mcg; pregnant women, 30 mcg; lactating women, 45 mcg; men, ages 19-50, 35 mcg; men ages 51+, 30 mcg.
Fluoride	
Exercise-related function	None known.
Best food sources	Fluoridated water supplies.

Fluoride *(continued)*	
Side effects and toxicity	Large amounts are toxic and can cause mottling of teeth.
DRIs for adults	Women, 3 mg; pregnant women, 3 mg; lactating women, 3 mg; men, 4 mg.
UL for adults	10 mg.
Molybdenum	
Exercise-related function	Involved in the metabolism of fats.
Best food sources	Milk, beans, breads, and cereals.
Side effects and toxicity	Diarrhea, anemia, and depressed growth rate.
DRIs for adults	45 mcg.
UL for adults	2,000 mcg.

Of these women, 81 percent reported that they did not menstruate for at least two months before a contest. The physical stress of training, the psychological stress of competition, the low-calorie diet, and the loss of body fat—these factors can all lead to a decrease in the body's production of estrogen. As in menopause, without enough estrogen, a woman stops menstruating. What's worse, no calcium can be stored in the bone when estrogen levels are low.

Of course, these women were very lean too. On average, they had 9 percent body fat. Extremely low body fat is another risk factor for loss of calcium from bones.

If your dietary practices regarding calcium mirror any of these, you must get calcium back into your diet by eating calcium-rich foods, namely, nonfat milk and dairy products.

If for some reason you cannot or will not drink milk, try nonfat yogurts. They are equally high in calcium, and often do not cause the intestinal problems that some people experience from milk. You can also obtain calcium from alternative sources if you are on a milk-free diet. Table 6.4 lists those sources.

Some people are lactose intolerant and can't digest milk. They lack sufficient lactase, the enzyme required to digest lactose, a sugar in milk that helps you absorb calcium from the intestine. If you are lactose intolerant, try taking an enzyme product such as Lactaid or DairyEase. These products replace the lactase you are missing and will digest the lactose

Table 6.4 Alternate Sources of Calcium for Milk-Free Diets

Food	Amount	Calcium (mg)	Calories
Collards, frozen, cooked*	½ c	179	31
Soy milk (fortified)	1 c	150	79
Mackerel, canned	2 oz.	137	88
Dandelion greens, raw, cooked*	½ c	74	17
Turnip greens, frozen, cooked*	½ c	125	25
Mustard greens, frozen, cooked*	½ c	76	14
Kale, frozen, cooked*	½ c	90	20
Tortillas, corn	2	80	95
Molasses, blackstrap	1 Tbsp.	176	48
Orange	1 lg.	74	87
Sockeye salmon, canned, with bone, drained	2 oz.	136	87
Sardines, canned, with bone, drained	2 med.	92	50
Boston baked beans, vegetarian, canned	½ c	64	118
Pickled herring	2 oz.	44	149
Soybeans, cooked	½ c	88	149
Broccoli, cooked	½ c	36	22
Rutabaga, cooked, mashed	½ c	58	47
Artichoke, cooked	1 med.	54	60
White beans, cooked	½ c	81	124
Almonds, blanched, whole	¼ c	94	222
Tofu	2 oz.	60	44

*Frozen, cooked vegetable greens are higher in calcium than fresh cooked greens. If you eat the fresh variety, you have to double your portion to get the same amount of calcium.

for you. Another option is Lactaid milk. Available at most supermarkets, Lactaid milk is pretreated with the lactase enzyme.

Calcium supplements may be in order, too—particularly because three of every four Americans are believed to be deficient in calcium. The best sources are calcium carbonate, calcium lactate, and calcium citrate malate.

The DRIs for calcium from food and supplements are as follows: women aged 19 to 50, 1,000 milligrams; women aged 51 to 70+, 1,200 milligrams; pregnant women, 1,000 milligrams; lactating women, 1,000 milligrams; men aged 19 to 50, 1,000 milligrams; and men aged 51 to 70+, 1,200 milligrams.

For the prevention and treatment of osteoporosis in postmenopausal women, many physicians recommend 1,500 milligrams daily. Table 6.5 illustrates how to get a day's worth of calcium from food.

If you have some calcium in your diet, don't take all 1,200 or 1,000 milligrams of calcium in a supplement. Too much calcium in the diet can cause kidney stones in some people.

A word to women: If you have irregular menstruation, no menstrual cycle, or stop menstruating before a contest, you should see a good sports medicine physician or a gynecologist who is familiar with your sport. Loss of estrogen production at an early age can have a critical impact on your bone health. It's possible for osteoporosis to develop at a very early age.

So take care of your inside while you are taking care of your outside. Add some dairy to your diet, and you'll be standing straight and tall for many years to come.

Table 6.5 A Healthy Day's Worth of Calcium

Food	Measure	Calcium (mg)	Calories
Orange juice, calcium fortified	1 c	300	112
Nonfat milk	1 c	301	86
Tofu	4 oz.	120	88
Low-fat yogurt, fruit	8 oz.	372	250
Mozzarella cheese, part-skim	1 oz.	229	73
Turnip greens cooked, chopped	1 c	250	50
Total		1,572	659

Iron

As a strength trainer or bodybuilder, you are constantly tearing down and rebuilding muscle tissue. This process can cause an additional need for iron, a mineral that is enormously essential to human health. What's more, there seems to be a common increase in iron losses from aerobic exercises that involve pounding of the feet, such as jogging, aerobic dancing, and step aerobics. Also at risk for low iron are women who exercise more than three hours a week, have been pregnant within the past two years, or eat fewer than 2,200 calories a day.

The major role of iron is to combine with protein to make hemoglobin, a special protein that gives red blood cells their color. Hemoglobin carries oxygen in the blood from the lungs to the tissues.

Iron is also necessary for the formation of myoglobin, found only in muscle tissue. Myoglobin transports oxygen to muscle cells to be used in the chemical reaction that makes muscles contract.

When iron is in short supply, your tissues become starved for oxygen. This can make you tire easily and recover more slowly.

The best sources of dietary iron are liver and other organ meats, lean meat, and oysters. Iron is found in green leafy vegetables, too, although iron from plant sources is not as well absorbed as iron in animal protein.

Strength trainers and other active people tend to shy away from iron-rich meats because of their high fat content. But you can beef up the iron in your diet without adding a lot of beef or animal fat. If you don't eat any meat at all, you must pay careful attention to make sure that you get what you need. Here are some suggestions:

1. Eat fruits, vegetables, and grains that are high in iron. You won't get as much iron as from animal foods, but the plant foods are the lowest in fat. Green leafy vegetables such as kale and collards, dried fruits like raisins and apricots, and iron-enriched and fortified breads and cereals are all good plant sources of iron.
2. Enhance your body's absorption of iron by combining high iron-containing foods with a rich source of vitamin C, which improves iron absorption. For example, drink some orange juice with your iron-fortified cereal with raisins for breakfast. Or sprinkle some lemon juice on your kale or collards.
3. Avoid eating very high-fiber foods at the same meal with foods high in iron. The fiber inhibits the absorption of iron and many other minerals. Avoid drinking tea and taking antacids with high-iron foods; they also inhibit absorption of iron.
4. Try to keep or add some meat to your diet. Lean red meat and the dark meat of chicken and turkey are highest in iron. Eating a three-

© iPhotoNews.com/Brooks

When you strength train, the tearing down and rebuilding of muscle tissue is constant, so you need ample iron to aid the process.

to four-ounce portion of meat three times a week will give your iron levels a real boost. And if you combine your meat with a vegetable source of iron, you will absorb more of the iron from the vegetables.

5. You might need an iron supplement. Eight milligrams for men and 18 milligrams for women 19 to 50 years old or 100 percent of the DRI for iron daily may be a big help. Don't pop huge doses of iron, though. The greater the amount of iron taken at one time, the less your body will absorb.

If you think you might be deficient in iron, talk to your physician or a registered dietitian who specializes in sports nutrition. Self-medicating with large doses of iron can cause big trouble and is potentially dangerous.

Zinc

Zinc, one of the antioxidant minerals, is important for hundreds of body processes, including maintaining normal taste and smell, regulating growth, and promoting wound healing.

My research has found that female bodybuilders, in particular, don't get enough zinc in their diets. Zinc is an important mineral for people who work out. As you exercise, zinc is helping to clear lactic acid buildup in the blood. In addition, zinc supplementation (25 milligrams a day) has been shown to protect immunity during periods of intense training.

Too much zinc might be a bad thing, however. It has been associated with lower levels of HDL cholesterol (the "good" kind) in people who exercise.

By eating zinc-rich foods, you can get just the right amount, which is 8 milligrams a day for women and 11 milligrams a day for men. The best sources of zinc are meat, eggs, seafood (especially oysters), and whole grains.

If you restrict your intake of meat, taking a one-a-day multiple vitamin will help fill in the nutritional blanks.

Magnesium

Magnesium, a mineral that is in charge of more than 400 metabolic reactions in the body, has been touted as an exercise aid. One study hints at a link between magnesium and muscle strength. A test group of men were given 500 milligrams of magnesium a day, an increase over the DRI of 400 milligrams. A control group took 250 milligrams a day, significantly less than the DRI. After both groups weight trained for eight weeks, their leg strength was measured. The supplemented men got stronger, whereas the control group stayed the same. But many researchers are not yet convinced that magnesium is a strength builder. They caution that the magnesium status of the subjects before the study was unknown. That's an important point, because supplementing with any nutrient in which you are deficient is likely to produce some positive changes in performance and health.

Specifically, magnesium promotes calcium absorption and helps in the function of nerves and muscles, including the regulation of the heartbeat. As I mentioned, the DRI for magnesium for men 19 to 30 is 400 milligrams a day, and for men 31 and older it is 420 milligrams per day. The DRI for women for this important mineral is 310 milligrams for women 19 to 30 and 320 milligrams for women 31 and older.

The use of laxatives and diuretics can impair magnesium balance. If you use these to make weight, beware that you can compromise your health and that you risk having nervous system complications from fluid and electrolyte imbalances.

The best dietary sources of magnesium are nuts, legumes, whole grains, dark green vegetables, and seafood. These foods should be plentiful in your diet. You can also supplement these foods with a one-a-day type multiple vitamin formulated with 100 percent of the DRI for magnesium.

Zinc-Magnesium Supplementation (ZMA)

One small study investigated the effects of a zinc-magnesium-vitamin B6 supplement on the muscle strength and functional power of college football players. Although the results of the supplemented group were positive, this research is preliminary and needs more follow-up to determine its validity. For more on zinc-magnesium as a muscle-building product, see page 170.

Vanadyl Sulfate

The supplement vanadyl sulfate is a commercial derivative of vanadium, a trace mineral found in vegetables and fish. The body needs very little vanadium, and more than 90 percent of it is excreted in the urine. At high doses, vanadium is extremely toxic and may cause excessive fatigue. To the knowledge of the medical community, no one has ever been diagnosed with a vanadium deficiency disease.

As a supplement, vanadyl sulfate is supposed to have a tissue-building effect by moving glucose and amino acids into the muscles faster and elevating insulin to promote growth. But the evidence for this has been

Quality Control

When you decide which vitamin and mineral supplements you need, stick to brands from well-known manufacturers. Avoid obscure, off-brand, or products from unknown international sources. There's so little regulation of the nutritional supplements industry that anything can be, or not be, in the products.

Products from unknown or nonestablished companies may have poor quality control and may not contain what is stated on the label. Lack of regulatory inspection can also lead to product contamination. These problems are less likely in products manufactured by recognized and well-established food supplement and pharmaceutical companies.

Other important tips: Identify companies that do research on their own products and ask your pharmacist for recommendations on good-quality supplements.

found only in rats. Still, vanadyl sulfate is being aggressively marketed as a tissue-building supplement for strength trainers and athletes.

But does it work the magic it promotes? A group of researchers in New Zealand asked the same question. In a 12-week study, 40 strength trainers (30 men and 10 women) took either a placebo or a daily dose of vanadyl sulfate in amounts matched to their weight (0.5 milligram per kilogram of body weight). So that strength could be assessed, the strength trainers performed bench presses and leg extensions in 1- and 10-repetition maximum bouts during the course of the experiment.

The findings of the study were that vanadyl sulfate did not increase lean body mass. There were some modest improvements in strength-training performance, but these improvements were short-lived, tapering off after the first month of the study. About 20 percent of the strength trainers experienced extreme fatigue during and after training.

In my opinion, there's no reason to supplement with vanadyl sulfate. You can get what it promises with the nutritional methods discussed elsewhere in this book.

Aspartates—A Special Type of Mineral Supplement

If you perform a lot of aerobic exercise, in addition to strength training, you may be interested in the use of aspartic acid salts for increasing endurance. The potassium and magnesium salts of aspartic acid, an amino acid composed of various substances, are known as aspartates. Aspartate supplements are usually available in health food stores and sport fitness centers.

The feeling of fatigue you get during intense exercise is caused by a combination of factors, and one factor may be the increased rate of ammonia production by the body. Aspartates turn excess ammonia, a by-product of exercise, into urea, which is consequently eliminated from the body.

Studies have shown that potassium and magnesium aspartates increase the endurance of swimming rats. Scientists speculate that the aspartates counteract energy-sapping increases in ammonia concentration.

But what about human exercisers? One study looked into this. Seven healthy men, all competitors in various sports, were tested on a bicycle ergometer. At intervals during a 24-hour period before the test, four of the men took a total of five grams of potassium aspartate and five grams of magnesium aspartate. The others took a placebo.

During the test, the men pedaled at a moderately high intensity. The researchers took blood samples before, during, and after the test. A week later, the men participated in the same experiment but the conditions were reversed.

In the aspartate-supplemented group, blood ammonia concentrations were significantly lower than in those of the placebo group. Plus, endurance was boosted by about 14 percent in the aspartate group. On average, the aspartate group cycled a total of 88 minutes before reaching exhaustion, whereas the other group cycled about 75 minutes until exhaustion. The researchers noted that "the results of this study would suggest that potassium and magnesium aspartate are useful in increasing endurance performance."

Of course, this is only one study, and aspartates have not been widely researched in exercise science. Supplementing may or may not be useful. If you want to try it, proceed with caution. Excess potassium or magnesium in the system may lead to water retention and mineral imbalances.

Sport Nutrition Fact vs. Fiction:

Chromium and Muscle Building

The mineral chromium has been hyped as a safe alternative to anabolic steroids and as a muscle-building agent.

Is there some hard fact behind the hype? Let's take a look.

Chromium is an essential trace mineral that helps the hormone insulin do one of its main jobs—transport glucose into cells. Chromium is also involved in the cellular uptake of amino acids. Its advocates say increased doses of chromium can thus stimulate a higher-than-normal uptake of amino acids, increasing the synthesis of more muscle mass. But that's quite a leap of faith. The exact way chromium works in the body is not entirely known.

What we do know about chromium is that you can lose it in urine as a result of exercise. Plus, a diet overloaded with simple sugars can force chromium from the body, too. However, the very small quantities of chromium we need for good health can be easily obtained from a good diet. Dietary sources include brewer's yeast, whole grain cereals, meats, raw oysters, mushrooms, apples with skins, wine, and beer.

As for whether chromium supplementation (namely chromium picolinate) builds muscle mass, the evidence is conflicting. Some studies show that it does, others show it doesn't, and still others show no change. Most of the studies to date have been very poorly designed, they used inaccurate methods of measuring body composition, and they failed to assess chromium status before the research.

The best and most well-controlled study to date was conducted several years ago at the University of Massachusetts. Thirty-six football players were given either a placebo or 200 micrograms of chromium picolinate daily for nine weeks during spring training. During that period, they worked out with weights and ran for aerobic conditioning. Before, during, and after supplementation, the researchers assessed the players' diet, urinary chromium losses, girth of various body parts, percentages of body fat and muscle, and strength. Percentages of body fat and muscle were measured by underwater weighing, one of the most precise ways to measure body composition. The findings: Chromium supplementation did not help build muscle, enhance strength, or burn fat.

Some words of warning about supplementation: A study released in 1995 suggested that supplementation with chromium picolinate may damage chromosomes, the bodies inside the cell nucleus that carry our genes. In the laboratory, researchers injected hefty amounts of chromium picolinate into hamster cells in dishes—about 3,000 times the normal safe amount you'd see in people supplementing with 200 micrograms a day. The chromosomes broke, and such breakage can lead to cancer. Other forms of chromium, namely chromium nicotinate and chromium chloride, did not cause this damage. Defenders of chromium picolinate responded by pointing out that the study was meaningless, because such huge doses of chromium were used.

What's more, chromium causes the body to excrete other trace minerals and interferes with the metabolism of iron. Given these drawbacks and the fact that chromium picolinate doesn't live up to its claims, supplementation is walking a nutritional tightrope at best.

7 Muscle-Building Products

You train hard. You're building body-hard muscle. Still, you want to know: Isn't there something else—besides intense workouts and healthy food—that can help you make gains a little faster, something that will give you a muscle-building edge, with less effort?

Definitely. You can do several things to pack on lean muscle. Unfortunately, not all of them are safe or legal. Anabolic steroids, though approved for medical use and available by prescription only, are among the most abused drugs among athletes. "Anabolic" means "to build," and anabolic steroids tend to make the body grow in certain ways. They do have muscle-building effects, but they're dangerous and life-threatening. Once practiced mainly by elite athletes, anabolic steroid abuse has spread to recreational and teen athletes and is now a national health concern. Research shows that among teenagers, 40 percent of kids under age 15 have tried anabolic steroids. Table 7.1 lists some of the dangers associated with these drugs.

A trend related to anabolic steroid abuse is the use of androstenedione and others of its ilk, a precursor or building block to testosterone. Testosterone is the male hormone responsible for building muscle and revving up the sex drive. Although legal, androstenedione is not without side effects. These include acne, hair loss in genetically susceptible people, abnormal growth of breast tissue (gynecomastia), negative blood cholesterol profiles that can lead to the increased risk of heart disease, and the potential reduction of testosterone output if these supplements are used for a long time. Use of this family of compounds may still result in a positive drug test.

Table 7.1 Health Dangers of Anabolic Steroids	
Liver disease	Masculinization in women
High blood pressure	Muscle spasms
Increased LDL cholesterol	Headache
Decreased HDL cholesterol	Nervous tension
Fluid and water retention	Nausea
Suppressed immunity	Rash
Decreased testosterone	Irritability
Testicular atrophy	Mood swings
Acne	Heightened or suppressed sex drive
Gynecomastia	Aggressiveness
Lowered sperm count	Drug dependence

In addition to using steroids and androstenedione, athletes use other types of drugs, including stimulants, pain killers, diuretics, and drugs that mask the presence of certain drugs in the urine. Synthetic growth hormone (GH) is used by athletes as well, because they believe it will increase strength and muscle mass. GH has many horrible side effects, including progressive overgrowth of body tissues, coronary heart disease, diabetes, and arthritis. GH is one of more than 100 drugs that has been banned by the International Olympic Committee. The full list of banned substances appears in table 7.2. Notice that not one of these substances is nutritional; they are drugs and not food substances.

My advice is to forget health-destroying drugs. There are some natural aids you can use to enhance muscle-building, give you an extra edge in training, and generally keep your body in healthy balance.

Sport Supplements: Sorting Through the Confusion

On average, exercisers and athletes spend $45 million on sport supplements—a sum that's growing every year. And with so many supplements

Table 7.2 Drugs Banned by the International Olympic Committee
Stimulants
Ameneptine, amfepramone, amiphenazole, amphetamine, bambuterol, bromantan, caffeine, carphedon, cathine, cocaine, cropropamide, crotethamide, ephedrine, ethamivan, etilamphetamine, etilefrine, fencamfamin, fenethylline, fenfluramine, formoterol, heptaminol, mefenorex, mephentermine, mesocarb, methamphetamine, methoxyphenamine, methylenedioxyamphetamine, methylephedrine, methylphenidate, nikethamide, norfenfluramine, parahydroxyamphetamine, pemoline, pentetrazol, phendimetrazine, phentermine, phenylephrine, phenylpropanolamine, pholedrine, pipradrol, prolintane, propylhexedrine, pseudoephedrine, reproterol, salbutamol, salmeterol, selegiline, strychnine, terbutaline
Narcotics
Buprenorphine, dextromoramide, diamorphine (heroin), hydrocodone, methadone, morphine, pentazocine, pethidine
Anabolic Agents
Androstenediol, androstenedione, bambuterol, boldenone, clenbuterol, clostebol, danazol, dehydrochlormethyltestosterone, dehydroepiandrosterone (DHEA), dihydrotestosterone, drostanolone, fenoterol, fluoxymesterone, formebolone, formoterol, gestrinone, mesterolone, methandienone, methenolone, methandriol, methyltestosterone, mibolerone, nandrolone, 19 norandrostenediol, 19 norandrostenedione, norethandrolone, oxandrolone, oxymesterone, oxymetholone, reproterol, salbutamol, salmeterol, stanozolol, terbutaline, testosterone, trenbolone
Diuretics
Acetazolamide, bendroflumethiazide, bumetanide, canrenone, chlorthalidone, ethacrynic acid, furosemide, hydrochlorothiazide, indapamide, mannitol (by intravenous injection), mersalyl, spironolactone, triamterene
Masking Agents
Bromantan, diuretics (see above), epitestosterone, probenecid
Peptide Hormones, Mimetics, and Analogues
ACTH, erythropoietin (EPO), hCG*, hGH, insulin, IGF-1, LH*, clomiphene*, cyclofenil*, tamoxifen*

(continued)

Table 7.2 (Continued)

Beta-Blockers
Acebutolol, alprenolol, atenolol, betaxolol, bisoprolol, bunolol, carteolol, celiprolol, esmolol, labetalol, levobunolol, metipranolol, metoprolol, nadolol, oxprenolol, pindolol, propranolol, sotalol, timolol

*Prohibited in males only.

on the market, how do you know which ones will help you, hurt you, or just waste your money?

With many products, the real hazards and nutritional implications are not based on what the supplement does, but what it doesn't do, and what other avenues of support it may impede. I call this the "laetrile effect."

For background, laetrile (technically known as amygdalin) is derived primarily from apricot pits and almonds. In the 1920s, a theory was formulated that laetrile could kill cancer cells. In the 1960s and 1970s, it became a popular cancer treatment promoted by nonmedical practitioners. Because it was not an approved medical treatment, patients seeking the cure had to travel to Mexico to acquire treatment. By 1982, medical science proved that laetrile was not an effective cancer treatment.

But in most cases, people who sought (and still seek) laetrile treatment did so by delaying standard medical treatment and at large financial expense, with no beneficial results, but usually without harm from the treatment. However, by foregoing more proven treatment, these patients lost time, and their disease advanced. In some cases, the laetrile treatment was harmful and even deadly.

And so it is with many sport supplements. Looking for a shortcut, athletes and exercisers spend time and money on supplements that don't work, while delaying the use of proven methods—namely good nutrition and intense training—to support their goals. Worst yet, some supplements can be harmful, even deadly.

To help you sort through the confusion regarding sport supplements, I have developed a rating system for strength-training supplements and herbal supplements based on the concept of the "laetrile effect":

Definitely worth it. This supplement meets its marketing claims.

Possibly useful. There is not yet enough research backing this supplement, although available data look promising.

Wasting your time. An abundance of negative data exists on this supplement.

Potentially harmful. This supplement does not meet marketing claims and is potentially harmful.

Now, here's a round-up of various sport supplements on the market, categorized according to this rating system.

Definitely Worth It

The products in this category have numerous research studies that back up the marketing claims. In the right setting, these products work.

Carbohydrate/Protein Sport Drinks

Unimaginable as it may seem, it is within your control to retool your body for more lean muscle and less fat—and do it naturally—all with a simple formulation. Here's how: Immediately after your workout, drink a liquid carbohydrate supplement that contains protein, and you'll jump-start the muscle-building process, plus boost your energy levels.

This simple formula is 12 ounces of carbohydrates and protein in liquid form taken immediately after your strength-training routine. This is the time your body is best able to use these nutrients for muscle firming and fat burning. The supplement I use with my clients is one of my Kleiner's Muscle-Building formulas, featured in chapter 16. For a long time now, I've used these formulas with many of my bodybuilding clients and soon started observing some major shifts in their body composition, from less fat to more muscle.

How It Works

But why? How does this formula help muscles get stronger and firmer? Exercise, of course, is the initial stimulus. You challenge your muscles by working out, and they respond with growth. But for muscle building to take place, muscles need protein and carbs in combination to create the right hormonal climate for muscle growth.

What happens is this: Protein and carbohydrates trigger the release of the hormones insulin and GH in your body. Insulin is a powerful factor in building muscle, among many other functions. It helps ferry amino acids into cells, reassembles those amino acids into body tissue, and prevents muscle wasting and tissue loss.

GH increases the rate of protein production by the body, spurring on muscle-building activity. It also promotes fat burning. Both hormones are directly involved in muscle growth. So you see: Your body is primed for growth, thanks to this simple muscle-gain formula.

Scientific Proof

Exploding research into the effect of carb-protein supplements on athletes and exercisers supports what I've observed for years. Here are some examples:

- In one scientific study, 14 normal-weight men and women ate test meals containing various amounts of protein (in grams): 0 (a protein-free meal), 15.8, 21.5, 33.6, and 49.9, along with 58 grams of carbohydrate. Blood samples were taken at intervals after the meal. The protein-containing meals produced the greatest rise in insulin compared with the protein-free meal. This study points out that protein clearly has an insulin-boosting effect.
- In another study, nine experienced male strength trainers were given either water (which served as the control), a carbohydrate supplement, a protein supplement, or a carbohydrate/protein supplement. They took their designated supplement immediately after working out and again two hours later. Right after exercise and throughout the next eight hours, the researchers drew blood samples to determine the levels of various hormones in the blood, including insulin, testosterone (a male hormone also involved in muscle growth), and GH.

The most significant finding was that the carbohydrate/protein supplement triggered the greatest elevations in insulin and growth hormone. Clearly, the protein works hand in hand with postexercise carbs to create a hormonal climate that's highly conducive to muscle growth.

More Energy

If you supplement with a carb/protein beverage after your workout, you'll notice something else. That "something else" is higher energy levels. Not only does this nutrient combination stimulate hormone activity, it also starts replenishing muscle glycogen. That means more muscle energy. The harder you can work out, the greater your muscular gains.

When protein is added to the supplement mix, your body's glycogen-making process accelerates—faster than if you just consumed carbs by themselves.

Some intriguing research proves this point. In one study, nine men cycled for two full hours during three different sessions to deplete their muscle glycogen stores. Immediately after each exercise bout and again two hours later, the men drank either a straight carb supplement, a straight protein supplement, or a carbohydrate/protein supplement. By looking at actual biopsy specimens of the muscles, the researchers observed that the rate of muscle glycogen storage was significantly faster when the carb/protein mixture was consumed.

Why such speed? It's well known that eating carbs after prolonged endurance exercise helps restore muscle glycogen. When protein is consumed along with carbs, there's a surge in insulin. Biochemically, insulin is like an acceleration pedal. It races the body's glycogen-making motor—in two ways. First, it speeds up the movement of glucose and amino acids into cells, and second, it activates a special enzyme crucial to glycogen synthesis.

In another study, a group of athletes performed enough exercise to deplete their glycogen reserves. Afterwards, part of the group consumed a carb/protein supplement; the other consumed a six percent glucose-electrolyte solution. Both groups exercised again. Endurance-wise, the carb/protein-supplemented group outlasted the other group by 66 percent.

In a similar study, eight endurance-trained cyclists performed two two-hour exercise bouts designed to deplete their glycogen stores. After exercise and again two hours later, they consumed either a carb/protein supplement or a carb-only formula. The carb/protein formula contained 53 grams of carbohydrate and 14 grams of protein; the carb formula, 20 grams of carbohydrate. The effects of the carb/protein supplement were quite remarkable: Glucose levels rose by 17 percent, and insulin levels increased by 92 percent. Furthermore, there was a 128 percent greater storage of muscle glycogen when athletes took the carb/protein supplement compared with when they supplemented with the carb-only formula.

Scientific research indicates that for hard trainers the optimum combination of protein and carbs after exercise is 1.5 grams of a high-glycemic index carb per kilogram of body weight with 0.5 grams of protein per kilogram of body weight.

Creatine

Quite probably, creatine is the most important natural fuel-enhancing supplement yet to be discovered for strength trainers. Unlike a lot of supplements, creatine has been extensively researched. Exciting experiments show that creatine produces significant improvement in sports that require high levels of strength and power, including strength training, rowing, and cycling sprints. Another big plus for creatine: Several creatine supplementation studies have shown gains in body mass averaging two to four pounds. It was once thought that this increase was mostly water weight gain. But now we're seeing that a significant amount of the gain is pure muscle, and only a small portion is water.

Not a Gimmick

Creatine received the following endorsement from a review article in the *International Journal of Sport Nutrition*, a respected publication in sports nutrition: "Creatine should not be viewed as another gimmick supplement; its ingestion is a means of providing immediate, significant performance improvements to athletes involved in explosive sports."

Sound good? You bet. Who wouldn't prefer a bona fide natural supplement like creatine over synthetic, dangerous compounds like steroids? Creatine is the ticket to greater strength and improved muscularity.

How It Works

Creatine is a substance produced in the liver and kidneys—at a rate of about 2 grams a day—from arginine, glycine, and methionine, three nonessential amino acids. About 95 percent of the body's creatine travels by the blood to be stored in the muscles, heart, and other body cells. Inside muscle cells, it's turned into a compound called creatine phosphate (CP). CP serves as a tiny energy supply, enough for several seconds of action. CP thus works best over the short haul, in activities such as strength training that require short, fast bursts of activity. CP also replenishes your cellular reserves of ATP, the molecular fuel that provides the power for muscular contractions. With more ATP around, your muscles can do more work.

You "load" creatine into your muscles, just as endurance athletes do with carbs. Consequently, you can push harder and longer in your workouts, because creatine boosts the pace of energy production in your muscle cells. Creatine supplementation doesn't build muscle directly. But it does have an indirect effect: You can work out more intensely, and this translates into muscle gains.

How Much?

Creatine supplements clearly swell the ranks of creatine in your muscles. This gives the working muscles another fuel source, in addition to glycogen from carbohydrates. The question is, how much creatine do you need? You do get creatine from food—roughly one gram a day. But that's not enough to enhance strength training performance. You need more.

Creatine usually comes in a powdered form as creatine monohydrate. Scientific research shows taking four 5-gram doses a day (that's about a teaspoon) for five days will do the trick (or 0.3 gram per kilogram of body weight per day). From there, 2 grams a day—about half a teaspoon (or 0.03 gram per kilogram of body weight per day)—will keep your muscles saturated with enough extra creatine.

The logic that if a small dose is good, a large dose is better isn't a good idea. The body has a ceiling on the amount of creatine that it will store in the muscles. If you keep taking more, creatine will not continue to load in the muscles.

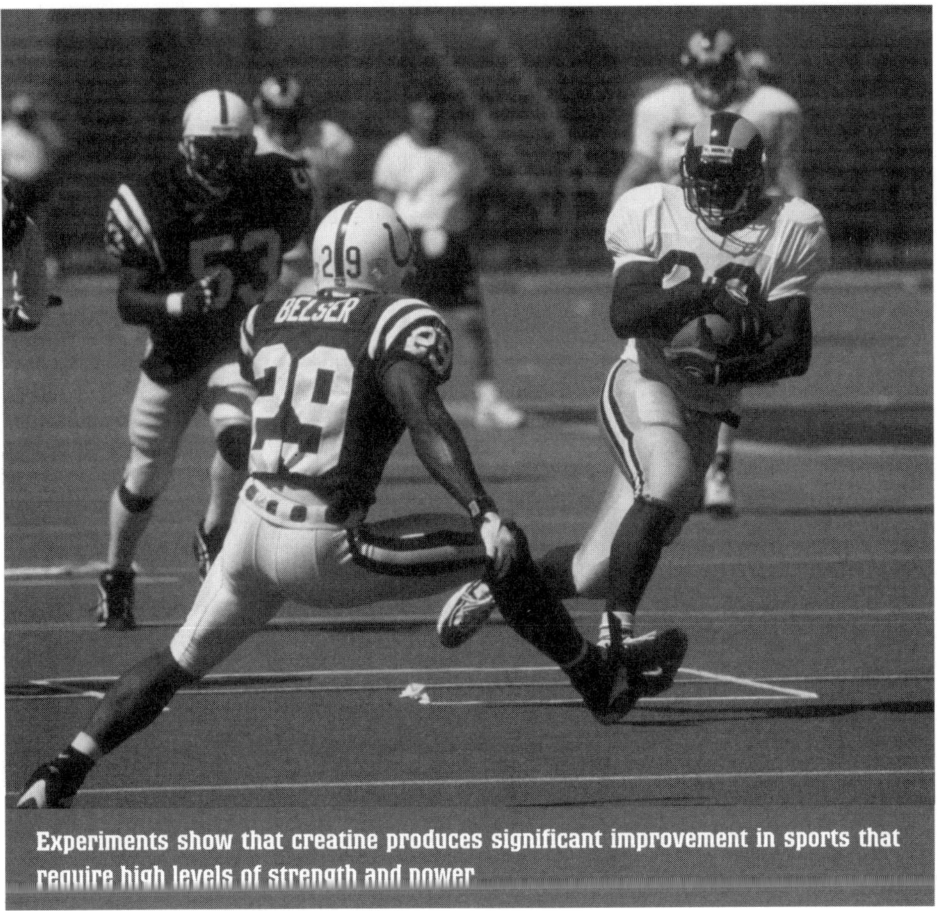

Experiments show that creatine produces significant improvement in sports that require high levels of strength and power.

The only known side effect associated with creatine intakes of 1 to 10 grams per day is water weight gain. In addition, one report suggests that some people may experience muscle cramping and possibly muscle tearing when supplementing with creatine. However, these claims are without studies and are unsubstantiated.

While loading with creatine, make sure to drink extra water. This may control any cramping that may occur. And you're asking for trouble if you belt down daily dosages of 40 grams or more. Such high doses may cause possible liver and kidney damage, according to some reports. Check with your physician before supplementing with creatine.

Supercharge: Creatine With Carbs

Here's an important fact about creatine supplementation: Creatine works best in combination with a liquid carbohydrate supplement. In fact, this combination boosts the amount of creatine accumulated in muscles by as much as 60 percent!

That's the key finding of a recent study. Investigators divided 24 men (average age was 24) into experimental and control groups. The control group took five grams of creatine in sugar-free orange juice four times a day for five days. The experimental group took the same dose of creatine followed 30 minutes later by 17 ounces of a solution containing carbs. Muscle biopsy specimens taken after the five-day test period showed that both groups had elevated creatine levels—but with one dramatic difference. Creatine levels in the experimental group were 60 percent higher than in the control group. There were also higher concentrations of insulin in the muscles of the experimental group.

The implications of this study to strength trainers, athletes, and exercisers are enormous. Just think: By supplementing with creatine and carbs at the same time, you're super-charging your body. With more creatine in your muscles, the more power you have to strength train.

The fact that the creatine/carb combo increases insulin is equally important. Insulin increases the uptake of glucose, which is ultimately stored as glycogen in the liver and muscles for fuel. The more glycogen you can stockpile, the more energy you'll have for exercise—including aerobics. The creatine/carb combo is a bona fide energy booster for all types of exercise activity.

Creatine is nontoxic, and studies have been unable to find any negative side effects to its use. But if you take too much at once, you can experience an upset stomach.

Creatine is ill advised if you have pre-existing kidney disease (for example, renal dialysis or kidney transplant patients). Thus, people with kidney disease should not supplement with creatine. Always consult your physician before supplementing.

Weight Gain Powders

You've seen them: huge cans brightly labeled with alluring product descriptions such as "weight gainer," "solid mass," "lean mass enhancer," or "muscle provider." These products belong to a group of supplements known as "weight gain powders." Most contain various concoctions of carbohydrate, protein, amino acids, vitamins, minerals, and other ingredients thought to enhance performance. The manufacturers of these products claim that their specific formulations will help you pack on muscle.

But do they? Actually, no one knows for sure. But in 1996, a group of researchers at the University of Memphis put two weight gain powders to the test. One was Gainers Fuel 1000, a high-calorie supplement that adds about 1,400 calories a day to the diet (290 grams of carbohydrate, 60 grams of protein, and 1 gram of fat). Although the supplement contains many other ingredients, it's formulated with two minerals that have been hyped as muscle builders: chromium picolinate and boron.

Chromium picolinate's link to muscle growth has to do with the fact that it increases the action of insulin, a muscle-building hormone. But that's where the association ends. There's no valid scientific evidence that chromium directly promotes muscle-building. (For more on chromium picolinate, see chapter 6.)

Boron has been touted as a supplement that promotes muscle growth, too, by increasing the amount of testosterone circulating in the blood. But experiments have failed to verify this claim. In one recent study, 10 male bodybuilders took 2.5 milligrams of boron daily for seven weeks, while nine male bodybuilders took a placebo. Both groups performed their regular bodybuilding routines for the entire seven weeks. The results were interesting: Lean mass, strength, and testosterone levels increased in all 19 men to the same relative degree. Boron supplementation didn't make a bit of difference. It was the training, pure and simple, that did the trick.

Back to the study on weight gain powder: The second supplement investigated was Phosphagain. It adds about 570 calories a day to the diet (64 grams of carbohydrate, 67 grams of protein, and 5 grams of fat). As with most weight gain powders, Phosphagain contains lots of other ingredients that are rumored to build muscle. Among the most notable are creatine (see the previous section), taurine, nucleotides, and l-glutamine. An amino acid found in muscles, taurine has been found in animal studies to enhance the effectiveness of insulin. Nucleotides are the building blocks of RNA and DNA; in Phosphagain, they are derived from the RNA in yeast. Nucleotides are fundamental to metabolism and integral to the cell division and replication involved in growth and development. As for l-glutamine, an amino acid, it theoretically regulates the water volume in cells and the protein-making process in muscles.

To check the effects of Gainers Fuel 1000 and Phosphagain on muscle growth, the University of Memphis researchers selected 28 strength-trained men, all about the same age (average age was 26). None was currently taking anabolic steroids, nor did they have a history of steroid use. All the subjects had been training for an average of six years.

The researchers assigned them to one of three groups: (1) a third of the men took a maltodextrin supplement three times a day (maltodextrin is a carbohydrate derived from corn); (2) a third took two servings of Gainers Fuel 1000 daily according to the manufacturer's directions; and (3) the remaining third took three servings a day of Phosphagain, according to the manufacturer's directions.

The subjects took their supplements with their morning, midday, and/or evening meal. None knew which supplement they were taking. They all continued their normal workouts and diets during the course of the study. In addition, they were told to not take any other supplements two weeks before the study and until the study was over.

Before, during, and after the study, the researchers analyzed the subjects' body composition using some of the most accurate and sophisticated technologies available. This was a very well-designed and well-controlled study.

Here's a summary of what the researchers discovered:

- Both the maltodextrin supplement and the Gainers Fuel 1000 promoted modest gains in muscle mass in combination with a strength training program.
- In the group that supplemented with Gainers Fuel 1000, fat weight and percent body fat increased significantly.
- Phosphagain supplementation was more effective in promoting muscle gains than either maltodextrin or Gainers Fuel 1000 during strength training. In fact, muscle gains were "significantly greater" with Phosphagain, according to lead researcher Dr. Richard Kreider. The men who supplemented with Phosphagain did not gain any additional fat.

Now before you draw your own conclusions, let me emphasize: It's still up in the air as to exactly which ingredients in Phosphagain were responsible for these results. More tests are needed on weight gain powders in general, as well as on the individual ingredients they contain, to confirm these findings. But, carbs with some protein (weight gain powders contain both), taken at the proper times, are important supplements to a muscle-building diet. Also, the creatine in Phosphagain could have been a factor in the results.

Glucose-Electrolyte Solutions

Glucose-electrolyte solutions do two things: Replace water and electrolytes lost through sweat and supply a small amount of carbohydrate to the working muscles. Most drinks are formulated with about 6 to 8 percent of carbohydrate. The carb is either glucose, a simple sugar; fructose, a fruit sugar; sucrose, ordinary table sugar (a blend of glucose and fructose); maltodextrin, a complex carbohydrate derived from corn; or a combination of these.

Because they contain carbs, these drinks benefit athletes competing in events that last an hour or longer. What happens is this: The carbs in these drinks decrease the use of muscle and liver glycogen stores. During competition, athletes can thus run, bike, or swim longer because the supplemental carbs have spared stored glycogen.

There's no evidence showing that electrolytes improve exercise performance. They're not required in supplemental amounts, unless you have a mineral deficiency identified by your physician or your daily sweat losses total more than 3 percent of your body weight (4.5 pounds in a 150-pound athlete). Endurance and ultraendurance athletes are among those who do need to replace electrolytes. But if you're eating a balanced diet rich in complex carbs, you're getting your fill of these minerals.

In addition to their ability to replenish fluids, electrolytes, and carbs, glucose-electrolyte solutions may strengthen your immune system. This amazing news comes from Appalachian State University, where researchers put two groups of marathoners on some rather high-intensity treadmill exercise for two and a half hours. One group drank 25 ounces of a glucose-electrolyte solution (Gatorade) 30 minutes before exercise, 8 ounces every 15 minutes during exercise, and a final 25 ounces over a six-

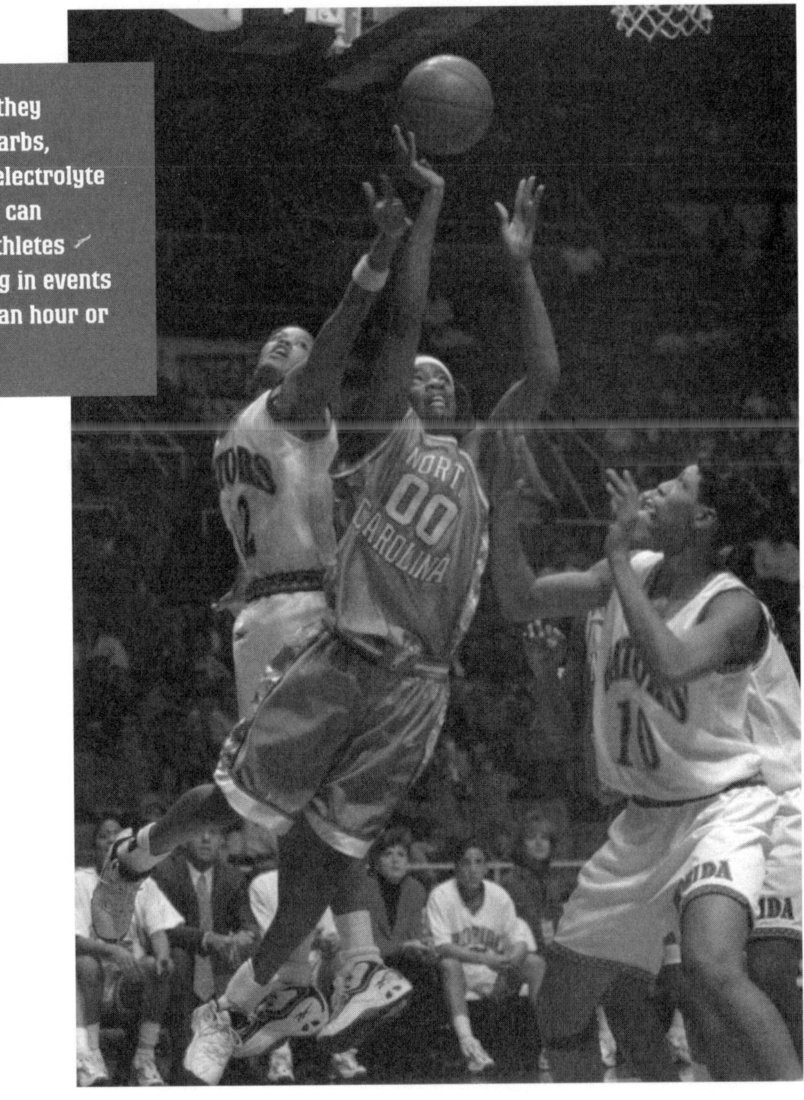

Because they contain carbs, glucose-electrolyte solutions can benefit athletes competing in events that last an hour or longer.

hour recovery period. The other group replenished fluids on the same schedule but with a noncarbohydrate placebo solution.

The researchers took blood samples from the marathoners and found that the Gatorade-drinkers had lower levels of cortisol in their blood than the other exercisers did. Cortisol is a hormone that suppresses immune response. The head of the research team, David Nieman, PhD, was quoted in *Runner's World* as saying: "It seems that when blood glucose level stays up, cortisol level stays down, thus immune function remains relatively strong."

Because this is just one study, there are obviously no final and complete answers on the glucose-immunity connection. This research is intriguing, nonetheless.

Glucose-electrolyte solutions are designed primarily for endurance athletes. But they have application for strength trainers, too—in two important ways. First, if you're training intensely for 45 minutes or more, extra fluid and fuel means more energy. A study conducted by Dr. Greg Haff at Appalachian State University examined the muscle glycogen levels and performance effect of supplementing with a glucose beverage or placebo just before and during a resistance exercise bout. There was significantly less muscle glycogen degradation in the supplemented group vs. the placebo group (15 percent vs. 19 percent) after resistance exercise. Although this group of researchers has previously reported improvements in successive bouts of resistance exercise when subjects were supplemented with a glucose beverage, in this study no improvements in the single bout of resistance exercise were observed.

Second, if you train aerobically—particularly in the heat—these supplements prevent electrolyte and fluid depletion.

The best time to swill one of these drinks is during an aerobic workout or during any period of exertion, especially if you're exercising or working in hot weather. That's when fluid loss is greater than any other time of the year. You can lose more electrolytes too, although the concentration of these minerals in sweat gets weaker the fitter you are. You also burn more glycogen working out in the heat—another good reason to quench your body with a glucose-electrolyte solution.

Caffeine

Caffeine, a drug consumed in coffee, tea, soda, or over-the-counter pharmaceutical preparations, can have a wide range of effects, depending on your sensitivity to it. You might feel alert and wide awake, or get the jitters. Your heart might race, or you might race to the bathroom, because caffeine is a diuretic.

Caffeine lingers in the body, so even small amounts can accumulate over time. It has a half-life of four to six hours—meaning that it takes that long for the body to metabolize half the amount consumed. Because of its half-life, caffeine can become counterproductive. If you drink small amounts during the day, these add up, and you eventually reach a point at which your body has more caffeine than it can handle. The consequence is that by increasing anxiety or restlessness, caffeine reduces the body's ability to function. Other unwanted side effects include upset stomach, irritability, and diarrhea.

Caffeine also inhibits the absorption of thiamin (a vitamin important for carbohydrate metabolism) and several minerals, including calcium and iron. In fact, women who consume caffeine regularly (two or more cups a day) and have a low intake of calcium in their diet (less than 600 milligrams a day) may run a greater risk of osteoporosis or brittle bone disease developing.

In the United States, about 52 percent of all adults drink beverages containing caffeine each day. Many are athletes and exercisers who believe that caffeine can enhance performance. For the most part, studies have shown that caffeine does have some value, although its performance-enhancing effects are as unpredictable as its physical effects.

How It Works

Most of the research with caffeine has focused on endurance sports. The main finding is that for many endurance athletes, caffeine may extend performance.

There are three theories that offer possible explanations. The first and probably most plausible theory has to do with caffeine's ability to enhance fat use for energy. Caffeine stimulates the production of adrenaline, a hormone that accelerates the release of fatty acids into the bloodstream. At the beginning of exercise, the muscles start using these available fatty acids for energy while sparing some of your muscle glycogen.

The second theory goes like this: Caffeine may directly affect skeletal muscle by altering key enzymes or systems that regulate carbohydrate breakdown within the cells. But the research here has been conflicting and inconclusive.

The third theory states that caffeine, because of its effect on the central nervous system, might have the psychological effect of making athletes feel they are not working as hard, or it may somehow maximize the force of muscular contractions. This theory has been difficult to substantiate, however.

Caffeine Use in Power Sports

Until recently, it was believed that caffeine doesn't help you much if your sport skills relate mainly to strength and power. But Dr. Larry Spriet and his colleagues at the University of Guelph in Ontario might disagree. They have looked into the effect of caffeine on power sports. In one study, 14 exercisers did three bouts of exercise as hard as they could. Each bout was separated by six minutes of rest. The first two exercise bouts lasted two minutes each, and bout three was performed to exhaustion. The exercisers were tested twice, once with caffeine and once with a placebo. In bout three, they were able to exercise longer with caffeine (4.93 minutes with caffeine compared with 4.12 minutes with the placebo). Caffeine clearly boosted performance in short-term, intense exercise.

But how? The mechanism isn't exactly clear, but the researchers were able to rule out one possibility. By taking blood samples and muscle biopsy specimens, they found that in this instance caffeine did not spare muscle glycogen, as was previously thought.

Well-Trained Athletes Do Best

Studies also show that caffeine works best as a power booster if you're well conditioned. Proof of this comes from experiments with swimmers, whose sport is anaerobic, as well as aerobic. Highly trained swimmers improved their swimming velocity significantly after consuming 250 milligrams of caffeine, then swimming at maximal speed. Untrained, occasional swimmers didn't fare as well. The same group of researchers had previously conducted experiments with untrained subjects who cycled against resistance after supplementing with caffeine. Again, caffeine didn't provide much of a performance boost in untrained individuals.

The Final Word on Caffeine

Caffeine may give you a kick for exercise (especially if you're in super shape), although no one has pinpointed exactly why and how. If you want to judge caffeine's effect on your own performance, start off with a little bit—maybe a cup or half a cup of coffee—before your workout. An eight-ounce cup of coffee contains between 100 and 150 milligrams of caffeine. See what happens, and compare it to the workouts when you don't consume caffeine beforehand. Overall, laboratory studies suggest that supplementing with doses of 3 to 6 milligrams per kilogram of body weight 30 to 60 minutes before exercise can enhance both power and endurance exercise in well-trained individuals. However, study results in the laboratory might not be the same as results in the real world of the gym.

Keep in mind, too: Caffeine may aggravate certain health problems, such as ulcers, heart disease, high blood pressure, and anemia, to name just a few. Stick to your doctor's advice. Above all, don't substitute caffeine for sound, commonsense nutritional practices for extending energy.

Possibly Useful

These products have some early research that looks promising, but there is not yet enough data for a definitive answer. In the end, they may or may not work.

Branched-Chain Amino Acids

The BCAAs include leucine, isoleucine, and valine. During endurance exercise, levels of these amino acids fall—a decline that may contribute to fatigue during competition. Emerging but limited research suggests that supplementation with BCAAs may enhance performance, particularly if you compete in endurance events. One study found that marathoners who consumed a sport drink containing BCAAs increased their performance by as much as 4 percent. Not all studies have shown a positive effect, however.

Here are some guidelines based on what is currently known about BCAA supplementation: Dosages of 4 to 21 grams daily during training and/or 2 to 4 grams per hour with a 6 to 8 percent glucose-electrolyte solution before and during prolonged exercise have been shown to improve physiological and psychological responses to training. In other words, athletes felt better mentally and physically during exercise.

According to Richard B. Kreider, PhD, writing in *Overtraining in Sport* (Human Kinetics, 1998): "In our view, the greatest potential application of BCAA supplementation is to help athletes tolerate training to a greater degree rather than a performance enhancement supplement."

Carnitine

Found in red meat and other animal products, carnitine is a proteinlike substance once thought to be an important vitamin. Now scientists know carnitine is not an essential nutrient, because the liver and kidneys can synthesize it without any help from food. Most people consume between 50 milligrams and 300 milligrams of this nutrient a day from food. Even if you don't eat that much, your body can produce its own from the amino acids lysine and methionine. About 98 percent of the body's carnitine is stored in the muscles.

Carnitine's main job in the body is to transport fatty acids into cells to be burned as energy. Because of this role, many theories have been floated regarding carnitine's potential benefit to exercisers. One theory is that carnitine boosts exercise performance by making more fat available to working muscles, thus sparing glycogen. Another theory has it that carnitine, because of its role in cellular energy processes, reduces the buildup of waste products such as lactic acid in the muscles, thereby extending performance.

Theories aside, what does scientific research show?

Numerous studies have evaluated the benefits of carnitine supplementation in both patient and athletic populations. With varying results, some studies indicate that carnitine (0.5 to 2 grams a day) may increase fat oxidation and improve cardiovascular efficiency during exercise.

Supplementation clearly improves performance in carnitine-deficient individuals and may be helpful for vegan athletes prone to low-muscle levels of carnitine. However, there is little support for otherwise well-nourished, healthy athletes to benefit from carnitine supplementation in either energy metabolism, exercise capacity, or body composition.

I see no real danger in trying carnitine. According to research, there are no ill effects with doses ranging from 500 milligrams a day to 6 grams a day for up to a month. But there is no reason to believe that more than 2 grams a day makes any difference. Large doses can cause diarrhea.

A word of caution: Some supplement preparations contain a mixture of l-carnitine and d-carnitine. The l-carnitine form appears to be safe; d-carnitine, on the other hand, can cause muscular weakness and excretion of myoglobin, the oxygen-transporting protein in the blood. So if you supplement with carnitine, use products that contain l-carnitine only.

Coenzyme Q10 (Ubiquinone)

Found in the mitochondria (energy factories) of cells, this nutrient plays a central role in a series of chemical reactions that transport oxygen and produce energy. It also works as an antioxidant and thus may help destroy free radicals, particularly during aerobic exercise.

In addition, supplemental coenzyme Q10 has been used successfully in patients with heart disease. As for its benefits for athletes and exercisers, the verdict is still out, even though I've placed it in the "possibly useful" category.

A few studies have shown that coenzyme Q10 may enhance aerobic performance in people who don't exercise. But in one study, trained triathletes took 100 milligrams of coenzyme Q10, 500 milligrams of vitamin C, 100 milligrams of inosine, and 200 International Units of vitamin E for four weeks. No change in their endurance capacity was found.

It is important to add that coenzyme Q10 in high doses may be harmful. In one study, supplementation with 120 milligrams daily for 20 days resulted in muscle tissue damage, possibly because of increased oxidation.

Glucosamine/Chondroitin Sulfate

The combo supplement of glucosamine sulfate and chondroitin sulfate is being sold as an arthritis cure. Although research into this combination is ongoing, there is good initial evidence that this supplement does help relieve the pain and ease the movement of arthritis sufferers—perhaps as effectively as NSAIDS without the long-term negative side effects.

One study of athletes with cartilage damage in their knees showed that 76 percent had complete resolution of symptoms and resumed full athletic training after 140 days of supplementation. However, there is no evidence demonstrating that glucosamine can repair damaged ligaments or tendons from sports-related injuries. More research is needed in this area, but supplementation with these compounds looks promising.

Glutamine

Glutamine is the most abundant amino acid in your body. Most of it is stored in your muscles, although rather significant amounts are found in your brain, lungs, blood, and liver. It serves as a building block for proteins, nucleotides (structural units of RNA and DNA), and other amino acids, and it is the principal fuel source for cells that make up your immune system.

Emerging evidence shows that glutamine may optimize recovery—in at least four possible ways. Glutamine spares protein, stimulates the formation of glycogen, protects immunity, and enhances protein synthesis.

During intense exercise, the muscles release glutamine into the bloodstream. This can deplete muscle glutamine reserves by as much as 34 percent. Such a shortfall can be problematic, because a deficiency of glutamine promotes the breakdown and wasting of muscle tissue. But if sufficient glutamine is available, muscle loss can be prevented.

Glutamine also stimulates the synthesis of muscle glycogen. In a study involving subjects who cycled for 90 minutes, intravenous glutamine, administered during a two-hour period after exercise, doubled the concentration of glycogen in the muscles. It's not clear exactly how glutamine works in this regard, though. Scientists speculate either that glutamine itself can be converted into muscle glycogen or that it may inhibit the breakdown of glycogen.

Glutamine is also the chief fuel source for cells that make up your immune system. As noted, strenuous exercise depletes glutamine, and researchers believe this shortage may be one of the reasons for the weakened immunity seen in hard-training athletes. Supplementing with glutamine may fend off infections that can sideline your training.

Glutamine assists with controlling hydration levels of cells, called cell volumization. By helping maintain cell volume, protein synthesis is stimulated and protein breakdown is decreased.

Glutamine thus may have benefits for anyone who wants to maximize performance, muscle repair, and immunity. The recommended dosage is between 5 and 15 grams a day.

Glycerol

Glycerol is a syrupy substance that causes your body to store water and curtail urine output. It is an ingredient in some sport drinks or available as a supplement you can add to water. A handful of studies indicates that glycerol supplementation can superhydrate your body. Research on whether glycerol supplementation actually enhances performance is equivocal, but one recent study in Australia showed enhanced fluid retention (600 milliliters) and improved endurance performance (5 percent) by cyclists in a hot environment when supplemented with glycerol.

The recommended dosage is one gram of glycerol per kilogram of body weight, with each gram diluted in 20 to 25 milliliters fluid (1 tablespoon + 1 to 2 teaspoons).

Beta-Hydroxy-Beta-Methylbutyrate

Found in grapefruit, catfish, and other foods, beta-hydroxy-beta-methylbutyrate (HMB) is a breakdown product of the branched-chain amino acid leucine. Your body produces it naturally from proteins containing leucine.

Studies show that HMB may be anticatabolic; that is, it inhibits the degradation of muscle and protein in the body. Preliminary research on HMB indicates that 1.5 to 3 grams a day of HMB can assist with increasing muscle mass, decreasing body fat, and boosting strength levels if you are just beginning a strength-training program. The benefits to well-trained athletes are less clear.

MCT Oil

MCT oil is a special type of dietary fat that is processed in the body much like a carbohydrate. Accordingly, it may help boost endurance. Case in point: At the University of Capetown Medical School in South Africa, researchers mixed 86 grams of MCT oil (nearly 3 tablespoons) with two liters of 10 percent glucose drink to see what effect it would have on the performance of six endurance-trained cyclists. The cyclists were fed a drink consisting of glucose alone, glucose plus MCT oil, or MCT oil alone. In the laboratory, they pedaled at moderate intensity for about two hours and then completed a higher intensity time trial. They performed this cycling bout on three separate occasions, so that each cyclist used each type of drink once. The cyclists sipped the drink every 10 minutes. Performance improved the most when the cyclists supplemented with the MCT/glucose mixture. The researchers did some further biochemical tests on the cyclists and confirmed that the combination spared glycogen while making fat more accessible for fuel. Thus, when combined with carbohydrate, MCT oil may improve aerobic endurance performance by sparing muscle glycogen.

MCT oil is reputed to help burn body fat and build muscle, but there are no data to support such claims of altering body composition. For more information on MCT oil, see chapter 4.

Protein Supplements

Protein supplements are a convenient way to consume high-quality proteins that are lactose- and/or fat-free, after workouts or between meals. A variety of these supplements are on the market. Each has some unique benefits to exercisers, strength trainers, and other athletes. Here's a rundown:

Bovine colostrum. A clear premilk fluid and life's first food for every newborn mammal, colostrum is loaded with growth factors, amino acids, and bioactive proteins that help the newborn develop in its first week of life.

Several brands are on the market. A new product called Intact, made from bovine colostrum, uses a low heat processing method that leaves all the growth factors, amino acids, and bioactive proteins intact, thus the name.

Studies have been conducted using this low-heat processed colostrum for its role on athletic performance. Two double-blind, placebo-controlled, randomized studies have shown promising results for strength and power improvements in repetitive bouts of exercise.

Two very recent studies presented at the 2001 Experimental Biology meetings are also of interest. Researchers at the University of Memphis looked at the body composition changes in 49 subjects participating in a standardized 12-week resistance training program while using either a carbohydrate-whey protein placebo, Intact bovine colostrum, or a vitamin-fortified Intact-creatine mixture. The study was conducted in a double blind and randomized manner.

Body composition was measured using DEXA, a highly accurate form of testing that uses low-dose radiation. Here are the results: Those who took the Intact and Intact-creatine had the greatest and most statistically significant gains in body mass and fat-free mass. The researchers concluded that bovine colostrum may be an effective source of protein for protein supplements.

A second study of the same subjects observed their training performance during the 12-week training program. Generally, the group on Intact performed better, with significant increases in bench press lifting volume (repetitions).

Although this research has yet to be fully published and the results are not conclusive, these preliminary studies are intriguing. Due to its naturally high content of insulin-like growth factors, colostrum is banned by the NCAA and USOC.

Colostrum is similar to whey protein in both protein efficiency ratio (3.0) (PER) and protein digestibility score (1.00) (PDCAAS). What's more, it is low-fat and lactose-free.

Egg protein. The protein obtained from egg whites (ovalbumin) is considered the reference standard with which to compare proteins. Egg protein was traditionally the protein of choice for supplements but is rather expensive. The PER of egg protein is 2.8; the PDCAAS, 1.00.

Soy protein. Despite lacking the amino acid methionine, soy is an excellent source of quality protein. Soy protein concentrate (70 percent protein) and isolate (90 percent protein) are particularly good protein sources for vegetarians. Soy protein isolate also contains isoflavone glucosides, which have a number of potential health benefits. The PER of soy protein is 1.8 to 2.3; the PDCAAS, 1.00.

Whey protein. Whey is a component of milk that is separated from milk to make cheese and other dairy products. It is high in B-complex vitamins, selenium, and calcium. In addition, whey appears to boost levels of the antioxidant glutathione in the body. With higher levels, could you possibly ward off oxidative stress?

Yes—says at least one study. Twenty athletes (10 men and 10 women) supplemented with a whey protein supplement (20 grams a day) for three months. A control group supplemented with a placebo.

Researchers assessed the athletes' power and work capacity during bouts of cycling. Both aspects of physical performance increased significantly in the whey-supplemented group, whereas there was no change in the placebo group. The researchers concluded that prolonged supplementation with a product designed to shore up antioxidant defenses resulted in improved performance.

Along with colostrum, whey protein represents the highest quality protein available in supplements. It is digested rapidly, allowing for fast uptake of amino acids. Also available are whey protein hydrolysate, ion exchange whey protein isolate, and cross-flow microfiltration whey protein isolate. Among these, there are subtle differences in the amino acid profiles, fat content, lactose content, and ability to preserve glutamine. It is unclear whether these small differences would have any impact on exercise performance.

Ribose

Found in every cell of your body, ribose is a simple sugar that forms the carbohydrate backbone of DNA and RNA, the genetic material that controls cellular growth and reproduction, thus governing all life. Ribose is also involved in the production of ATP, the main energy-producing molecule of all living cells, and is one of its structural components. Cells need ATP to function properly.

Normally, your body can produce and recycle all the ATP it needs, especially when there is an abundant supply of oxygen. But under certain circumstances—namely ischemia (lack of blood flow to tissues) and strenuous exercise—ATP cannot be regenerated fast enough, and energy-producing compounds called adenine nucleotides may be lost from cells. This can impair muscle function and tax strength, because cells need adenine nucleotides to produce sufficient amounts of ATP.

In animal research, ribose supplementation increased the rate of nucleotide synthesis in resting and exercising muscles of rats by three to four times. Other animal studies have found that ribose can restore nucleotides to near normal within 12 to 24 hours.

Some medical studies indicate that ribose supplementation (10 to 60 grams a day) can increase ATP availability in certain patients and protect against ischemia in others. But what about athletes and exercisers? Does ribose, now marketed as a sport supplement, have any benefit?

Two abstracts of research presented at the 2000 American College of Sports Medicine meeting have convinced me to move ribose from the "wasting your time" category to the "possibly useful" category.

In one very small study, six subjects consumed 2 to 10 grams of ribose. As a result, their blood glucose levels were maintained over 120 minutes, whereas placebo takers experienced no such benefit. What this study hints at is that ribose may make more energy (blood glucose) available to working muscles.

The results of the second study were a little more convincing. This study investigated whether short-term ribose supplementation improved anaerobic performance in eight young men compared with a taste-matched placebo. Subjects performed a series of six 10-second cycle sprints, separated by 60-second rest periods.

There were two familiarization rides before the series of six, and then four depletion rides and two posttest rides. Four 8-gram doses were given over a period of 36 hours, with a final dose given 120 minutes before posttesting.

In four of six sprints, values for peak power were improved by 2.2 to 7.0 percent, and overall power improved by 2.0 to 10 percent. The researchers are now hoping to confirm these results in a larger study.

Both studies indicate that quite possibly, ribose taken before, during, and after hard exercise may help energize muscles and enhance power.

Supplemental ribose is available in sport drinks, energy bars, or in tablets or powder form. The usual recommended dosage is 3 to 5 grams daily as maintenance dose and 5 to 10 grams daily for hard-training athletes.

As a way to restore muscular energy, ribose looks promising. So stay tuned: There is much more to be learned about this intriguing new supplement—and what it holds for athletes and exercisers.

Taurine

One of the most abundant amino acids in the body, taurine is found in the central nervous system and skeletal muscle and is very concentrated in the brain and heart. It is manufactured from the amino acids methionine and cysteine, with help from vitamin B6. Animal protein is a good source of taurine, but it is not found in vegetable protein.

Taurine appears to act on neurotransmitters in the brain. There have been reports on the benefits of taurine supplementation in treating epilepsy to control motor tics, such as uncontrollable facial twitches. Taurine's effectiveness in epilepsy is limited, however, because it does not easily cross the blood-brain barrier.

With high-intensity exercise, blood levels of taurine increase, possibly due to its release from muscle fibers. Because of its association with neurotransmitters in the brain, taurine has recently been advocated as a supplement to enhance attention, cognitive performance, and feelings of well-being. One study investigated these issues with a supplement containing caffeine, taurine, and glucuronolactone (a natural detoxifier derived from carbohydrate metabolism), and found that these ingredients had positive effects upon human mental performance and mood. But because a combination of ingredients was tested, there's no way of knowing how much of an effect was contributed by taurine alone. Research into taurine is very limited, and many more studies need to be done to verify its benefits. However, due to the possible effectiveness of supplemented taurine in other populations, it is a supplement to watch.

Zinc-Magnesium

Zinc and magnesium are mineral elements required in adequate amounts to maintain health and physiologic function, and promote increased energy expenditure and work performance. Both of these nutrients can be lacking in the diets of athletes. I have documented this fact in female bodybuilders and others have seen it in high school football players. One study presented as an abstract only was conducted to evaluate the effects of zinc-magnesium supplementation on muscle attributes of football players. Over a period of eight weeks, college football players supplemented with 30 milligrams of zinc monothione aspartate, 450 milligrams of magnesium aspartate, and 10.5 milligrams vitamin B6, or placebo. The supplement-takers increased their strength at 180 degrees and 300 degrees by 8.9 percent and 7.9 percent, compared to the placebo group.

At this time, this is the only study, and it has not been published in manuscript form for thorough peer review, but it is intriguing in light of the functions of both zinc and magnesium, and the level of dietary intake observed in some athletes. This is a supplement to watch.

Wasting Your Time

These products have either no scientific data, negative data, poor studies, or only animal studies to support their claims.

Conjugated Linoleic Acid

Derived from safflower oil, this supplement is promoted as a fat-burning, muscle-toning, energy-boosting agent. A magazine that was considering running an ad for conjugated linoleic acid (CLA)-containing products sent me the ad for my opinion. I pointed out that the claims regarding reduced body fat and improved muscle tone were not true, unless "in rats" was added to the copy. Animal studies do indicate that CLA may promote fat burning, increase bone mass, and enhance immune function. Few human studies have been done, however. The few available studies indicate that CLA does not promote fat loss in humans but may improve bone mass and immune status.

Inosine

Inosine is a natural chemical that improves oxygen use, possibly by forcing additional production of ATP, the direct source of energy used for all physiological processes. However, there is no research that supports claims that supplemental inosine increases physical power.

Pyruvate

Pyruvate, or more specifically pyruvic acid, is made naturally in the body during carbohydrate metabolism and is involved in energy-producing reactions that occur at the cellular level. Pyruvate is also found in many foods in tiny amounts. The dietary supplements sold as pyruvate are derived from pyruvic acid, which is bonded to a mineral salt, usually calcium, sodium, or potassium.

Studied in animals and humans for more than 25 years, pyruvate may produce some desirable metabolic effects. Research with supplemental pyruvate indicates that calcium pyruvate (6 to 25 grams a day) with or without dihydroxyacetone phosphate (DHAP) (16 to 75 grams a day) promoted significant fat loss in obese people on low-calorie diets. However, little data support that the dosages currently marketed to promote fat loss (0.5 to 2 grams a day) affect fat loss or improve exercise performance.

New on the supplement scene are products that pair pyruvate with another energizing nutrient, creatine. Pyruvate and creatine function differently in the body but may work together. However, there is not yet enough research to support the use of such a combo supplement.

Tryptophan

Tryptophan is an amino acid supplement used by athletes to increase strength and muscle mass, although it does neither. Other people have used tryptophan to relieve insomnia, depression, anxiety, and premenstrual tension. In 1989, thousands of Americans developed a crippling illness called eosinophilia-myalgia syndrome after taking tainted tryptophan made by a Japanese chemical company. Although some recovered rapidly after stopping the supplements, 31 people died.

Others had lingering damage, including inflammation, muscle pain and fatigue, scarring of connective tissue around muscle, and deterioration of nerves and muscle. Unfortunately, there aren't many effective treatments for this syndrome, particularly in its later stages, and many victims become permanently disabled.

As a result of this scare, tryptophan was yanked from the market. I think this sad story underscores one of the biggest problems with supplements today: As a consumer, you can't distinguish between a contaminated product and a pure one, because there's no regulation, product testing, or quality control applied to these products.

Potentially Harmful

These products have been shown to cause harm and are not worth the risk.

Amino Acids

Amino acid supplements are heavily marketed to bodybuilders and other strength-training athletes with claims that they build muscle as a safe alternative to steroid drugs. But these supplements are bought not only by bodybuilders but also by average exercisers lured by promises that amino acids, the building blocks of protein, build lean mass and burn fat.

Amino acids are nitrogen-containing compounds, and their use is believed to cause nitrogen retention in the body. Supposedly, nitrogen retention initiates protein formation at the cellular level, and ultimately, muscle growth.

However, no data support claims for increased muscle growth and strength or decreased body fat. Taken in excess, amino acids may cause gastrointestinal distress and may block the absorption of other amino acids.

Bee Pollen

Supplements sold as bee pollen are actually a loose powder of bee saliva, plant nectar, and pollen compressed into tablets of 400 to 500 milligrams or poured into capsules. Bee pollen also comes in pellets to be sprinkled on foods.

Bee pollen is rich in amino acids, with a protein content that averages 20 percent but ranges from 10 to 36 percent. Ten to 15 percent is simple sugars. There are traces of fats and minerals in bee pollen.

Bee pollen has been marketed as an athletic supplement for improving physical performance. Some European studies find benefits, but American studies do not. Much of the disagreement rests on the design of the experiments. Most studies use pure sources of pollen extract from a single manufacturer, and these are not available to the average consumer.

Can bee pollen hurt you? Possibly. It does contain pollen so you could have an allergic reaction if you're prone to allergies, or worse, death from anaphylactic shock.

Dehydroepiandrosterone

Dehydroepiandrosterone (DHEA) is everywhere—pharmacies, grocery stores, health food stores, department stores. Promoted as an antiaging product, DHEA is probably the most talked about, most hyped supplement on the shelves. Near-magical properties have been attached to DHEA, ranging from increased sex drive to higher energy levels. Bodybuilders, strength trainers, and other athletes take it with the hope that it will build muscle and burn fat.

DHEA is a steroid that's naturally secreted by the adrenal glands. In fact, it's the most abundant steroid in the bloodstream, concentrated mostly in brain tissues. Because DHEA levels decline steadily with age, there's a lot of speculation that it may postpone, even reverse, some of the effects of aging.

When taken as a supplement, DHEA breaks down and is converted to both estrogen and testosterone. The fact that DHEA turns into testosterone, a muscle-building steroid, makes it very appealing to bodybuilders and other athletes who want to build muscle. But there's no real evidence to support this. As with all anabolic steroids, DHEA has side effects. Among them: excessive hair growth in women and breast enlargement in men.

A major issue with DHEA is that there have been no long-term human experiments with it. As with most of these overhyped supplements, DHEA has been tested mostly in rats. Extrapolating results from rat studies to humans is just too much of a stretch. Long-term, large-scale, and properly controlled studies are needed on DHEA. At this point, the benefits of DHEA are all speculation. Don't take it, even in small doses. Once you start tinkering with your hormonal system, you're flirting with physiological disaster.

Dimethylglycine, Vitamin B15

A dietary supplement rather than a vitamin, dimethylglycine (DMG) claims to increase aerobic power and endurance. There are no studies to substantiate these claims, however. What most people don't realize is that DMG and supplements containing it may cause chromosome damage in cells.

Gamma Butyrolactone

Gamma butyrolactone (GBL) has been sold in some health food stores, gyms, and fitness centers, as well as through the Internet. The substance

Table 7.3 Rating the Supplements

Supplement	Definitely worth it	Possibly useful	Wasting your time	Potentially harmful
Carbohydrate/protein sport drinks	•			
Creatine	•			
Weight gain powders	•			
Glucose-electrolyte solutions	•			
Caffeine	•			
BCAAs		•		
Carnitine		•		
Coenzyme Q10		•		
Glucosamine/chondroitin sulfate		•		
Glutamine		•		
Glycerol		•		
HMB		•		
MCT oil		•		
Protein supplements		•		
Ribose		•		
Taurine		•		
Zinc-magnesium		•		
CLA			•	
Inosine			•	
Pyruvate			•	
Tryptophan			•	
Amino acids				•
Bee pollen				•

(continued)

Table 7.3 (Continued)

Supplement	Definitely worth it	Possibly useful	Wasting your time	Potentially harmful
DHEA				•
DMG				•
GBL				•
Plant sterols				•

claims to build muscle, improve physical performance, and act as an aphrodisiac.

Although labeled as a dietary supplement, GBL and products containing it are illegal drugs marketed under various trade names, including Renewtrient, Revivarant, Blue Nitro, GH Revitalizer, Gamma G, and Remforce.

The FDA has issued a recall on products containing GBL because of at least 55 adverse events, including one death.

Plant Sterols

These substances are naturally occurring steroids extracted from plants. Some of the major plant sterols promoted to exercisers, strength trainers, and athletes include gamma oryzanol, found in rice bran oil; Smilax, an herbal extract that is advertised as a natural form of testosterone; beta-sitosterol, a lipid extract; and ferulic acid, another type of lipid extract. There is, however, no data supporting claims for increased muscle mass and decreased body fat. Some people may be sensitive to these substances, which can cause allergies, and possibly, anaphylactic shock.

Diet Is Key

Building fit, firm muscle—is it as easy as just exercising and supplementing? No, there's a lot more to it than that. You can't neglect a good diet. Refer to the sample strength-training diets in chapters 11 through 14. Above all, eat enough quality calories each day to fuel your body for exercise and activity.

8 Performance Herbs

Herbs are the most popular self-prescribed medication. They now come in capsules, tablets, liquids, and powders. Americans spend almost $700 million a year on them, and there's a lot of promotion around herbs as bodybuilding supplements. Yet there's little evidence that herbs can help you, and they may even do harm.

An herb is a plant or a part of a plant valued for its medicinal qualities, its aroma, or its taste. Herbs and herbal remedies have been around for centuries. Even Neanderthal man used plants for healing purposes. About 30 percent of all modern drugs are derived from herbs.

Natural, But Not Always Safe

It's a common but dangerous notion to think that because herbs are natural, they are safe. What separates plant-derived drugs from herbal supplements is careful scientific study. Makers of herbal supplements in the United States are not required to submit their products to the FDA, so there is no regulation of product quality or safety. Without the enforcement of standards, there is a meager chance that the contents and potency described on labels are accurate.

Herbs are classified as food supplements by the FDA. Labeling them as medicines would require stringent testing to prove their safety and effectiveness. This costs millions of dollars per herb, an investment few manufacturers are willing to make.

Fortunately for consumers, supplements can no longer be labeled with unsubstantiated claims. The latest government regulations require that the supplement industry abide by the same food-labeling laws that govern packaged foods. This means that any supplement bearing a health claim must support the claim with scientific evidence that meets government approval. Any product marketed as a way to cure, modify, treat, or prevent disease is regulated as a drug by the FDA.

It's not uncommon to have an allergic reaction to drugs, even though these medicines have been tested and manufactured with strict safeguards. Therefore, it is even more likely that untested herbs, which are consumed in large amounts, may also produce allergic reactions. These reactions can sometimes be fatal.

Herbs can interact with prescribed medications, too. If you're taking any medications, you should consult your physician, pharmacist, or dietitian before using any herbal supplement.

In addition, if you're scheduled for surgery and supplementing with herbs, let your physician know well in advance of your operation. Certain herbs, particularly gingko biloba, garlic, ginger, and ginseng, interfere with normal blood clotting and can lead to excessive blood loss during surgery. Mood-boosting herbs such as St. John's wort and kava-kava dangerously heighten the sedative effects of anesthesia.

Pregnant and nursing mothers should avoid all herbal preparations. Ask your physician or dietitian about specific herbal teas, because even these can cause harmful reactions to a developing baby or nursing infant.

Don't give herbal supplements or remedies to children, either. There is virtually no medical information about the safety of herbs for children. Your best intentions could be terribly harmful.

Because there's no universal quality-control regulation of the industry, the danger of chemical contamination of herbal supplements is real. Were the plants sprayed with any chemicals before harvesting or processing? Other toxic contaminants may enter the product during processing, as well. Products that are purchased by mail order from other countries are even more questionable.

What's on the Market?

The following is a rundown of well-known herbs, either sold alone or found in fitness supplements as part of the formulation. According to current sport science research, some are definitely worth it, and others are possibly useful. Many herbs are a waste of your time and money, and several are downright dangerous.

Definitely Worth It

Much of this research has been conducted outside the United States, but experts agree that these products have been well-tested for their efficacy.

Buchu

Derived from the shrub native to South Africa, the leaves of this herb are usually made into a tea and other supplement forms. Buchu is a mild diuretic, and in that regard, may help rid your body of excess water weight. It is also an antiseptic that fights germs in the urinary tract.

Buchu is generally considered safe, although herbalists recommend taking no more than two grams two or three times a day.

Fo-Ti

Ancient Chinese herbalists swore that this member of the buckwheat family is one of the best longevity promoters ever grown. As herbalists see it, fo-ti exhibits different properties, depending on the size and age of its root. A fist-size 50-year-old plant, for example, keeps your hair from turning gray. A 100-year-old root the size of a bowl preserves your cheerfulness. At 150 years old and as large as a sink, fo-ti makes your teeth fall out so that new ones can grow in. And a 200-year-old plant restores youth and vitality. Or so the folk tales go.

Fo-ti also has a reputation as a good cardiovascular herb. Supposedly, it lowers cholesterol, protects blood vessels, and increases blood flow to the heart. Fo-ti does act as a natural laxative, however. It's probably a safe herb in that regard.

Guarana

Guarana is a red berry from a plant grown in the Amazon valley. It contains seven times as much caffeine as the coffee bean and is widely sold in health food stores as a supplement to increase energy. The supplement is made from the seeds of the berry.

Guarana is used in a number of natural weight-loss supplements, often combined with ephedra. The combination is believed to increase thermogenesis (body heat) and thus stimulate the metabolism. Guarana may also cause your body to lose water, because the caffeine it contains is a diuretic. As for a possible performance benefit, guarana has been shown to increase blood glucose in animals. Whether that holds true for humans, however, remains to be seen.

A note of caution: If you're sensitive to caffeine, it's best to leave guarana alone.

Maté

Another caffeinated herb is maté. Touted as a natural upper, it has a caffeine content of 2 percent.

Maté is found in some natural weight-loss supplements, because it is believed to help control appetite. The herb also has a mild diuretic effect and thus may produce temporary water weight loss. Medical experts say the herb is relatively safe when taken in small quantities for short periods of time.

Possibly Useful

The research on these products is still not clear on whether the claims made about these herbs are true. Maybe; maybe not.

Ciwujia

Ciwujia is the Chinese term for eleuthero, also known as Siberian ginseng. According to noted herbalist and author Christopher Hobbs, L.Ac., writing in his book *Ginseng: The Energy Herb* (Botanica Press, 1996): "With over 35 years of intense clinical and practical research behind it, eleuthero is taken by millions of Russians daily. It is used by the Russian Olympic team, especially weight lifters and runners. The extract was used by cosmonauts to adapt to radically different conditions in outer space. Among others, mountain climbers, sailors, and factory workers all use eleuthero regularly to increase adaptability, reduce sick days, and promote increased endurance."

Ciwujia is the herbal constituent of the popular supplement Endurox. Studies of Endurox conducted at the Institute of Nutrition and Food Hygiene in Beijing, China, found that men in a 2-week or 10-day exercise program who took 800 milligrams daily cut their lactate levels by 33 percent, increased fat burning by 30 to 43 percent, lowered their heart rates, and boosted oxygen intake (a 4.6 percent increase) per heart beat. These findings led the researchers to speculate that the supplement's active ingredient, ciwujia, shifts the body's fuel source during exercise from carbohydrates to fat.

At least one study, however, has found that Endurox has little significant metabolic or performance benefits. In this placebo-controlled study, 10 men were given 400 milligrams of a placebo or 800 milligrams of Endurox daily for seven days and tested on cycle ergometers. After a one-week washout period, the protocol was switched; those taking the placebo took Endurox and vice versa. Researchers checked heart rate, aerobic capacity, and lactate levels but could find no differences between the ciwujia-supplemented group and the placebo group.

The research is conflicting, but ciwujia may be worth a try. With ciwujia extracts, doses of between 500 milligrams to 2,400 milligrams daily—usually before working out—are typically recommended by manufacturers.

Echinacea

Echinacea is a member of the sunflower family. There are three species used medicinally—*purpurea*, *angustifolia*, and *pallida*. The German Commission E, Germany's equivalent to our FDA, has approved *Echinacea purpurea* as supportive therapy for colds and chronic infections of the respiratory tract. The Commission's monographs, a publication describing scores of herbs and their therapeutic applications, notes that echinacea preparations increase the number of white blood cells in the body. White blood cells destroy invading organisms, including cold viruses.

Weakened immunity is often seen in athletes and highly active people—which is why many sport scientists recommend supplementing with echinacea.

Dosages of 900 milligrams daily have been shown to help. But a good rule of thumb is to follow the dosage instructions on the label.

Don't supplement with echinacea if you have an autoimmune disease such as lupus or a progressive illness such as multiple sclerosis, because the herb may overstimulate your immune system and do further damage. Also, don't take echinacea orally for longer than eight weeks.

Green Tea

Green tea is derived from the leaves and leaf buds of an evergreen plant native to Asia. An extract standardized for a beneficial group of chemicals called polyphenols is made from the tea and put into capsules or used as a filler in some natural diet supplements.

Green tea is of interest to fitness-minded people because it may help encourage weight loss. Researchers in Switzerland found that certain natural chemicals called catechins in green tea increased fat burning and stimulated thermogenesis, the calorie-burning process that occurs as a result of digesting and metabolizing food.

The study involved 10 healthy men who ranged from lean to mildly obese. They were randomly assigned to one of three treatments: green tea extract (270 milligrams of epigallocatechins and 150 milligrams of caffeine), caffeine (150 milligrams), or a placebo. The levels of catechins and caffeine in the green tea extract equated amounts normally consumed in Asian countries (about three cups daily).

Those who took the green tea extract used up more energy from fat stores, plus increased their metabolism by 4 percent. The researchers attributed this benefit to the epigallocatechins, not to the caffeine, because the caffeine dose was too small to exert any meaningful effect. Furthermore, researchers speculated that epigallocatechins inhibit an enzyme that degrades the brain chemical norepinephrine, which is involved in stimulating the metabolism.

What does this mean to you? Suppose, for example, you're eating roughly 1,500 calories and drinking three cups of green tea daily. You'd effortlessly expend an additional 60 calories a day.

Although more research into the antiobesity actions of green tea is needed, it's worth drinking for other reasons. Research has found that the natural chemicals in green tea may protect against periodontal disease, some cancers, and heart disease. Unless you're sensitive to caffeine, green tea or extracts containing it are very safe and probably beneficial to health.

Wasting Your Time

These products don't have enough research to back up the marketing claims.

Burdock

This relative of the dandelion was used by the ancient Greeks as a healing remedy and throughout the Middle Ages as an important medicine. Certain constituents of burdock that may fight bacteria and fungus have been isolated by researchers. Today, its leaves and seeds are formulated into herbal preparations.

Burdock is often called a blood purifier, a diuretic, a treatment for skin diseases such as acne and psoriasis, and a diaphoretic (sweat producer). None of these claims has been verified scientifically, and no solid evidence exists that burdock has any useful therapeutic activity. In addition, there have been reports of poisonings caused by burdock tea contaminated with the harmful herb belladonna.

Canaigre

Any herbal product marketed as wild red American ginseng or wild red desert ginseng is actually an herb called canaigre. But in no way is it related to ginseng, either botanically or chemically. The herb is deceptively promoted as a less expensive American alternative to bona fide ginseng.

Native to the southwestern United States and Mexico, canaigre has been recommended by herbal enthusiasts for a variety of problems ranging from lack of energy to leprosy. Trouble is, canaigre is potentially cancer-causing because of its high content of tannin. I can think of no rational reason to use canaigre therapeutically. There's another side to the herb, though: It's useful for tanning leather and dyeing wool.

Citrus Aurantium (Bitter Orange, Synephrine)

Citrus aurantium is the botanical name of the Chinese fruit zhishi. An alkaloid called synephrine is extracted from this fruit and used as an ingredient in numerous fitness supplements.

Synephrine is a chemical cousin to ephedrine (an alkaloid found in the herb ephedra) but has few of ephedrine's adverse side effects. This is because synephrine, unlike ephedrine, does not easily cross the blood–brain barrier and therefore cannot stimulate the central nervous system. (See the section later on ephedra.)

Synephrine is thought to suppress the appetite, increase the metabolic rate, and help burn fat by stimulating the action of fat-burning enzymes inside cells. Ephedrine is believed to stimulate fat cells in much the same manner. To date, though, there are no published studies on synephrine as a fat burner.

My advice is to proceed with caution until more is known about the safety of citrus aurantium and its active component, synephrine.

Cordyceps

Cordyceps is a mushroom native to mountainous regions of China and Tibet, and it is unusual in that it grows on caterpillar larvae.

This mushroom has been used for centuries in China as a food and as a tonic to boost immunity, alleviate fatigue, fight old age, and strengthen the lungs, kidneys, and reproductive system. It is more of a folk remedy than a proven medicine.

Cordyceps is available as a performance supplement, believed to open up breathing passages to let more oxygen circulate. With more oxygen available to cells, endurance increases. The effects of Cordyceps on performance are untested, however.

Although Cordyceps is described as safe and gentle, very little information exists on its safety.

Damiana

Damiana comes from the leaves of a Mexican shrub. Around the turn of the century, it was touted as a powerful aphrodisiac. But any such effects were actually caused by the presence of other drugs in the preparation. Closer scientific scrutiny of damiana revealed that it has no aphrodisiac properties or any beneficial physiological action whatsoever.

Gotu Kola

A member of the parsley family, gotu kola is a common weed, usually found growing in drainage ditches in Asia and orchards in Hawaii.

A known effect of this herb is that it fights water retention by helping the body eliminate excess fluid. It is also a central nervous system stimulant and believed to be a lipotropic, or fat-burning, herb.

Gotu kola is also a constituent of numerous cellulite-fighting supplements. It is thought to strengthen and regenerate the connective tissue between veins and thus help improve the underlying integrity of the skin. However, *The PDR for Herbal Medicines* does not cite research supporting any of these claims for gotu kola.

Because of its stimulating effect, gotu kola should be avoided if you have any chronic medical conditions. Side effects may include insomnia and nervousness.

Pau d'Arco

The name refers to the bark of various species of trees. As an herbal agent, pau d'arco is found as a tea or in cosmetic preparations.

It's often billed as a cancer cure. Indeed, the bark contains a tiny amount of lapachol, an agent shown in research to have anticancer properties. But when given in therapeutic doses, lapachol produces unbearable side effects.

Other disease-fighting benefits have been attributed to pau d'arco, but all are unproven. Pau d'arco is potentially toxic and not to be fooled with.

Sassafras

Usually found as a tea, this well-known herb sounds like a cure-all. It has been promoted as a stimulant, a muscle relaxant, a sweat producer, a blood purifier, and a treatment for rheumatism, skin diseases, and typhus. None of these benefits has been supported or even documented by medical science.

Even if there were some therapeutic effect, it could come with a deadly price. Sassafras contains safrole, an oil once used in root beer. This oil is cancer causing, as are other agents in sassafras. So it's little wonder that sassafras and safrole were banned by the FDA in the early 1960s from use as flavors or food additives. Because of the harmful properties of sassafras, I wouldn't recommend that sassafras tea be consumed at all, even in small amounts or weak concentrations.

Saw Palmetto

Saw palmetto, an herb sold as the ripe or dried berries of the fan palm, has an interesting background. In Germany, it's one of several plants approved to help men with benign prostatic hypertrophy (BPH), an enlargement of the prostate gland. Purportedly, saw palmetto helps increase urinary flow, cuts the frequency of urination, and makes it easier to pass urine. Many herbal medicines containing saw palmetto are marketed throughout the world.

When saw palmetto was injected into young female mice, their estrogen activity—the hormone responsible for development of breasts and other secondary sex characteristics—speeded up. But taking saw palmetto by mouth is another matter. Its active ingredients dissolve in water. What's more, the body doesn't absorb saw palmetto well. So there's no real therapeutic benefit.

Tribulus Terrestris

The strength-training herb of the moment is tribulus terrestris, also known as puncture weed. This herb is believed to be a natural steroid that increases testosterone, enhances muscle mass, and boosts strength.

Unfortunately, it does none of these. That's the finding of a recent study performed at the University of Nebraska. Investigators gave 15 strength trainers (men) either a placebo or tribulus terrestris (3.21 milligrams per kilogram of body weight) for eight weeks. During the experimental period, the subjects engaged in a strength-training program. By the end of the eight-week period, investigators could find no significant changes in body composition, endurance, or strength.

Tribulus terrestris is often recommended as part of a natural steroid "stack," taken with other supposedly natural anabolics and natural hormones. Another recent study substantiated the ineffectiveness of this approach. For eight weeks, men took either a placebo or a combination of the following: 200 milligrams of androstenedione (a precursor or building block to testosterone), 150 milligrams of DHEA (a hormone that is converted to testosterone in the body), 750 milligrams of tribulus terrestris, 625 milligrams of chrysin (a plant constituent believed to enhance immunity), 300 milligrams of indole-3-carbinol (a plant chemical involved in immunity), and 540 milligrams of saw palmetto. The subjects engaged in strength training three times a week throughout the experimental period. However, the stack did not increase testosterone. Nor did it improve strength-training performance.

White Willow Bark

Derived from the willow trees native to central and southern Europe, white willow bark contains an active ingredient called salicin. Salicin is a natural anti-inflammatory agent related to the compound used to make aspirin—which is why white willow bark has often been dubbed the "natural aspirin." The extract of the bark has been used for centuries to relieve pain and reduce fever.

Today, white willow bark extract is available in capsules, liquid extracts, and tea. You often find it as an ingredient in natural weight-loss supplements containing the herb ephedra. The idea behind this formulation is that white willow bark, as a natural form of aspirin, is thought to regulate body temperature and thus preserve the thermogenic effect of ephedra. Although studies have been done showing that aspirin appears to enhance the metabolic effects of ephedra, no research has yet shown that white willow bark extract does the same.

Potentially Harmful

These products have been shown to cause harm and are not worth the risk.

Ephedra (Ma Huang)

The world's oldest known cultivated plant, ephedra is a short-acting stimulant also known as ma huang, Chinese ephedra, or Mormon tea. Ephedra contains ephedrine alkaloids, which are stimulant compounds that exert a number of effects. Cold remedies also contain ephedrine.

Ephedra is found in many herbal remedies marketed for weight loss, making it a popular supplement for bodybuilders, exercisers, and athletes. The herb may encourage weight loss in two specific ways. First, the ephedrine alkaloids act on the appetite control center of the brain to suppress appetite. Second, ephedrine resembles our body's own stimulant, adrenaline, which among other functions, liberates fat from cells to be used as energy.

Accompanying ephedra in many of these formulations are caffeine-containing agents, such as guarana, green tea, or yerba mate. Like ephedrine, caffeine is believed to stimulate the production of fat-releasing adrenaline. And when combined with ephedra, caffeine reportedly doubles thermogenesis (the creation of body heat). Studies in Denmark showed that a drug made of ephedrine and caffeine was helpful in promoting weight loss; however, the combination produced central nervous system side effects such as agitation.

Ephedrine and caffeine have been tested against dexfenfluramine (Redux), which has been removed from the market. In the most overweight people, the ephedrine/caffeine combo was found to be 29 percent more effective for weight loss than dexfenfluramine.

To burn fat, some bodybuilders and exercisers use something called a "caffeine/ephedrine/aspirin stack." This is a combination of the three agents, usually 20 milligrams of ephedrine, 200 milligrams of caffeine, and 300 milligrams of aspirin. Including aspirin supposedly regulates body temperature to preserve the thermogenic effect. This combination also seems to curb appetite.

A 1993 study looked into the effectiveness of the caffeine/ephedrine/aspirin combo on weight loss. Over an eight-week period, people taking the combination lost nearly 12 pounds—without exercising or cutting calories. Those given a placebo didn't do as well.

The caffeine/ephedrine/aspirin may be risky, however, because ephedra has so many troublesome side effects (see later). Caffeine may aggravate certain health problems, such as ulcers, heart disease, high blood pressure, and anemia, to name just a few. Aspirin can upset your stomach.

Ephedra has lots of side effects, including nervousness, agitation, and rapid heartbeat. It can make the heart race and blood pressure soar. Because of these effects, people with heart conditions, high blood pressure, or diabetes should stay away from it. When abused, ephedra and its active compound ephedrine can be lethal.

In an attempt to curb the health problems associated with ephedra and supplements containing it, the FDA has been keeping close tabs on the herb. Since 1994, the agency has received and investigated more than 800 complaints of health problems associated with the use of ephedrine-containing products. Among the most serious: heart attacks, stroke, and death. Most occurred in young to middle-aged, otherwise healthy adults using the products for weight control and increased energy. Toward the end of 2000, the FDA warned the public to stop using ephedrine and products formulated with it.

Worth emphasizing, too: Ephedrine is banned by the National Collegiate Athletic Association and the International Olympic Committee.

Ginseng

Used for thousands of years in the Orient as a tonic to strengthen and restore health, ginseng has more recently been touted as a performance-boosting herb for exercisers and athletes.

For background, ginseng comes from the root of a medicinal plant in the ginseng family (Araliaceae). There are various types of ginseng, including those in the Panax classification and a botanical cousin called Siberian ginseng, or "eleuthero," for short.

Panax ginseng and eleuthero are approved medicines in Germany. In fact, the German Commission E states in its monographs that these ginsengs can be used "as a tonic for invigoration and fortification in times of fatigue and debility, for declining capacity for work and concentration, also during convalescence."

In the United States, the FDA considers ginseng a food. According to one nutritional analysis, 100 grams of Panax ginseng root contain 338 calories, 70 grams of carbohydrate, appreciable amounts of vitamins A, B1 (thiamin), B2 (riboflavin), B12, C, and E, as well as the minerals niacin, calcium, iron, and phosphorus.

The main active constituents of the Panax species are plant steroids called ginsenosides. Eleuthero's active constituents are plant steroids known as eleutherosides, which differ in chemical structure from ginsenosides but have similar properties. The mechanisms of action of these chemical components are complex, but scientists theorize that they increase the size of the mitochondrion (the energy factory of the cell), stimulate the production of adrenal hormones, and enhance the transmission of brain chemicals called neurotransmitters, among other functions.

In herbal medicine, all ginsengs are considered to be "adaptogens." Coined by a Soviet scientist in 1947, the term refers to a class of agents that build resistance to physical stress, enhance performance, extend endurance, and stimulate the body's recovery power after exercise.

Russian scientists were the first to discover that many plants in the Araliaceae family, including ginseng, are adaptogens, and in the early 1950s the scientists pioneered their use as therapeutic agents. Studies of ginseng continue to this day, making ginseng among the most researched herbs in the world.

Ginseng's performance benefits were initially studied in animals. Taken together, these studies have found that ginseng can extend endurance, spare carbohydrates during prolonged exercise, and accelerate recovery after exercise.

The performance-enhancing effects of ginseng in humans have been explored rather extensively, though studies have often yielded mixed results.

In one study, researchers administered 100 milligrams of a standardized Panax ginseng extract (4 percent ginsenosides) to 20 athletes (18 to 31 years old) twice a day for nine weeks. Supplementation significantly increased the subjects' aerobic capacity, reduced their blood lactate levels (a measure of muscle fatigue) during recovery from exercise, and lowered their heart rates, during and after intense exercise.

These findings hint that ginseng may improve the body's ability to process oxygen during exercise and accelerate muscular and cardiovascular recovery afterward. Worth noting, however, is that this particular study did not use a placebo or use control subjects. Thus, the true clinical significance of the findings is unclear.

In another study, subjects pedaled to exhaustion after seven days of taking ginseng (8 or 16 milligrams per kilogram of body weight daily), or a placebo. No significant performance-boosting effects were noted. Nor were any observed in a three-week trial in which 20 men and 8 women supplemented with 200 milligrams of Panax ginseng (7 percent ginsenosides) or a placebo daily and were tested on ergometers.

In another study, supplementation with 200 milligrams or 400 milligrams of a standardized Panax ginseng extract had no effect on the aerobic capacity, heart rate, lactate levels, or perceived exertion of 36 healthy men who were asked to engage in an eight-week aerobic exercise program.

Clearly, there is conflicting research on ginseng. Still, how do you make sense of the data?

The most valid explanation is the wide variability found among commercial ginseng products. An analysis of 24 roots and products (including softgels, tablets, dry-filled capsules, and teas) showed great variations in the concentrations of ginsenosides. Another study revealed that ginseng products vary in content even across lots of the same brand, and that some products contain no ginsenosides at all. In addition, the chemical composition of commercial ginseng products varies according to the age of the root, its cultivation, the part of the root used, and manufacturing methods.

It can be difficult to know what you're buying. And taking ginseng is a questionable practice. There are known side effects of large doses and long-term use: high blood pressure, nervousness, insomnia, low blood pressure, sedation, painful breasts, breast nodules, and vaginal bleeding. In addition, ginseng reacts with many drugs. Talk to your physician and pharmacist about potential interactions with any medications you're taking. Proof of ginseng's reported benefits is still sketchy. Until more studies are done in the United States, I'd leave this herb on the shelves.

Yohimbe

Yohimbe is an herb derived from the bark of an evergreen grown in West Africa. It is best known for its aphrodisiac properties, because it stimulates erection. An extract of the herb yohimbine is available as a prescription drug for treating erectile dysfunction.

Yohimbine stimulates the release of noradrenaline (norephedrine), a hormone that raises body temperature and helps liberate fatty acids from cells to be burned as fuel. When subjects on a 1,000-calorie-a-day diet supplemented with yohimbine hydrochloride (a prescription medicine), they lost an average of 7.8 pounds in three weeks compared with a control group that lost 4.8 pounds. Whether the whole herb yohimbe produces the same effect is unclear. Still, the herb is included in some natural weight-loss formulas.

Yohimbe is considered a dangerous herb, even by herbalists' standards. It can cause anxiety, elevated blood pressure, irregular heartbeats, headaches, painful erections, flushing, hallucinations, kidney failure, seizures, and death.

It's best to avoid supplements containing the herb yohimbe. In fact, the American Botanical Council, which promotes herbal supplements, has recommended that consumers avoid it. Further, the FDA considers it to be potentially unsafe.

Precautions

If you're still curious and want to try an herbal supplement, do it with care by following these few precautions: Start with low doses. More is not necessarily better and could be dangerous. Take only one type of supplement at a time. Allow at least 24 hours in between supplements before changing the dosage or starting something new. Keep empty bottles on hand for a while; in case of an adverse reaction, you can provide information about the supplement to your doctor.

Sports Nutrition Fact vs. Fiction:

Functional Foods—The New Training Staple?

If you've ever bitten into a sport bar, swilled a glass of calcium-fortified orange juice, or slurped a soup beefed up with herbs such as St. John's wort or echinacea, you've feasted on something called a "functional food."

Technically, the term "functional food" refers to a food product that enhances performance or is beneficial to health. In its position paper on functional foods, the American Dietetic Association formally defines these products as "any modified food or food ingredient that may provide a health benefit beyond the traditional nutrients it contains."

Products that fit this definition include the following:

- **Foods in which sugar, fat, sodium, or cholesterol have been reduced or eliminated.** Fat-free cheese, reduced-sugar jam, or low-sodium soup are all examples. Functional foods like these are beneficial to people on restricted diets and may be helpful in preventing or controlling obesity, cardiovascular disease, diabetes, and high blood pressure.
- **Foods in which naturally occurring ingredients have been increased.** Breakfast cereal and pasta that have been enriched with additional fiber or vitamins are good examples. Foods modified in this way can play an important role in preventing disease.
- **Foods enhanced with nutrients not normally present.** Folic acid–enriched bread and soups or soft drinks spruced up with therapeutic herbs are good examples. Enriched foods help people take in higher levels of health-protective nutrients and can be important in maintaining general wellness.
- **Probiotic yogurt and other dairy products to which special healthy bacteria have been added as a part of the fermentation process.** These foods are believed to enhance healthy flora in the intestines, which improve digestion and prevent disease.
- **Sport foods targeting the nutrient and energy needs of athletes and exercisers.** These include sport drinks with added electrolytes; protein powders formulated with creatine, amino acids, and other nutrients; and sport bars packed with vitamins, minerals, or herbs. Functional foods like these are designed to provide energy, enhance muscle growth, and replenish nutrients lost during exercise.

Table 8.1 Rating the Herbal Supplements

Supplement	Definitely worth it	Possibly useful	Wasting your time	Potentially harmful
Buchu	•			
Fo-ti	•			
Guarana	•			
Maté	•			
Ciwujia		•		
Echinacea		•		
Green tea		•		
Burdock			•	
Canaigre			•	
Citrus aurantium			•	
Cordyceps			•	
Damiana			•	
Gotu kola			•	
Pau d'arco			•	
Sassafras			•	
Saw palmetto			•	
Tribulus terrestris			•	
Ephedra				•
Ginseng				•
Yohimbe				•

So, should you incorporate these foods into your diet, if you're not already doing so?

Answer—yes, particularly if convenience is important and you're trying to enhance muscular health, strength, and growth. Sport foods, in particular, can help you achieve those goals. However, think of functional foods as supplements to your diet rather than substitutes for real food. Ultimately, the best way to fuel your body is always by eating a varied, nutrient-rich diet of low-fat proteins and dairy products, fruits, grains, and vegetables.

Part III

Plans

Here's where you put your knowledge to work. You have the foundation, the information, and hopefully, the inspiration. Now put it all into practice, designing your own personalized Power Eating plan. To begin with, determine your goals: Do you want to maintain, build, taper, or cut? Are you in your off-season trying to gain, or approaching a championship and planning for a peak? With the information here, you can figure your calories and map out your protein, carbohydrate, and fat needs based on your personal goals, just as I would if you came to my office. I've kept no top-level professional secrets from these pages. It's all here.

Once you've designed your diet, have some fun with the recipes in chapter 16. This section includes my special power drinks, which I created for the clients and teams I've worked with over the years. These drinks can be used in place of liquid formula supplements. Add powdered supplements to them for an extra boost. My family and I particularly enjoy the smoothies, and we make them daily. They're a great way to sneak in fruit servings. Don't miss the power breakfasts, either. They will give your day a tasty and energy-charged start.

Most of all, train hard and POWER EAT!

9 Planning a Peak

Perhaps you've decided to fine-tune your physique to look more trim, fit, and muscular. Maybe you desire to take your strength training up a notch—to competitive bodybuilding, powerlifting, or weightlifting. Or perhaps you're already a competitive strength trainer who's searching for that extra edge. No matter what your ambition, proper nutrition is the key.

You may not realize it, but the same nutritional techniques that work for bodybuilders and other athletes can also be applied to exercisers and recreational strength trainers. That's because the goals are generally the same: increasing muscularity (degree of muscular bulk), etching in definition (absence of body fat), and training for symmetry (shape and size of your muscles in proportion to each other).

Whether you're trying to get in shape for swimsuit season or preparing for a bodybuilding competition, you strive to reduce body fat, but without sacrificing muscle mass, to reveal as much muscular definition as possible. Or perhaps one of your chief goals is building strength and muscle mass—either for looks and health or because you're a competitive powerlifter and weightlifter. In these cases, your goal is to lift as much weight as possible when you train and/or compete.

If you're a competitor, you'll be required to "make weight" to qualify for a specific weight class. Thus, you must focus on gaining and preserving muscular weight, as well as on losing body fat to achieve your contest weight. Diet therefore plays a critical role in precontest preparation for all competitive strength trainers who want to achieve peak shape.

Until quite recently, most strength athletes partitioned their diets into two distinct phases: a "bulking phase," in which the competitor eats huge amounts food without much regard to fat content or other sound nutrition practices; and the "cutting phase," in which drastic measures such as starvation-type dieting and drugs are used to lose weight rapidly in the weeks before a contest. Even if you're not a competitor, you've probably done something similar: bulking up in the winter, then crash dieting to get in shape for summer.

Unless sound nutritional practices are followed, the cutting phase, much like a crash diet, can be unhealthy, rigid, monotonous, and risky to performance. Bulking up, in particular, tends to pile on fat pounds, which are that much harder to lose when it comes time to get in shape or prepare for competition.

Today though, more strength athletes choose to stay in competition shape year round. That way, it's easier to lose body fat because there's less to lose, and the process of cutting up is much safer and more successful.

This chapter discusses a step-by-step diet strategy called "tapering" that lets you lose maximum body fat, retain hard-earned muscle, and perform at your very best level. This strategy works for exercisers, bodybuilders, and strength athletes—anyone who wants to become lean and muscular. The end of the chapter covers key issues for bodybuilders, powerlifters, and weightlifters.

Step 1: Plan Your Start Date

The length of time you spend dieting depends on how out of shape you are to begin with. If you've let yourself get too fat by bulking up, then you'll really have to stretch your dieting out by several months.

A caution for bodybuilding competitors: Don't start your dieting too close to your contest either. You'll be too tempted to resort to crash dieting. This can result in loss of muscle, decreased strength and power, low energy, moodiness or irritability, and low immunity. Losing lots of fat in a short period of time is virtually impossible for most people, anyway. Physiologically, no one can lose more than four pounds of fat a week even by total fasting. Take a gradualistic approach to dieting.

Start your diet or contest preparation about 10 to 12 weeks before your competition. During this period, make slight adjustments in your calorie and nutrient intake, as well as in your aerobic exercise level. In addition, supplement with creatine and take a carbohydrate/protein supplement immediately after your training session, as suggested in chapter 7.

Step 2: Figure Out a Safe Level of Calorie Reduction

Getting cut is absolutely essential to achieving physique perfection, as well as for competitive success in a sport such as bodybuilding. One way

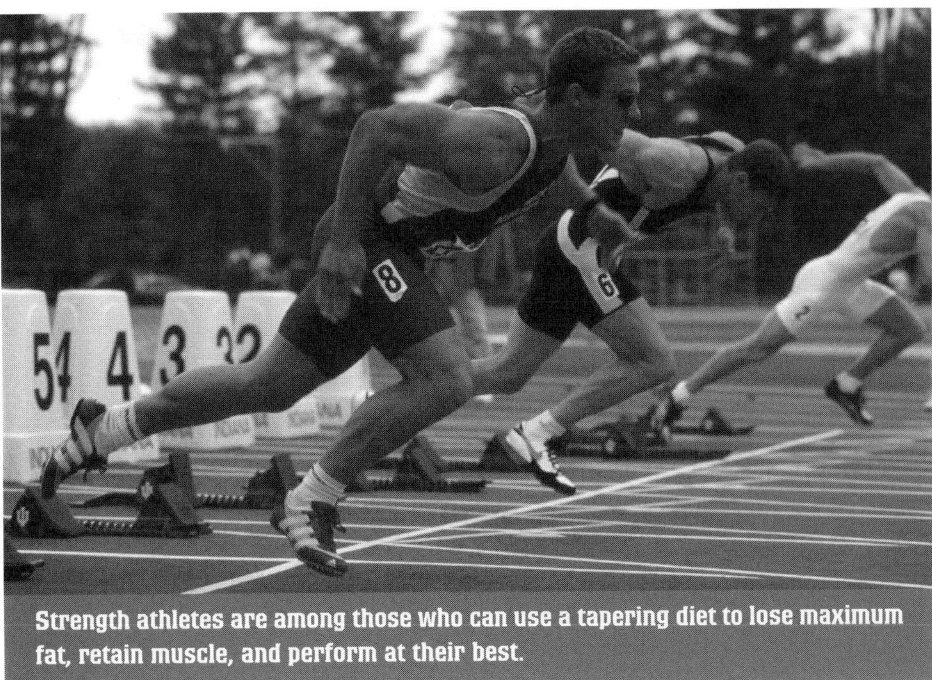

Strength athletes are among those who can use a tapering diet to lose maximum fat, retain muscle, and perform at their best.

to begin this process is by slightly reducing your caloric intake. By consuming fewer calories, you can gradually reduce body fat to lower levels. But you don't want to cut calories too much. A drastic reduction in calories will downshift your RMR—for two reasons. The first has to do with the thermic effect of food (TEF), the increase in your RMR after you eat a meal as food is digested and metabolized. Eating more calories increases the thermic effect of food and along with it the RMR. Likewise, cutting calories decreases the TEF, as well as the RMR. Without enough calories to drive your metabolic processes, it becomes harder for your body to burn calories to lose body fat.

Second, long periods of calorie deprivation—that is, diets under 1,200 calories a day—lower your RMR as a result of something called the "starvation adaptation response." This simply means that your metabolism has slowed down to accommodate your lower caloric intake. Your body is stockpiling dietary fat and calories rather than burning them for energy. You can actually gain body fat on a diet of 1,200 calories or less a day.

The starvation adaptation response has been observed frequently in undernourished endurance athletes. In a study of triathletes, researchers found these athletes weren't consuming enough calories to fuel themselves for training and competition. When calories were increased, the athletes' weight stayed the same. This occurred because their RMRs returned to normal with the introduction of ample calories. So to keep your metabolism running in high gear, you have to eat enough calories to match your energy requirements.

While dieting, reduce your calories by up to 500 each day. A reduction like this won't adversely affect your RMR. At the same time, increase your aerobic exercise to burn up to 500 calories a day. Both adjustments should allow for an energy deficit of 1,000 calories a day. A pound of fat is equal to 3,500 calories, so with a deficit of 1,000 calories, you should lose one to two pounds of body fat a week—a safe rate of fat loss that should successfully help you get tapered and cut by your deadline.

You may want to reduce your caloric intake by only 250 calories, depending on how much fat you need to lose in the allotted time and how efficiently your body burns fat.

Another way to figure out how many calories you need to lose body fat is the calories per kilogram of body weight per day method. These calorie levels have been calculated from research and observation of highly muscled athletes doing rigorous exercise. If you are not in this category, you will need to drop your calorie intake by about 5 to 10 calories per kilogram to achieve similar results. You generally need about 38 to 44 calories per kilogram of body weight a day to maintain your weight or higher (50 to 60 calories if your training program includes aerobics). To lose body fat, drop down to 30 to 35 calories per kilogram of body weight a day. Don't go any lower than that, however, because you risk losing muscle.

You might wonder: Why can't I just crash diet for a few weeks to get in shape? After all, I'm training hard with weights. Shouldn't strength training protect me from losing muscle?

As logical as the argument sounds, scientific research proves otherwise. Case in point: In one study, overweight women were divided into two groups: a diet-only group or a diet-plus-strength-training group. The experimental diet provided only 800 calories a day, and the study lasted four weeks. Now, the intriguing news: Both groups lost roughly the exact same amount of weight (11 pounds). Even the composition of the lost weight was the same. All the women lost eight pounds of fat and three pounds of muscle. Bottom line: Strength training didn't preserve muscle even under low-calorie dieting conditions.

The implications are clear: In just four short weeks, you can lose precious muscle if you crash diet. Watch how low you go, calorie-wise. Research with bodybuilders confirms that you can lose muscle on calories as low as 18 per kilogram of body weight a day in just seven days.

Step 3: Increase Your Aerobic Exercise

To sculpt a fit physique, increase the intensity and duration of your aerobic exercise. Aerobic exercise stimulates the activity of a fat-burning enzyme, technically known as "hormone-sensitive lipase," which breaks down stored fat and moves it into circulation to be burned for energy. Aerobic exercise also increases $\dot{V}O_2max$—the capability to process oxygen and transport it to body tissues. Fat is burned most efficiently when there's sufficient oxygen available.

If you put a lot of effort into your aerobics, you may not have to reduce your calories. That's the conclusion of a recent study from West Virginia University. Women of normal weight were able to decrease their body fat within three months simply by exercising aerobically four days a week for about 45 minutes each time at a heart rate of between 80 to 90 percent of their maximum. They didn't have to cut calories, yet still lost plenty of body fat.

Some good news: The better trained you are aerobically—and the leaner you are—the better your body can burn fat for energy. By increasing $\dot{V}O_2max$ and thus available oxygen to tissues, aerobic exercise enhances the ability of your muscles to combust fat as fuel. At the cellular level, the breakdown of fat speeds up, and it's released faster from storage sites in fat and muscle tissue.

There's no doubt about it: Aerobic exercise is a miracle worker when it comes to fat burning. Stay aerobically fit and lean year round, and you'll have no trouble shedding those last few parcels of pudge.

Step 4: Eat More Protein

To shed body fat, you should be eating at least 1.8 to 2.0 grams of protein per kilogram of body weight a day. This level will help you maintain muscle mass. Increasing your protein intake during a time of calorie reduction helps protect against muscle loss. The extra protein can be used as a backup energy source in case your body needs it.

Step 5: Time Meals and Exercise for Greater Fat-Burning

Want to maximize fat-burning during aerobic exercise? Then don't eat a high-carb meal (especially one that contains high-glycemic foods) within three to four hours of exercising. This recommendation is the exact opposite of what I'd tell an endurance athlete, or a strength trainer during the regular training period. But read on.

Preworkout carbs curtail your fat-burning ability during the first 50 minutes of moderate-intensity exercise. What happens is this: Carbs trigger the release of insulin into the bloodstream. Insulin keeps the fat-burning enzyme, hormone-sensitive lipase, from breaking down stored fat for energy. In the absence of carbs, your body is thus more likely to draw on its fat reserves for energy. You can get leaner as a result.

Eat a little protein in the preworkout period, instead of carbs, if your body needs some extra nutrient energy. Protein does not inhibit the fat-breakdown process during exercise like carbohydrate does. However, eliminating preworkout carbs is a practice that should be followed only when you're trying to burn an optimum amount of body fat.

Step 6: Don't Neglect Carbs

As far as the rest of your diet is concerned, don't cut your carbs too much—or else you're going to be really sluggish and out of sorts, because a carb-needy body adversely affects your energy levels and mood. Clearly, it's critical to have some carbohydrates in your diet throughout the tapering phase.

With the recommended increase in your protein intake, your total calories might look something like this: protein, 20 to 25 percent; carbohydrate, 60 to 65 percent; and fat, 15 to 20 percent. As long as you do not cut calories too drastically, you'll still have enough carbs to support your training requirements.

Step 7: Lower Your Fat Intake

Watch your fat intake, too. As I explained in chapter 4, fat in the diet turns into fat on the body more easily than carbohydrate does. Thus, it becomes even more critical to avoid high-fat foods during your tapering phase. Make whole grains, pastas, beans, vegetables, and fruits the mainstays of your diet, and you'll automatically eat a low-fat diet. This low-fat diet should contain much more unsaturated than saturated fat. See chapter 4 for how to calculate the fat content in your diet.

Step 8: Space Your Meals Throughout the Day

Your body will better use its calories for energy, rather than deposit them as fat, if you eat several small meals throughout the day. Most bodybuilders and other strength athletes eat five, six, or more meals a day. Spacing meals in this manner keeps you well-fueled throughout the day. Plus, the more times you eat, the higher your metabolism stays—thanks to the thermic effect of food. In other words, every time you eat, your metabolism accelerates. For best results, don't consume more than 400 to 500 calories at one sitting. Eating multiple meals throughout the day is a good dietary practice to follow, whether or not you're dieting for competition.

Step 9: Supplement Prudently

There are some real nutritional horror stories among people who crash diet or diet stringently for contests. They tend to suffer deficiencies in calcium, magnesium, zinc, vitamin D, and other nutrients. Generally, these occur because dieters and bodybuilders eliminate dairy foods and red meat while dieting. You really don't need to shy away from these foods, however. Red meat can be included in your diet as long as it's lean and cooked appropriately. Nonfat dairy foods, an important source of body-strengthening minerals, can be included in your diet too. Neither of these foods will make you gain fat, as long as you eat them in moderation.

Because calories are cut during diets, supplement with an antioxidant vitamin/mineral formula that contains 100 percent of the DRI for all essential nutrients. This type of supplement will help cover your nutritional bases. See chapters 6 and 7 for additional supplement recommendations.

Step 10: Watch Your Water Intake

Fitness-conscious people live in dread of water retention, medically known as edema. True, water retention can keep you from looking lean even after you've pared down to physique perfection. Water can swell up in certain areas, and you look "fat" even though it's only water weight.

How can you prevent water retention? Ironically, the best defense is to drink plenty of water throughout your tapering period. This means drinking between 8 and 10 cups, or more, of pure water daily. With ample fluid, your body automatically flushes itself of extra water.

Conversely, not drinking enough water can make your body cling to as much fluid as it can, and you'll end up bloated. Dehydration can sap your energy too. Low on fluids, you won't be able to work out as intensely.

Besides drinking plenty of water, follow these strategies to prevent water retention.

Moderate Your Sodium Intake If You're "Sodium Sensitive"

An essential element in our diets, sodium has gained a very bad reputation. Our bodies have a minimum requirement of 500 milligrams a day. The body tightly regulates its electrolyte levels, including sodium. Decreasing sodium levels really doesn't have much of an effect. Your body holds on to the exact amount of sodium it needs, even if you reduce your intake. It's essential to consume the minimum requirement to maintain fluid balance and electrolyte balance. Otherwise, nerve and muscle function will be impaired, and exercise performance will definitely diminish. Some bodybuilders have passed out just before their competition because of dehydration and possible electrolyte imbalance.

If you're "sodium sensitive"—that is, sodium does cause you to retain water—you probably should reduce your intake slightly. Don't go to extremes, though. Simply avoid high-sodium foods, such as snack foods, canned foods, salted foods, pickled foods, cured foods, and lunch meats. Certainly don't add any extra salt to your food. This is the key. But eliminating natural, whole foods because of their sodium content is usually unnecessary.

To maintain a low-sodium diet, concentrate your food choices on whole grains, fresh fruits and vegetables, nonfat dairy foods, and unprocessed meats.

Diuretics flush sodium and other electrolytes from your body, causing life-threatening imbalances. Avoid diuretics at all cost. And stay away from illegal drugs if you're a competitor. Their use is unethical and unhealthy.

Eat Vegetables That Are Naturally Diuretic

Some foods naturally help the body eliminate water. These include asparagus, cucumbers, and watercress. You might try eating these while dieting, especially if water retention is a concern.

Don't Let Up on Your Aerobics

Aerobic exercise improves the resiliency and tone of blood vessels. Unless blood vessels are resilient, water can seep from them and collect in the tissues. Water retention is the result. A regular program of aerobics helps prevent this.

For Powerlifters and Weightlifters Only

As a powerlifter or weightlifter, you probably don't care much about getting ripped. Rather, you want to be as strong and as powerful as possible in your weight class. Here's what you should do to go strong for training and competition.

Load Your Muscles With Energy Sources

Carbohydrates and creatine are your best bets. Stay on a high-carb diet, supplemented with creatine. Take your creatine with carbs, as recommended in chapter 7, to supercharge your muscles with energy. Of the numerous studies now being published on creatine, this supplement is proving to be a sure thing for boosting strength and power.

You don't need to "carbohydrate load." There's no scientific evidence showing that this method has any performance-enhancing benefit for strength athletes. Simply maintain a high-carb diet throughout your training and competition preparation. Going into competition well fueled is critical.

Up Your Aerobics If You Need to Make Weight

While maintaining your high-energy diet, increase your aerobics. This will help you lose fat to qualify for your weight class. You may need to decrease your calories slightly too. If so, give yourself plenty of time to make weight—at least 10 to 12 weeks. If your contest is fast approaching, you can cut your calories down to 30 per kilogram of body weight a day. That will result in a three- to four-pound weight loss a week. But keep in mind that you may lose some muscle mass too.

Power Profiles

Couple's Fitness

Sometimes, good nutrition can turn back the clock—or at least, it feels that way.

Looking and feeling younger—that's the best way to describe the experience of Al and Joyce, a retired couple in their early 50s. Their goals were to lose body fat and gain more energy. However, they experienced much more.

After following the Power Eating Diet, Al lost 25 pounds and reduced his body fat percentage from 18 percent to 11 percent. Joyce lost 10 pounds. On purpose, both trimmed down slowly, over a time period of many months. In addition, Al improved his cholesterol profile significantly.

"Everyone tells us that we are getting younger. I didn't feel or look this good when I was in my 20s," Al said.

Both Al and Joyce ski eight hours a day, four days a week during ski season. In the spring and summer, they hike instead of ski, using heavy backpacks. They have also begun a serious strength-training program on my recommendation.

Added Al: "When I skied prior to starting Power Eating, I would be exhausted by the end of the day. Now I never feel tired."

If you do cut to 30 calories per kilogram of body weight a day, stay on this regimen for no longer than seven days. Prolonged restrictive dieting slows your RMR—and your ability to burn fat.

Avoid Dangerous Make-Weight Practices

Before a meet, it's fairly common for some lifters to exercise in rubberized suits or sit in steam and sauna baths for extended periods—all without drinking much water. This practice can lead to dehydration so severe that it can harm the kidneys and heart. Dehydrated lifters usually do poorly in competition.

Nor is fasting a good idea, even for a day or two. You'll lose water rapidly—and with it, the health problems caused by dehydration. Glycogen depletion sets in too, making it virtually impossible to perform well on competition day.

Toward Physique Perfection!

If you follow these guidelines as best you can, you'll be amazed by how easy dieting can be. Within just a few months, you'll achieve superb condition. So get started—off with the body fat, and on with the muscle!

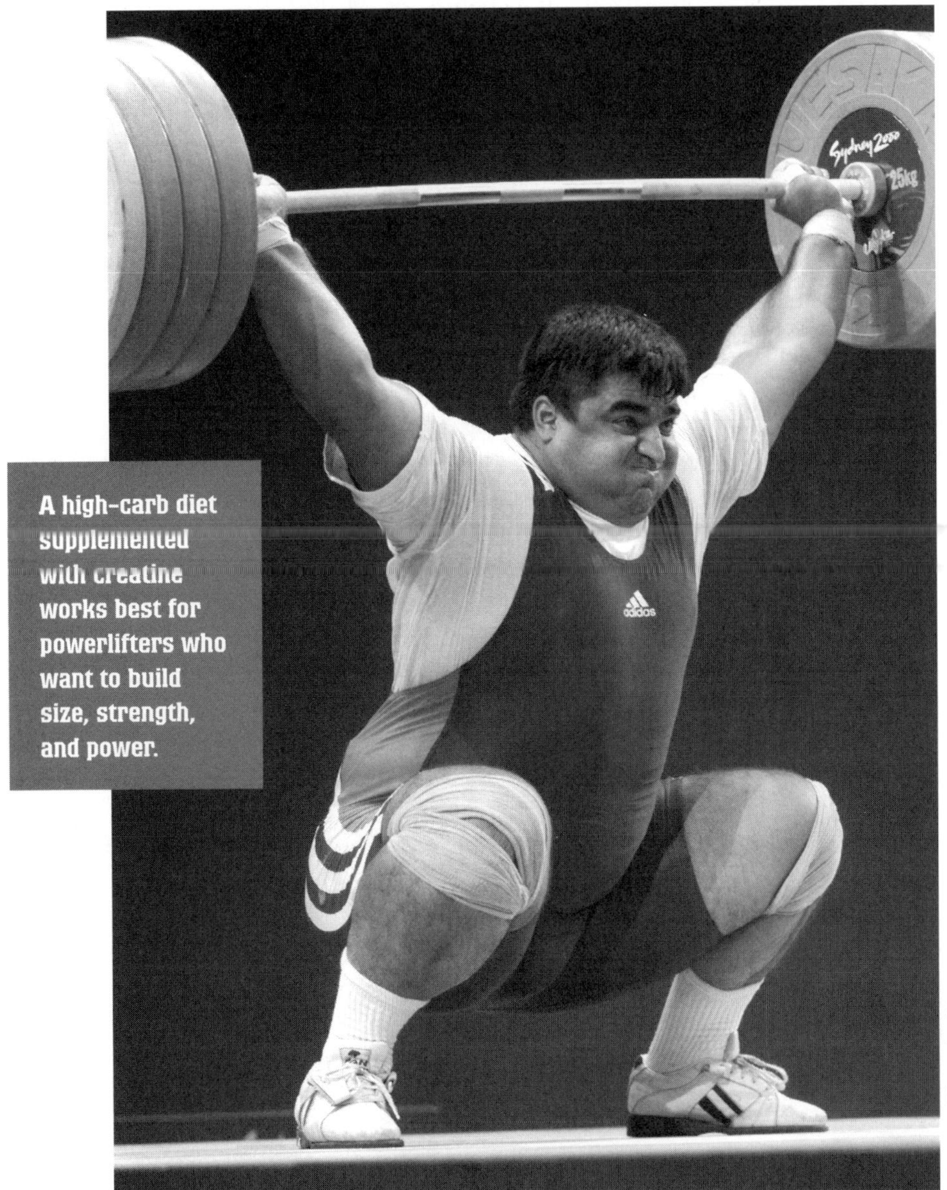

A high-carb diet supplemented with creatine works best for powerlifters who want to build size, strength, and power.

Sport Nutrition Fact vs. Fiction:

Insulin: A Magic Bullet?

One of the most powerful and multifunction hormones in the human body is insulin. It increases the uptake and use of glucose by cells, including muscle cells. It has an anabolic (tissue-building) effect on the body by promoting protein formation. It joins forces with human growth hormone to promote growth. And, on the downside, it promotes fat synthesis.

Medically, the drug insulin is used to treat diabetes, a complex disease in which the pancreas does not produce enough insulin (a condition known as type I diabetes), or the body doesn't use it properly (type II diabetes). Type I diabetic patients require injections of insulin. Diabetes, in general, is the seventh leading cause of death in the United States, and about 11 million people have it.

In bodybuilding circles, insulin got a lot of attention in the '80s when an insulin-dependent diabetic bodybuilder won several major contests and came to prominence. Nondiabetic, healthy bodybuilders started experimenting with insulin to see whether it would spark muscle growth. Thus, insulin joined the ranks of chemical muscle-building aids.

Bodybuilders and other strength athletes assumed that if insulin increased the body's use of glucose, then it could maximize glycogen storage. Wrong—there is no scientific evidence backing this. It is well known that you can stockpile plenty of glycogen with a high-carbohydrate diet. Nor is there any evidence that insulin promotes muscle growth.

Fooling around with insulin is downright dangerous. Injections of insulin, or any other synthetic hormone for that matter, can throw your natural hormonal balance out of whack and lead to a whole host of medical problems. Plus, there's the danger of insulin shock, which occurs when too much insulin is injected. You could become unconscious or have a seizure. Another complication is hypoglycemia, in which blood sugar drops dangerously low. Symptoms include tremors and sweating and, in extreme cases, convulsions, and loss of consciousness.

Unless you are being treated for type I diabetes, leave insulin alone. Combined with hard-work training in the gym, the new nutritional discoveries now available to strength trainers and other athletes are all you need to build a winning physique.

10 Building Your Power Eating Plan

To help you map out your own power eating diet, sample maintenance, building, tapering, and cutting diets are included in the subsequent chapters. All the sample diets are based on the needs of a 120-pound (54.5 kilogram) woman and a 180-pound (81.8 kilogram) man. Some numbers are rounded to the nearest 10 or 100 to make the diet user-friendly. To change pounds to kilograms, divide pounds by 2.2.

The Power Eating plan is based on several strategies. I first determine the proper calorie level for the goal of the plan and then the right distribution of protein, fat, and carbohydrate to meet that goal. Menu development is based on a food group plan that I have tweaked just a bit to meet what I think is the current state-of-the-science. Food groups force you to have variety in your diet, and at the same time allow you to personalize your program through food choices and exchanges between food groups. Use the sample diets as a starting point and then add or subtract servings to meet your protein, carb, and fat needs.

There are a lot of examples of fat servings, and this is done purposely to give you the freedom to personalize your plan. Nonfat milk and very lean and lean protein sources are the primary choices included in the meal plans. This is to accommodate adding healthier fats such as vegetable oils, nuts, and seeds in place of animal fats that are higher in saturated fats. You will also count any lowfat or fat-free protein supplements as very lean protein servings.

To use more medium-fat protein sources such as whole eggs and soy products, as well as the occasional high-fat protein source, just exchange one very lean protein serving plus one fat serving for one medium-fat protein serving. Exchange one lean protein serving plus one fat serving for one high-fat protein serving. Refer to the "Your Diet Plan" chart to become proficient at food group exchanges. Remember that you can easily determine your fat grams once you have calculated your total calories, protein, and carbohydrate needs. All the leftover calories are fat calories. Divide fat calories by 9 to get your total fat grams per day.

Notice that alcoholic beverages are listed as fat servings in the chart of food groups and serving sizes. Alcohol is metabolized more similarly to fat than any of the other macronutrients. Remember that too much alcohol on a regular basis will slow your training, halt your fat loss, and even impair your health and safety.

Other carbohydrates are what I call a "sugary" food category. They do not contain any fat, but they are pure carbohydrates, many of which are high-glycemic index carbs. You will find sport drinks in this food group, as well.

Your Diet Plan

This chart shows the amount of nutrients in one serving from each food group. Once you have calculated your daily nutrient and calorie needs, use this chart to design your diet. Make sure that you select from all of the food groups to ensure a well-balanced diet. Add liquid supplements to meet additional carbohydrate, protein, and calorie needs. Refer to the charts on serving size guidelines on pages 209 through 215 for a representation of foods and serving sizes for each food group.

Food groups	Carbohydrate (g)	Protein (g)	Fat (g)	Calories
Starch	15	3	1 or less	80
Fruit	15	—	—	60
Milk				
Nonfat	12	8	0–3	90
Low-fat	12	8	5	120
Other carbohydrates	15	—	—	60
Vegetables	5	2	—	25

Food groups	Carbohydrate (g)	Protein (g)	Fat (g)	Calories
Meat and meat substitutes				
Very lean	—	7	0–1	35
Lean	—	7	3	55
Medium	—	7	5	75
Fat	—	—	5	45

Adapted from *Exchange Lists for Meal Planning*. American Diabetes Association, the American Dietetic Association. 1995.

Know Your Portions

A portion is the amount of food used to determine the numbers of servings for each food group. It is not always the amount of food that you would think of as a serving, however. For example, one portion of pasta is just a half cup. But if you have pasta for dinner, you would likely eat at least one cup. One cup of pasta equals two servings from the bread and cereal group.

Learning the portion sizes for servings is the foundation of success. It is the method by which calorie control is built into the Power Eating Plan. If you are eating portions that are too large or too small, the plan will not work. Look at the following chart for a listing of foods and serving sizes for each food group. In the beginning, you should refer to this chart frequently, as well as weigh and measure foods to get a handle on portion sizes. After a few weeks, you will be able to do it on your own.

Milk, Yogurt, and Cheese Group

A portion equals 90–120 calories.
Each portion contains 0–3 grams of fat.

Food	Size of one portion
Nonfat milk or plain nonfat yogurt	1 cup
Evaporated skim milk	1 cup
Nonfat dry milk	⅓ cup

Food	Size of one portion
Nonfat or low-fat soy or rice milk, fortified with calcium and vitamins A & D	1 cup
Buttermilk	1 cup
Low-fat or nonfat cottage cheese	½ cup
Ricotta cheese	2 oz.
Low-fat or nonfat hard cheese (cheddar, Swiss)	1 oz.
American cheese	1 slice
Low-fat or nonfat ice cream or frozen yogurt	½ cup
Low-fat or nonfat fruit-flavored yogurt	1 cup
Low-fat or nonfat pudding	½ cup

Fruit Group

A portion contains 60 calories.
Each portion contains 0 grams of fat.

Food	Size of one portion
Most fruits, whole	1 medium
Most fruits, chopped or canned in own juice	½ cup
Melon, diced	1 cup
Berries, cherries, grapes (whole)	¾ cup
Fruit juice	½ cup
Banana	1 small
Grapefruit, mango	½
Plums	2 each
Apricots	4 each
Strawberries (whole)	1¼ cup
Kiwi	1 each

Food	Size of one portion
Prunes, dried	3 each
Figs	2 each
Raisins	2 Tbsp.
Juice—cranberry, prune, fruit blends (100% juice)	⅓ cup
Cranberry juice cocktail (reduced calorie)	1 cup

Vegetable Group

Each portion contains 25 calories.
Each portion contains 0 grams of fat.

Food	Size of one portion
Most cooked vegetables	½ cup
Most raw leafy vegetables	1 cup
Sprouts	1 cup
Most other raw vegetables, chopped or sliced	1 cup
Vegetable juice	6 oz.
Vegetable soup	1 cup
Tomato sauce	½ cup
Salsa (made without oil)	3 Tbsp.

Bread, Cereal, Rice, and Pasta Group

Each portion has 60–100 calories.
Each portion contains 0–1 gram of fat.

Food	Size of one portion
Bread	1 slice
Pita	1 oz.
Bagel, English muffin, bun	½ small (1 oz.)
Roll	1 small

Food	Size of one portion
Cooked rice, cooked pasta	½ cup
Tortilla	6-inch round
Crackers, large	2, or 3-4 small
Croutons	⅓ cup
Pretzels, nonfat chips	1 oz.
Rice cakes	2 each
Cooked cereal	½ cup
Cold cereal, unsweetened	1 cup
Granola	¼ cup
Corn, green peas, mashed potato	½ cup
Corn on the cob	1 medium
White or sweet potato baked with skin	1 small

Meats, Poultry, Fish, Dry Beans, and Eggs Group

Each protein portion contains about 35–75 calories. Very lean servings contain 35 calories and 0–1 gram of fat; lean, 55 calories and 3 grams of fat; and medium-fat, 75 calories and 5 grams of fat.

Food	Size of one portion
Very lean	
White meat skinless poultry	1 oz.
White fish	1 oz.
Fresh or canned tuna in water	1 oz.
All shellfish	1 oz.
Beans, peas, and lentils	½ cup
Cheeses and processed sandwich meat with 1 gram of fat	1 oz.
Egg white	1 each

Food	Size of one portion
Lean	
Select or choice grades of lean beef, pork, lamb, or veal trimmed to 0 fat	1 oz.
Dark meat skinless poultry or white meat chicken with skin	1 oz.
Oysters, salmon, catfish, sardines, tuna canned in oil	1 oz.
Processed sandwich meat with 3 grams of fat	1 oz.
Parmesan cheese	1 oz.
Medium-fat	
Most styles of beef, pork, lamb, veal—trimmed of fat, dark meat poultry with skin	1 oz.
Ground turkey or chicken	1 oz.
Cheese with 5 grams of fat	1 oz.
Cottage cheese 4.5% fat	1/4 cup
Whole egg	1 each
Regular soy milk	1 cup
Tempeh	4 oz. or 1/2 cup
Tofu	4 oz. or 1/2 cup

Other Carbohydrates

Each serving of other carbohydrates contains 15 grams of carbohydrates and 60 calories. Some foods listed are more than 1 serving. You can substitute or exchange these foods based on the number of servings.

Food	Number of servings
Angel food cake, unfrosted, 1/12 cake	2
Hard candy, 3 small	1
Cookie, nonfat, 2 small	1

Food	Number of servings
Cranberry sauce, jellied, ¼ cup	1 ½
Frozen fruit bars, 100% juice, 1 bar (3 oz.)	1
Fruit snacks, chewy (pureed fruit concentrate), 1 roll (3 oz.)	1
Fruit spreads, 100% fruit, 1 Tbsp.	1
Gatorade sport drink, 1 cup	1
Gelatin, regular, ½ cup	1
Gingersnaps, 3 small	1
Granola bar, nonfat, 1 bar	2
Ice cream, nonfat, no sugar added, ½ cup	1
Jam or jelly, regular, 1 Tbsp.	1
Pudding, regular (made with low-fat milk), ½ cup	2
Pudding, sugar-free (made with low-fat milk), ½ cup	1
Salad dressing, nonfat, ¼ cup	1
Sherbet, sorbet, ½ cup	2
Soda pop, 12 oz.	3
Syrup, light, 2 Tbsp.	1
Syrup, regular, 2 Tbsp.	1
Syrup, regular, ¼ cup	4
Yogurt, frozen, nonfat, no sugar added, ½ cup	1
Yogurt, nonfat with fruit, 1 cup	3
Yogurt, nonfat, no sugar added, 1 cup	1 ½

Fats and Oils

Each portion contains 45 calories.
Each portion contains 5 grams of fat.

Food	Size of one portion
Oil, butter, margarine, full-fat mayonnaise	1 tsp.
Diet margarine	1 tsp.
Cream cheese, whipped cream, sour cream	1 Tbsp.
Cream cheese, whipped cream, sour cream (low-fat or nonfat)	1 Tbsp.
Salad dressing (full-fat)	1 Tbsp.
Salad dressing (low-fat or nonfat)	1 Tbsp.
Avocado	1/8 medium
Olives	8
Nuts	6–10
Seeds	1 Tbsp.
Peanut butter and other nut butters	1 Tbsp.
Equivalent to 2 fat servings:	
Regular beer or wine	6 oz.
Light beer	8 oz.
Liquor	1 oz.

Power Profiles

A Winning Formula

A championship high school football team in Pennsylvania was accused by the local newspaper of taking creatine—even performance-enhancing drugs—because the players had gotten so big. But when confronted with these accusations, the coach replied, "All we are using is Dr. Susan Kleiner's Power Eating Diet. That is our winning formula."

This high school has won five state football championships through 2000—four in the past four years. They just won their fourth championship in a row. Since 1998, I have been working with the strength coach on nutrition strategies for the players. The players have more energy, endurance, muscle, and power during training, practices, and games. The team is now ranked 13th in the nation.

11 Maintenance Plan

The following maintenance diet is designed for exercisers, bodybuilders, recreational strength trainers, powerlifters, and weightlifters.

Power Eating Maintenance Diet

	Men	Women
Calories/kg	44	38–44
Calories/lb	20	17–20

Power Eating Nutrients for Maintenance

	180-lb man (3,600 calories)	120-lb woman (2,400 calories)
	Grams	Grams
Protein 1.4 g/kg 0.64 g/lb	115	76
Carbohydrate 7 g/kg 3.2 g/lb	573	382
Fat (g)	94	63

57

Maintenance Diet

Food Groups	Number of Servings
Breads, cereals	9
Fruit	5
Nonfat milk	2
Other carbohydrates	8
Vegetables	5
Protein sources	
Very lean	2
Lean	2
Fat	9

Menu	Food Group Servings
Breakfast	
1 bagel	2 breads
1 cup orange juice	2 fruits
10-oz. latte	1 milk
2 tsp. butter	2 fats
water	water
Snack	
2 granola bars	2 other carbohydrates 2 fats
water	water
Lunch	
1 cup tomato soup with 4 crackers	2 breads
½ cup fresh fruit	1 fruit
1 ½ cups tossed salad	3 vegetables
1 oz. grilled chicken	1 lean protein
2 Tbsp. regular or 4 Tbsp. reduced-fat salad dressing	2 fats
water	water

2,400 Calories

Menu	Food Group Servings
***Preworkout snack**	
2 slices bread	2 breads
1 Tbsp. honey	1 other carbohydrate
2 tsp. peanut butter	1 fat
water	water
Workout	
16-oz. sport drink	2 other carbohydrates
water	water
Postworkout snack	
High-Calcium Smoothie (minus ½ cup frozen fruit and ½ Tbsp. protein powder)—see chapter 16	2 fruits 1 milk 2 other carbohydrates 2 very lean proteins
Dinner	
1 ½ cups whole wheat pasta	3 breads
1 cup fat-free pasta sauce	2 vegetables
1 100% fruit juice frozen bar	1 other carbohydrate
1 oz. ground round or ½ cup tofu (1 lean protein + ½ fat)	1 lean protein
6 oz. red wine	2 fats
water	water

Note on the preworkout snack: *Your preworkout snack should be eaten two to three hours before your workout.*

Maintenance Diet

Food Groups	Number of Servings
Breads, cereals	12
Fruit	6
Nonfat milk	2
Other carbohydrates	16
Vegetables	8
Protein sources	
Very lean	2
Lean	2
Medium-fat	3
Fat	12

Menu	Food Group Servings
Breakfast	
1 bagel	2 breads
1 cup orange juice	2 fruits
1 Tbsp. butter	3 fats
2 sugar packets	2 other carbohydrates
coffee	
water	water
Snack	
1 cup nonfat yogurt with fruit	5 other carbohydrates
2 granola bars	2 fats
water	water
Lunch	
2 cups rice	4 breads
2 cups stir-fried vegetables	4 vegetables
3 oz. pork	3 medium-fat proteins
1 Tbsp. vegetable oil	3 fats
water	water

3,600 Calories

Menu	Food Group Servings
***Preworkout snack**	
2 slices bread	2 breads
2 Tbsp. honey	2 other carbohydrates
4 tsp. peanut butter	2 fats
water	water
**Eat this snack two to three hours before your workout.*	
Workout	
32-oz. sport drink	4 other carbohydrates
water	water
Postworkout snack	
Kleiner's Muscle-Building Formula II (see chapter 16)	3 fruits 2 milks 2 other carbohydrates 2 very lean proteins
Dinner	
2 cups whole wheat pasta	4 breads
1 slice watermelon	1 fruit
1 cup fat-free pasta sauce	4 vegetables
1 cup steamed asparagus	
2 oz. ground round or 1 cup tofu (2 lean proteins + 1 fat)	2 lean proteins
1 tsp. olive oil drizzled on asparagus	3 fats
6 oz. red wine	
water	water

12 Building Plan

My Building Diet is designed for exercisers, bodybuilders, powerlifters, weightlifters, and other serious strength trainers who are interested in building quality muscle. The larger you are and the greater your muscle mass, the more calories it will take for you to build muscle. If you are not seeing gains at these caloric levels, increase your calories by 250 to 500 per day by primarily increasing carbohydrates, and secondarily increasing fats. If you are cross-training with intense aerobic exercise, increase your carbohydrate intake to 9 to 10 grams per kilogram of body weight per day.

Power Eating Building Diet

	Men	Women
Calories/kg	52+	44-52
Calories/lb	24+	20-24

Power Eating Nutrients for Building

	180-lb man (4,250 calories)	120-lb woman (2,800 calories)
	Grams	Grams
Protein **1.6 g/kg** **0.73 g/lb**	131	87
Carbohydrate **8 g/kg** **3.6 g/lb**	654	436
Fat (g)	123	79

Building Diet

Food Groups	Number of Servings
Breads, cereals	11
Fruit	6
Nonfat milk	2
Other carbohydrates	9
Vegetables	5
Protein sources	
Very lean	2
Lean	2
Fat	12

Menu	Food Group Servings
Breakfast	
1 bagel	2 breads
1 cup orange juice	2 fruits
10-oz. latte	1 milk
2 Tbsp. 100% fruit spread	2 other carbohydrates
2 tsp. butter	2 fats
water	water
Snack	
2 granola bars	2 other carbohydrates
	2 fats
water	water
Lunch	
1 cup tomato soup with 4 crackers	2 breads
½ cup fresh fruit	1 fruit
1 ½ cups tossed salad	3 vegetables
1 oz. grilled chicken	1 lean protein
2 Tbsp. regular or 4 Tbsp. reduced-fat salad dressing	2 fats
water	water

2,800 Calories

Menu	Food Group Servings
***Preworkout snack**	
2 slices bread	2 breads
1 Tbsp. honey	1 other carbohydrate
4 tsp. peanut butter	2 fats
water	water
** Eat this snack two to three hours before your workout.*	
Workout	
16-oz. sport drink	2 other carbohydrates
water	water
Postworkout snack	
High-Calcium Smoothie (minus ½ cup frozen fruit and ½ Tbsp. protein powder)—see chapter 16	2 fruits 1 milk 2 other carbohydrates 2 very lean proteins
Dinner	
2 cups whole wheat pasta	5 breads
1 slice Italian bread	
1 slice watermelon	1 fruit
1 cup fat-free pasta sauce	2 vegetables
1 oz. ground round or ½ cup tofu (1 lean protein + ½ fat)	1 lean protein
2 tsp. olive oil for dipping the bread	4 fats
6 oz. red wine	
water	water

Building Diet

Food Groups	Number of Servings
Breads, cereals	14
Fruit	11
Nonfat milk	2
Other carbohydrates	15
Vegetables	6
Protein sources	
Very lean	3
Lean	3
Medium-fat	3
Fat	16

Menu	Food Group Servings
Breakfast	
1 bagel	2 breads
1 cup orange juice	4 fruits
4 Tbsp. raisins	
¼ cup lowfat cottage cheese*	1 very lean protein
½ Tbsp. butter (for bagel)	5 fats
18 almonds	
2 sugar packets	2 other carbohydrates
coffee	
water	water
**Mix raisins and almonds with cottage cheese.*	
Snack	
1 cup nonfat yogurt with fruit	5 other carbohydrates
2 granola bars	2 fats
water	water
Lunch	
2 cups rice	4 breads
1 medium-large banana	2 fruits

4,250 Calories

Menu	Food Group Servings
Lunch ***(continued)***	
2 cups stir-fried vegetables	4 vegetables
3 oz. pork	3 medium-fat proteins
1 Tbsp. vegetable oil	3 fats
water	water
***Preworkout snack**	
2 slices bread	2 breads
2 Tbsp. honey	2 other carbohydrates
4 tsp. peanut butter	2 fats
water	water
** Eat this snack two to three hours before your workout.*	
Workout	
32-oz. sport drink	4 other carbohydrates
water	water
Postworkout snack	
Kleiner's Muscle-Building Formula II (see chapter 16)	3 fruits 2 milks 2 other carbohydrates 2 very lean proteins
Dinner	
2 cups whole wheat pasta 1 small or ½ cup sweet potato 1 slice Italian bread	6 breads
1½ cups fresh pineapple	2 fruits
1 cup fat-free pasta sauce	2 vegetables
3 oz. ground round or 1½ cup tofu (3 lean proteins + 1½ fats)	3 lean proteins
2 tsp. olive oil for dipping bread 6 oz. red wine	4 fats
water	water

Power Profiles

Are you a "hard-gainer"—unable to put on any appreciable muscle weight no matter how hard you try?

That was the case of Scott E., a 44-year-old business executive who at 6' 3" and 177 pounds had not been able to gain weight in 20 years. To make matters worse, he had no appetite, plus he had stomach problems caused by stress, infections, and overtreatment with antibiotics. I placed him on my Power Eating Building Diet.

Before beginning this diet, Scott was consuming only about 2,800 calories a day and not enough vitamins, minerals, or fluids. I increased his calories to 3,560 calories daily, plus added more protein (113 grams daily) and carbs (570 grams daily). He started supplementing with a good antioxidant, began eating multiple meals throughout the day, and consumed healthier fats from fish and plant sources. He also decreased his alcohol intake.

In addition, I recommended that Scott supplement with Kleiner's Muscle-Building Formula, take 400 milligrams of vitamin E, and continue taking acidophilus, a supplement that restores intestinal flora after antibiotic treatment. I also suggested that Scott try a natural supplement, PRELIEF, to help reduce stomach irritation.

In only six weeks, Scott's energy levels soared, and he felt energetic enough to begin a regular exercise program. He gained 15 pounds of pure muscle—with no increase in his waist measurement. Scott felt that the PRELIEF helped him eat the extra calories without stomach irritation.

As Scott put it: "In the first three weeks, I gained 14 pounds, from 180 to 194. To put this in perspective, I have not weighed over 184 in 20 years and have been trying to gain weight for the past two to three years."

What's more, most of his stomach problems were resolved.

13 Tapering Plan

My Tapering Diet is designed for exercisers, bodybuilders, athletes, and virtually anyone who wants to lose body fat in a safe, controlled manner—without losing precious muscle. Caloric levels differ for men and women because it is more difficult for women to lose fat than it is for men.

Power Eating Tapering Diet

	Men	Women
Calories/kg	38	35
Calories/lb	17	16

Power Eating Nutrients for Tapering

	180-lb man (3,100 calories)	120-lb woman (1,900 calories)
	Grams	Grams
Protein **2.0 g/kg** **0.91 g/lb**	164	109
Carbohydrate **6 g/kg for men** **5 g/lb for women**	491	273
Fat (g)	53	41

Tapering Diet

Food Groups	Number of Servings
Breads, cereals	7
Fruit	4
Nonfat milk	2
Other carbohydrates	4
Vegetables	5
Protein sources	
Very lean	4
Lean	5
Fat	3

Menu	Food Group Servings
Breakfast	
1 bagel	2 breads
½ cup crushed pineapple	1 fruit
½ cup 4.5% fat cottage cheese (spread on bagel with crushed pineapple and broil for 2 minutes)	2 lean proteins
water	water
Snack	
10-oz. latte	1 milk
3 oz. (17 count) grapes	1 fruit
water	water
Lunch	
½ cup split pea soup (low-sodium)	2 breads
1 small whole wheat roll	
1½ cups tossed salad	3 vegetables
2 oz. grilled chicken	2 very lean proteins
1 Tbsp. regular or 2 Tbsp. reduced-fat salad dressing	1 fat
water	water

1,900 Calories

Menu	Food Group Servings
***Preworkout snack**	
celery sticks	1 vegetable
1 Tbsp. honey	1 other carbohydrate
2 tsp. peanut butter (mixed with honey and spread on celery)	1 fat
water	water
** Eat this snack three to four hours before your workout.*	
Workout	
water	water
Postworkout snack	
High-Calcium Smoothie (minus ½ cup frozen fruit and ½ Tbsp. protein powder)—see chapter 16	2 fruits 1 milk 2 other carbohydrates 2 very lean proteins
Dinner	
1½ cups whole wheat pasta	3 breads
½ cup nonfat pasta sauce	1 vegetables
⅓ cup frozen low-fat yogurt	1 other carbohydrate 1 fat
3 oz. ground round	3 lean proteins
water	water

Tapering Diet

Food Groups	Number of Servings
Breads, cereals	12
Fruit	6
Nonfat milk	3
Other carbohydrates	10
Vegetables	6
Protein sources	
Very lean	7
Lean	5
Medium-fat	1
Fat	3

Menu	Food Group Servings
Breakfast	
1 bagel	2 breads
1 cup orange juice	2 fruits
2 Tbsp. 100% fruit spread	2 other carbohydrates
1 egg (hard boiled, soft boiled, or fried in nonstick pan with 1 pump of cooking spray)	1 medium-fat protein
water	water
Snack	
protein-energy bar	2 breads 2 very lean proteins 1 fat
water	water
Lunch	
2 cups rice	4 breads
2 cups stir-fried vegetables	4 vegetables
4 fortune cookies	2 other carbohydrates

3,100 Calories

Menu	Food Group Servings
Lunch *(continued)*	
3 oz. shrimp	3 very lean proteins
2 tsp. vegetable oil	2 fats
water	water
***Preworkout snack**	
10-oz. latte	1 milk
2 slices raisin bread	2 breads
2 Tbsp. honey	2 other carbohydrates
water	water
** Eat this snack three to four hours before your workout.*	
Workout	
water	water
Postworkout snack	
Kleiner's Muscle-Building Formula II (see chapter 16)	3 fruits 2 milks 2 other carbohydrates 2 very lean proteins
Dinner	
2 cups whole wheat pasta	4 breads
1 slice watermelon	1 fruit
1 cup fat-free pasta sauce	2 vegetables
⅔ cup fat-free frozen yogurt	2 other carbohydrates
5 oz. ground round	5 lean proteins
water	water

Power Profiles

A Basketball Player Meets His Fitness Goals

Several years ago, I was asked to work with a 6' 11" 28-year-old basketball player after his physical conditioning and performance had markedly diminished over a period of a year.

At our initial meeting, he weighed 276 pounds and had 23 percent body fat. Seriously concerned about his condition and his performance, he reported that he had been desperately trying to lose weight, particularly because his contract required him to maintain a certain weight and body fat level. His initial goal weight was 261 pounds or 15 percent body fat; his ultimate goal was 257 pounds or 13 percent body fat.

His prior diet consisted of 1,700 calories, with 30 percent coming from protein, 27 percent from carbohydrates, 32 percent from fat, and 11 percent from alcohol. These are clearly not optimal percentages for an athlete, particularly one who is trying to lose weight and retain muscle.

Because of his poor diet, he was very fatigued, even unable to eat when he got home from practice. What's more, he was afraid to eat, fearing that food would show up the next day on the scale. He truly was in the beginning stages of an eating disorder. And the less he ate, the higher his body fat percentage climbed.

With only five weeks to go until his first goal weight deadline, I placed him on the Power Eating Tapering Diet. This initially included 4,019 calories (33 kcal/kg), 222 grams of protein, 603 grams of carbohydrate, and 80 grams of fat. In addition, he drank a gallon of fluid a day and supplemented with 500 milligrams of vitamin C and 800 milligrams of vitamin E. During his workout, he sipped a glucose-electrolyte solution (48 ounces); after his workout, he consumed a serving of Kleiner's Muscle Building Formula I or II.

After several weeks and seeing some success, I discontinued the glucose-electrolyte solution during his aerobic workouts. This was the only major change that I made. I also decreased his daily calories by 100 to activate further weight loss.

In five weeks, he made amazing progress, reaching 263.5 pounds and 12.75 percent body fat. A few weeks later, he weighed in at 261 pounds and 12.9 percent body fat.

14 Seven-Day Cutting Plan

To lean out—either for additional body fat reduction or for a bodybuilding competition—tweak your diet using my Seven-Day Cutting Diet. (It is particularly useful for bodybuilders who must lean out the week before a competition.) Women should reduce calories to 30 calories per kilogram of body weight per day, and men should reduce to 33 calories per kilogram of body weight a day. Use this approach only when absolutely necessary. Because women have more difficulty losing fat than men do, calorie levels are different here. Stay on this diet no longer than 14 days.

Power Eating Cutting Diet

	Men	Women
Calories/kg	33	30
Calories/lb	15	14

Power Eating Nutrients for Cutting

	180-lb man (2,700 calories)	120-lb woman (1,635 calories)
	Grams	Grams
Protein **2.0 g/kg** **0.91 g/lb**	164	109
Carbohydrate **5 g/kg for men** **4 g/lb for women**	409	218
Fat (g)	45	36

Cutting Diet

Food Groups	Number of Servings
Breads, cereals	7
Fruit	3
Nonfat milk	2
Other carbohydrates	2
Vegetables	4
Protein sources	
Very lean	4
Lean	5
Fat	2

Menu	Food Group Servings
Breakfast	
1 bagel	2 breads
½ cup crushed pineapple	1 fruit
½ cup 4.5% fat cottage cheese (spread on bagel with crushed pineapple and broil for 2 minutes)	2 lean proteins
water	water
Snack	
10-oz. latte	1 milk
water	water
Lunch	
½ cup split pea soup (low-sodium)	2 breads
1 small whole wheat roll	
1½ cups tossed salad	3 vegetables
2 oz. grilled shrimp	2 very lean proteins
1 Tbsp. regular or 2 Tbsp. reduced-fat salad dressing	1 fat
water	water

1,635 Calories

Menu	Food Group Servings
***Preworkout snack**	
1 slice bread	1 bread
1 oz. white meat chicken (make half sandwich with mustard and lettuce leaf)	1 lean meat
water	water
** Eat this snack three to four hours before your workout.*	
Workout	
water	water
Postworkout snack	
High-Calcium Smoothie (minus ½ cup frozen fruit and ½ Tbsp. protein powder)—see chapter 16	2 fruits 1 milk 2 other carbohydrates 2 very lean proteins
Dinner	
½ cup whole wheat pasta 1 slice Italian bread	2 breads
½ cup nonfat pasta sauce	1 vegetable
2 oz. ground round	2 lean proteins
1 tsp. olive oil for dipping bread	1 fat
water	water

Cutting Diet

Food Groups	Number of Servings
Breads, cereals	10
Fruit	5
Nonfat milk	3
Other carbohydrates	8
Vegetables	6
Protein sources	
Very lean	9
Lean	5
Fat	2

Menu	Food Group Servings
Breakfast	
1 bagel	2 breads
1 cup orange juice	2 fruits
2 Tbsp. 100% fruit spread	2 other carbohydrates
2 egg whites (can fry in nonstick pan with 1 pump of cooking spray)	1 very lean protein
water	water
Snack	
protein-energy bar	2 breads
	2 very lean proteins
	1 fat
water	water
Lunch	
1 cup rice	2 breads
1½ cups steamed vegetables	3 vegetables
4 fortune cookies	2 other carbohydrates

2,700 Calories

Menu	Food Group Servings
Lunch *(continued)*	
2 oz. stir-fried shrimp	2 very lean proteins
1 tsp. vegetable oil	1 fat
water	water
***Preworkout snack**	
10-oz. latte	1 milk
2 slices bread	2 breads
2 oz. white meat chicken	2 very lean proteins
water	water
* *Eat this snack three to four hours before your workout.*	
Workout	
water	water
Postworkout snack	
Kleiner's Muscle-Building Formula II (see chapter 16)	3 fruits 2 milks 2 other carbohydrates 2 very lean proteins
Dinner	
1 cup whole wheat pasta	2 breads
½ cup fat-free pasta sauce	3 vegetables
1 cup steamed asparagus	
⅔ cup fat-free frozen yogurt	2 other carbohydrates
5 oz. ground round	5 lean proteins
water	water

Special Advice to Competitors

Many strength athletes worry about being too full just as they go into competition. But it's critical to have enough fluid, calories, and nutrients to feel strong and look great. Probably the best way to do this is to use liquid meal-replacement supplements. These will charge you up but pass through your digestive system more quickly than solid foods.

Because each serving of meal-replacement supplement is about the number of calories as a small meal or snack, you should drink one 2½ to 3 hours before your competition. If you feel comfortable, you can also add some low-fiber foods throughout the day to increase your nutritional intake and avoid the boredom of just drinking. Then, eat a variety of foods after your competition to round out your nutrition for the day.

15 Customizing a Power Eating Plan

When strength-training athletes follow a healthy diet, they demonstrate what an amazing machine the human body is. Until recently, most sport scientists and physicians believed that strength training played a minor role in health maintenance. But now we know that, when combined with a healthful diet, strength training is essential not only for lifelong health but also for maintaining physical independence as we age.

Unfortunately, too many strength-training athletes use unhealthy dietary practices, and possibly even drugs, with the hope of cheating time and rapidly achieving their goals. They may cheat time in the short run, but in the long run they are cheating themselves out of living a long, healthy life. There's no question that by following a sophisticated, scientifically based, healthy diet plan, you can build tremendous strength and muscle. Other successful athletes have done it. It will take longer than if you followed illegal and unhealthy strategies, but you'll live to enjoy it and extend your playing life.

Personalizing the Plan

Even though you're an active person, you're still human, and your basic nutrient requirements are generally the same as the rest of the human race. Except, of course, for energy. To supply your body with the nutrients that you need every day, eat in virtually the same style as recommended in the USDA Food Guide Pyramid, but pump up the volume. In other words, to get all the calories you need, you'll probably need to eat more servings than recommended in the guide. As long as you eat a variety of foods from all the food groups and you consume enough calories to meet your daily needs, you'll most likely eat the amount of nutrients that your body requires. That's the whole concept behind the pyramid.

Depending on the total calories in your diet, the nutrients should fall at around 12 to 15 percent protein, 60 to 65 percent carbohydrates, and 20 to 25 percent fat during your training and maintenance phases. Tapering phases for bodybuilders or athletes trying to make weight will be different.

Learn to read labels. The nutrition facts labels on foods will tell you exactly how much protein, carbohydrate, and fat, and sometimes the types of fat, that are found in the food you're eating. You might also want to purchase a book or software that can give you the nutrient breakdown of foods.

Nutrition Facts

Serving Size 1/2 cup (114g)
Servings Per Container 4

Amount Per Serving

Calories 260 Calories from Fat 120

	% Daily Value*
Total Fat 13g	**20%**
Saturated Fat 5g	**25%**
Cholesterol 30mg	**10%**
Sodium 660mg	**28%**
Total Carbohydrate 31g	**11%**
Dietary Fiber 0g	**0%**
Sugars 5g	
Protein 5g	

Vitamin A 4%	Vitamin C 2%
Calcium 15%	Iron 4%

*Percent Daily Values are based on a 2000 calorie diet. Your daily values may be higher or lower depending on your calorie needs.

	Calories:	2000	2500
Total Fat	Less than	65g	80g
Sat. Fat	Less than	20g	25g
Cholesterol	Less than	300mg	300mg
Sodium	Less than	2400mg	2400mg
Total Carbohydrate		300g	375g
Dietary Fiber		25g	30g

Calories per gram:
Fat 9 • Carbohydrate 4 • Protein 4

If you're trying to achieve the greatest strength and muscle-gain goals, follow these guidelines when designing your diet:

1. Figure Out Your Calorie Needs Based on Present Body Weight

As your weight changes, energy and nutrients must be recalculated.

Training to maintain muscle: 44 calories per kilogram of body weight a day for men (3,608 calories a day for a 180-pound man). Women may be able to increase muscle at 44 calories per kilogram of body weight a day (2,398 calories for a 120-pound woman) and maintain at about 38 to 40 calories per kilogram of body weight a day (2,071 to 2,180 calories). The larger and more muscular a woman, the more calories she can handle for maintenance.

Some smaller women will need even fewer than 38 calories per kilogram per day to maintain weight. There is a lot of trial and error with women, because all the research has been done on men, and levels of activity vary widely. For the rest of the phases, women should generally choose the lower end of the calorie ranges. This diet is great for bodybuilders, powerlifters, and weightlifters, as well as for recreational strength trainers.

Building: 52 to 60 calories per kilogram of body weight a day, depending on intensity of training (4,264 to 4,920 calories for a 180-pound man; 2,834 to 3,270 calories for 120-pound woman). Start low and add as needed. As stated earlier, women will likely be able to build at 44 calories per kilogram of body weight a day (2,398 calories for a 120-pound woman). Smaller women should try slightly fewer calories to begin a building program and work up from there. This diet is good for all competitive and recreational strength trainers.

Tapering for competition (10 to 12 weeks of precontest dieting): 33 to 38 calories per kilogram of body weight a day (2,706 to 3,116 calories for a 180-pound man; 1,798 to 2,071 calories for a 120-pound woman). Because it's more difficult for women to lose fat than it is for men, women should choose the lower calorie range (decrease about 500 calories a day from maintenance caloric levels, and increase aerobic exercise to burn about 500 calories a day). Again, smaller women may need fewer calories. This recommendation is primarily for bodybuilders.

Cutting (7 to 14 days maximum): 30 calories per kilogram of body weight a day for women (1,635 calories for a 120-pound woman) and 33 calories per kilogram of body weight a day for men (2,706 calories for a 180-pound man). If you are a smaller woman who has been tapering on a lower calorie level, decrease recommended calories here as well. Use this approach only when absolutely necessary. This diet is only for bodybuilders or others trying to make a weight class—not for powerlifters or weightlifters.

For powerlifters and weightlifters trying to make a weight class: After dieting to build muscle, go back to the maintenance diet for two weeks before your meet, and use your goal weight for the calculations. This will allow for loss of body fat without loss of muscle, strength, or power. This strategy is also a good basic diet for the overweight strength trainer who wants to lose body fat.

2. Figure Your Protein Needs

Protein needs change with both energy intake and training goals. Make sure to cover your protein needs during all four diet strategies.

Bodybuilders

Maintenance: 1.4 grams per kilogram of body weight a day

Building: 1.6 grams per kilogram of body weight a day

Tapering: 2.0 grams per kilogram of body weight a day

Cutting: 2.0 grams per kilogram of body weight a day (2.2 for those eating mostly vegetarian)

Strength/speed athletes

Maintenance: 1.2 to1.4 grams per kilogram of body weight a day

Building: 1.4 to 1.6 grams per kilogram of body weight a day

Athletes who strength train in addition to their regular sport (cross-trainers): 1.4 to 1.6 grams per kilogram of body weight a day

3. Figure Your Carbohydrate Needs

Calculate your carbs as 7 to 10 grams per kilogram of body weight a day. Strength trainers only need closer to 8 grams per kilogram of body weight a day for maintenance and 9 grams per kilogram of body weight a day for building. Intense cross-trainers need closer to 10 grams per kilogram of body weight a day, and bodybuilders need 7 grams per kilogram of body weight a day for maintenance and 8 grams for building.

During tapering and cutting phases, women and men need different amounts of carbohydrates.

Tapering

Women: 5 g/kg/day

Men: 6 g/kg/day

Cutting

Women: 4 g/kg/day

Men: 5 g/kg/day

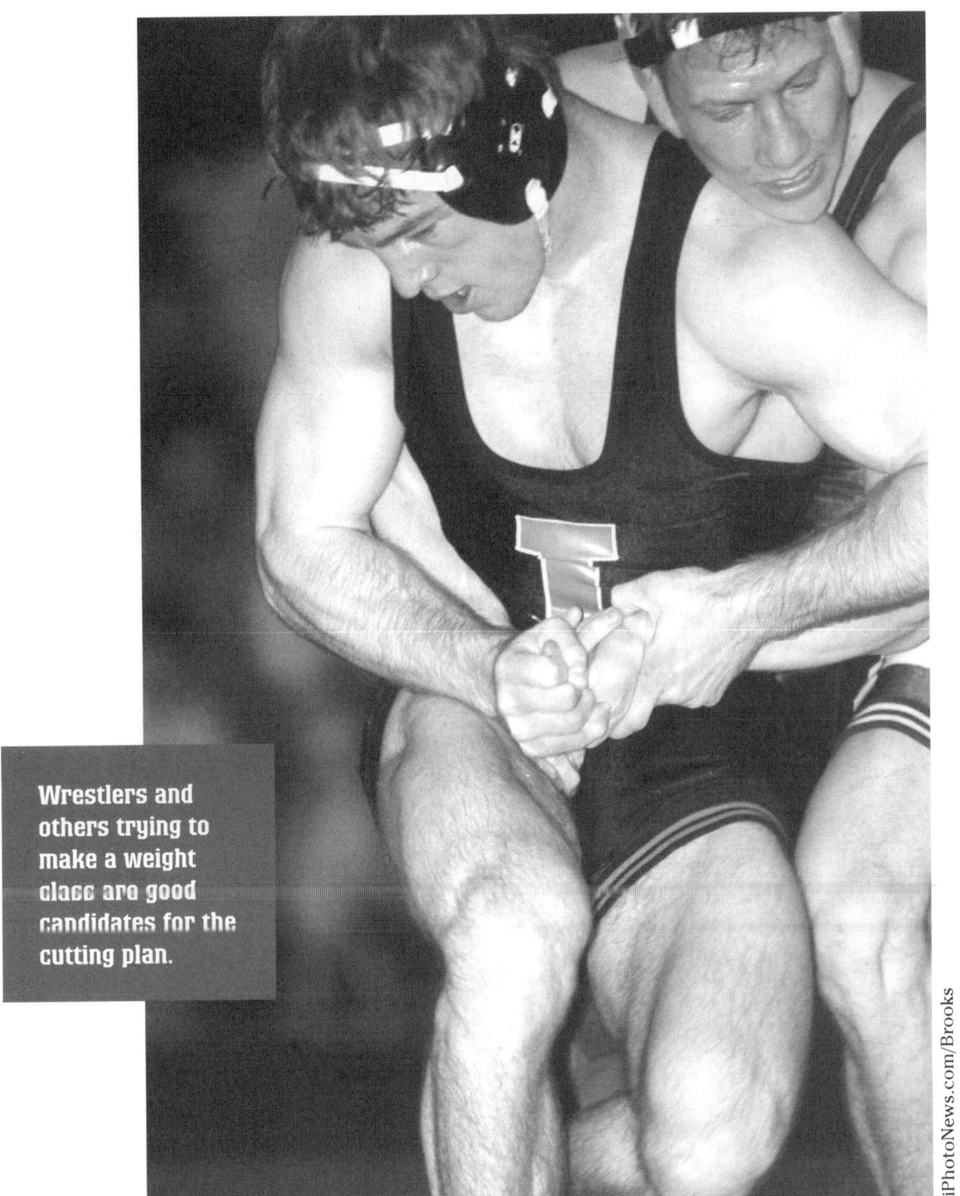

Wrestlers and others trying to make a weight class are good candidates for the cutting plan.

© iPhotoNews.com/Brooks

4. Figure Your Fat Needs

Basically, the rest of your calories will be 20 to 25 percent of your total calories. Fat sources should be predominantly monounsaturated and polyunsaturated, with much less saturated fat. Review chapter 4 to figure out grams of fat.

5. Fluid Intake

Drink a minimum of 8 to 12 cups of fluid daily. Consume more fluid in hot, humid weather or at high altitude and when you are exercising. Avoid caffeine and alcohol, which are dehydrating. Additional guidelines to follow:

- Fluids should be cool.
- For general exercise lasting less than an hour, water is sufficient for replacing lost fluids.
- If flavoring increases palatability, flavored unsweetened or lightly sweetened drinks should be used.
- For exercise lasting an hour or more or for high-intensity exercise lasting 45 minutes or more, carbohydrate-electrolyte sport drinks containing 4 to 8 percent carbohydrates (grams per 100 milliliter) are best. Carbohydrates can be glucose, sucrose, or maltodextrins. Fructose should not be the sole or primary carbohydrate, but it is acceptable in smaller amounts.
- Drink two cups of water two hours before exercise. Drink one cup (8 ounces) immediately before exercise.
- Drink 7 to 10 ounces every 10 to 20 minutes during exercise.
- Drink at least two to three cups of fluid for every pound of body weight lost during exercise.

6. Supplements

Liquid: Carbohydrate-electrolyte beverages (discussed previously).

Meal replacers: These are good to use as balanced snacks and after strength-training exercise to consume carbohydrate-protein combinations for potential muscle-building enhancement. They're also great to use on the day of contests to avoid looking or feeling too full. Don't forget to figure in the calories, protein, fat, and carbohydrate from these supplements into your dietary allowances.

Vitamins and minerals: One-a-day antioxidant multivitamin/mineral tablets may be unnecessary during maintenance and building phases but might be helpful during tapering, especially for women.

Vitamin E: A 200- to 400-International Unit supplement is recommended.

Calcium: For men and women who avoid dairy products because of taste or physical discomfort: 800 to 1,200 milligrams a day. It's best to try to get as much calcium as possible from food.

Creatine: This supplement is definitely worth a try, especially for full or partial vegetarians, because creatine is found naturally in meat. Follow dosing plan in chapter 7.

7. Time Your Meals Appropriately for Best Results

Eat small, frequent meals to promote calorie burning versus fat storage. Five to six meals a day are best—more if your calories are greater than 3,000 a day. Make sure to eat breakfast if you work out in the morning. Eat smaller meals in the evening. It's best to eat two to three hours before exercise. This meal should be high in carbs and low in fat (except when you're tapering).

Replace your glycogen stores by consuming high-glycemic index foods within 15 minutes to two hours after exercise.

Promote muscle building by consuming a carbohydrate-protein formula within 30 minutes and again two hours after strength-training exercise.

8. For Competitive Bodybuilders

Here's an at-a-glance review of guidelines to follow if you're preparing for a contest.

Tapering phase: Begin this phase 10 to 12 weeks before your contest. Decrease calories and increase aerobic exercise. The more aerobically fit you are, the more fat you'll be able to burn. Aerobic exercise should be part of your all-around program but is even more important now. During the tapering phase, reduce calories by reducing carbohydrates and fats. Avoid carbohydrates three to four hours before aerobic exercise to maximize your fat-burning potential.

Cutting phase (one to two weeks before your contest): If you're not looking as ripped as you would like to look, follow the 30 to 33 calories per kilogram per body weight a day cutting program for one week. This will allow for a final loss of three to four pounds, as long you keep your aerobic training intense. Make sure to increase your protein intake to 2.0 grams per kilogram of body weight a day. Drop calories by reducing carbs to 60 percent of total calories and by further reducing your fat intake.

Sticking to Your Plan

For these power-eating strategies to work, you have to stick to your plan. Design your diet with the foods that you like. Use the sample diets in chapters 11 through 14 to help you design your personal plan. If you don't like the foods you're supposed to eat, you won't stick to the plan. If you're

Power Profiles

Say Good-Bye to Yo-Yo Dieting

Here's a familiar story: Melody B., a 35-year-old female executive, was a yo-yo dieter who could never keep her lost weight off, despite a regular strength-training and aerobic exercise program.

At 5' 6" and 150 pounds, Melody had tried every fad diet, product, and diet drug there was—all to no avail. She was muscular, but her body-fat percentage was too high.

In just six weeks on the Power Eating Diet, Melody lost 1 percent of her body fat and one whole dress size. After this experience, she became so excited about fitness and nutrition that she started her own health and fitness promotion company.

After going on the diet, Melody had this to say: "Susan saved my life. Before, I couldn't go on any longer thinking about food all the time. Now I just know what to do and I do it, because it feels good."

using liquid supplements, try different brands and flavors, and find supplements that you like.

Pay attention to your body. Plan to eat when you're hungry. You might want to pick specific times of the day to eat rather than depending on the pace of each day. But also be aware of whether you are hungry or thirsty. Sometimes we confuse thirst with hunger. Keep food and drink on hand wherever you go. The most successful strength trainers always have a backpack full of food and drink that goes with them everywhere. This way, they can stick to their timed eating patterns, and if they get hungry, they're not dependent on vending machines or other snack foods that are high in fat and sodium.

During your tapering phase, you might find it difficult to eat at restaurants and especially difficult to travel. If you must do either, try to find restaurants that specialize in healthy fare. They should be able to easily adjust their menu to meet your personal needs. Don't forget to ask what is in the recipe. A menu description may be misleading. You can even ask for foods that are not on the menu. The restaurants may be able to accommodate your request.

Remember to always recalculate your requirements based on your present weight. If you have gained weight during a building or bulking phase and now want to taper, use your new weight rather than that of the prebulking phase.

No one can do this for you. You know that to get big and strong, you have to work your body hard. You also have to fuel your body to grow. And this is the best way. Plan your diet and stick to it. You'll be thrilled with how you feel, how you look, and how you perform.

Sport Nutrition Fact vs. Fiction: The Nutrition in Fast Foods

If yours is an on-the-go lifestyle, you probably have to order fast food every now and then. The key is to make the right choices—those that are low in fat and high in nutrition. Fortunately, fast-food restaurants today cater to the low-fat preferences of consumers.

To help you make healthy choices, table 15.1 lists some "best bets" at fast-food restaurants.

Here are some additional fast-food tips to keep you on track:

- Always order the regular-sized sandwiches because they are lower in fat.
- Instead of ordering a bigger sandwich, order a salad, lowfat milk, and low-fat frozen yogurt to complete your meal.
- Stay away from fried foods.
- Don't eat the high fat tortilla shells from taco salads.
- Request that sour cream and secret sauces be left off your order.
- Top your baked potato with chili instead of fatty cheese sauce.
- Whatever you order, order just one!

Table 15.1 Healthy Fast Food

Food	Calories	Percent of fat
Arby's		
Chocolate shake	451	23
Jamocha shake	368	26
Vanilla shake	330	31

(continued)

Table 15.1 (Continued)

Food	Calories	Percent of fat
Plain baked potato	240	7
Chicken fajita pita	272	31
Grilled chicken barbecue	378	34
Lite chicken deluxe	263	21
Lite ham deluxe	255	19
Lite roast beef deluxe	294	31
Lite roast turkey deluxe	260	17
French dip roast beef	345	32
Burger King		
Chocolate shake	409	24
Vanilla shake	334	27
Chocolate frozen yogurt	132	20
Vanilla frozen yogurt	120	23
BK broiler sandwich	267	32
Broiled chicken sandwich (no dressing)	140	26
McDonald's		
Shakes	320	5
Cheerios	80	11
Wheaties	90	10
English muffin with spread	170	21
Hotcakes with margarine and syrup	440	25
McDonaldland cookies	290	28
Soft-serve ice cream	140	29
Chunky chicken salad (no dressing)	150	24

Food	Calories	Percent of fat
Lite vinaigrette dressing (1 Tbsp.)	12	38
Hamburger	255	32
Pizza Hut		
Cheese pizza (2 medium slices)	518	35
Cheese pan pizza (2 medium slices)	492	33
Taco Bell		
Bean burrito	387	33
Chicken burrito	334	32
Combination burrito	407	35
Wendy's		
Apple Danish	360	35
Frosty (12 oz.)	340	26
Chili (small)	190	28
Chili (large)	290	28
Bacon and cheese baked potato	510	30
Broccoli and cheese baked potato	450	28
Plain baked potato	300	2
Caesar side salad	160	34
Grilled chicken sandwich	290	22
Subway		
Almost all selections at Subway restaurants are good choices EXCEPT the following high fat foods:		
6-inch cold subs		
Classic Italian BMT	450	42

(continued)

Table 15.1 (Continued)

Food	Calories	Percent of fat
Salads		
Seafood and crab	157	40
Steak and cheese	182	40
Cold cut trio	193	56
Tuna	198	55
Meatball	232	50
Classic Italian BMT	269	64
Super Subs		
Classic Italian BMT	668	53
Cold cut trio	517	42

16 Power Eating Recipes

Although there are many supplements on the market, I always like to use fresh ingredients whenever possible. These recipes have been designed for my strength training clients and teams over many years. Try them all to find which one will be your favorite.

Power Drinks

Kleiner's Muscle-Building Formula

8 ounces skim milk

1 packet Carnation Instant Breakfast

1 banana

1 tablespoon peanut butter

(Optional: Add 2 heaping tablespoons protein powder supplement or the equivalent of 25 grams of protein and 100 calories)

Blend until smooth.

One serving contains:

Nutrients	**Food group servings**
438 calories	1 milk serving
70 grams carbohydrate	2 other carbohydrate servings
17 grams protein	1 very lean protein serving
10 grams fat	2 fruit servings
6 grams fiber	2 fat servings

Kleiner's Muscle-Building Formula II

1 cup frozen strawberries

1 cup nonfat strawberry yogurt

1 heaping tablespoon protein powder supplement (or equivalent to 15 grams of total protein)

1 tablespoon honey

1 cup nonfat milk

1 cup calcium-fortified orange juice

Blend all ingredients together in blender until smooth.

One serving contains:

Nutrients	**Food group servings**
529 calories	3 fruit servings
100 grams carbohydrate	2 other carbohydrate servings
31 grams protein	2 nonfat milk servings
1 gram fat	2 very lean protein servings
4 grams dietary fiber	

Kleiner's Muscle Formula *PLUS*

2 packets Intact colostrum *or* 24 grams whey protein

1 cup frozen unsweetened strawberries

1 medium banana

1 cup nonfat vanilla soy milk fortified with calcium and vitamins A and D

1 cup orange juice fortified with calcium and vitamin C

Blend for 60 seconds until smooth.

One serving contains:

Nutrients	**Food group servings**
512 calories	4 fruit servings
90 grams carbohydrate	1 other carbohydrate serving
30 grams protein	1 nonfat milk serving
4 grams fat	3 very lean protein servings
8 grams dietary fiber	1 fat serving

Kleiner's Muscle Formula *PLUS Light*

1 packet Intact colostrum *or* 12 grams whey protein

1 cup frozen unsweetened strawberries

1 medium banana

1 cup nonfat vanilla soy milk fortified with calcium and vitamins A and D

1 cup orange juice fortified with calcium and vitamin C

Blend for 60 seconds until smooth.

One serving contains:

Nutrients	Food group servings
438 calories	4 fruit servings
87 grams carbohydrate	1 other carbohydrate serving
18 grams protein	1 nonfat milk serving
2 grams fat	1 very lean protein serving
8 grams dietary fiber	½ fat serving

Strawberry Banana Smoothie

1 packet strawberry Carnation Instant Breakfast Powder

1 cup low-fat strawberry banana yogurt

1 cup skim milk

2 ice cubes, crushed

Place all ingredients in a blender and process for 1 minute or until ice is blended. Drink immediately.

One serving contains:

Nutrients	Food group servings
470 calories	2 nonfat milk servings
91 grams carbohydrate	5 other carbohydrate servings
21 grams protein	1 very lean protein serving
2 grams fat	

High-Calcium Smoothie

One serving contains 600 mg calcium.

1 cup mixture of frozen mango, blueberries, strawberries, and raspberries

½ medium banana

½ cup nonfat vanilla yogurt

1 tablespoon nonfat dry milk powder

1 tablespoon milk-egg protein powder (equivalent of 13 grams of total protein)

½ cup nonfat milk

½ cup calcium-fortified orange juice

Blend all ingredients together in blender until smooth.

One serving contains:

Nutrients	**Food group servings**
478 calories	3 fruit servings
89 grams carbohydrate	2 other carbohydrate servings
28 grams protein	1 nonfat milk serving
<1 gram fat	3 very lean protein servings
7 grams dietary fiber	

Mocha Breakfast Smoothie

1 medium banana

1 low-fat coffee yogurt

2 tablespoons natural peanut butter

1 envelope chocolate instant breakfast mix

1 cup nonfat milk

10 to 12 ice cubes

Blend all ingredients together in blender until smooth. This recipe can be heated if you prefer a hot drink. For a warm drink, eliminate ice cubes. For a lower calorie beverage, make 1 recipe for 2 servings.

(continued)

Mocha Breakfast Smoothie (continued)

One serving contains:

Nutrients	**Food group servings**
722 calories	2 fruit servings
110 grams carbohydrate	4 other carbohydrate servings
33 grams protein	2 nonfat milk servings
21 grams fat	2½ very lean protein servings
7 grams dietary fiber	4 fat servings

Soyful Smoothie (Lactose-Free)

⅓ block soft tofu (5 ounces)

¾ cup frozen strawberries

½ medium banana

½ cup vanilla nonfat soy milk fortified with vitamins A and D and calcium

½ cup calcium-fortified orange juice

1½ tablespoons honey

Cream tofu in blender until smooth. Add the next five ingredients and blend until smooth.

One serving contains:

Nutrients	**Food group servings**
368 calories	4 fruit servings
76 grams carbohydrate	½ other carbohydrate serving
11 grams protein	½ nonfat milk serving
4 grams fat	1 medium-fat protein serving
5 grams dietary fiber	

Phytochemical Phenomenon Smoothie

This smoothie is a good source of antioxidant beta-carotene and other carotenes and phytochemicals important for boosting immune function and preventing cancer and heart disease.

2 cups mixture of frozen raspberries, peaches, and papaya

1 medium kiwifruit, peeled and quartered

1 cup nonfat apricot mango yogurt

1 cup pineapple juice

1 cup nonfat milk

Blend all ingredients together in blender until smooth. For a lower calorie beverage, make 1 recipe for 2 servings.

One serving contains:

Nutrients	**Food group servings**
700 calories	5 fruit servings
148 grams carbohydrate	3 other carbohydrate servings
20 grams protein	2½ nonfat milk servings
1 gram fat	
16 grams dietary fiber	

Zesty Citrus Smoothie

This smoothie will help replenish fluids and electrolytes, particularly on hot days.

2-inch piece of fresh ginger

zest of 1 large lemon (about 2 tablespoons)

1 cup lemon sorbet

2 cups cold unflavored sparkling water

2 tablespoons fresh lemon juice

1 tablespoon lime juice

⅛ teaspoon salt

4 tablespoons sugar

15 ice cubes

(continued)

Zesty Citrus Smoothie (continued)

Grate the ginger and squeeze out the juice. Blend the ginger juice with the remaining ingredients in a blender until mixture reaches the consistency of a frozen margarita drink. For a lower calorie beverage, make 1 recipe for 2 servings.

One serving contains:

Nutrients	**Food group servings**
460 calories	8 other carbohydrate servings
120 grams carbohydrate	
<1 gram protein	
3 grams dietary fiber	

Pina Colada Smoothie

1 cup nonfat milk

1 envelope vanilla Carnation Instant Breakfast powder

6 ounces low-fat pina colada yogurt

½ cup crushed pineapple in natural juice

2 tablespoons lite coconut milk

½ teaspoon rum extract

4 ice cubes

Place all ingredients in a blender and blend for 1 minute, or until smooth.

One serving contains:

Nutrients	**Food group servings**
455 calories	1 fruit serving
82 grams carbohydrate	2 other carbohydrate servings
21 grams protein	3 nonfat milk servings
5 grams fat	1 fat serving
1 gram dietary fiber	

Antioxidant Advantage

After intense exercise, your body needs to replace lost fluid and fuel, repair muscle tissue damage, and continue the process of building and strengthening muscles. This power drink will help you do it all.

1 cup nonfat milk

6 ounces strawberry-kiwi nonfat yogurt

½ cup frozen strawberries

1 whole kiwi, peeled

1 tablespoon lime juice

1 tablespoon honey

5 grams creatine monohydrate

Place all ingredients in a blender and blend for 45 seconds, or until smooth.

One serving contains:

Nutrients	**Food group servings**
380 calories	2 fruit servings
78 grams carbohydrate	1½ other carbohydrate servings
18 grams protein	2 nonfat milk servings
1 gram fat	
4 grams dietary fiber	

Cherry Cordial

1 cup nonfat milk

1 cup low-fat cherry yogurt

1 envelope chocolate Carnation Instant Breakfast powder

⅓ cup frozen cherries

Place all ingredients in a blender and blend for 45 seconds, or until smooth.

(continued)

Cherry Cordial (continued)

One serving contains:

Nutrients	**Food group servings**
551 calories	1 fruit serving
109 grams carbohydrate	4 other carbohydrate servings
21 grams protein	3 nonfat milk servings
4 grams fat	1 fat serving
3 grams dietary fiber	

Morning Pick-Me-Up

2 teaspoons Chai tea

2 cups nonfat milk

⅓ cup nonfat dry milk powder

1½ tablespoon honey

⅛ teaspoon nutmeg

4 ice cubes

Simmer the tea in milk for five to eight minutes. Cool in the refrigerator. Pour the milk into a blender, straining out the tea leaves. Add the remaining ingredients. Blend 1 minute or until smooth.

One serving contains:

Nutrients	**Food group servings**
350 calories	3 nonfat milk servings
62 grams carbohydrate	2 other carbohydrate servings
25 grams protein	
1 gram fat	

Caribbean Crush

11.5 ounces (1 can) papaya juice

⅓ cup crushed pineapple in natural juice

½ banana

4 tablespoons protein powder (21 grams)

6 ice cubes

Add all ingredients to blender and blend 1 minute or until smooth.

One serving contains:

Nutrients	Food group servings
423 calories	5 fruit servings
79 grams carbohydrate	3 very lean protein servings
23 grams protein	
2 grams fat	
6 grams dietary fiber	

Apple Pie A La Mode

1 cup unfiltered apple juice

½ cup unsweetened apple sauce

⅓ cup vanilla nonfat frozen yogurt

2 tablespoons toasted wheat germ

⅓ cup nonfat dry milk powder

1 tablespoon protein powder

Add all ingredients to blender and blend 1 minute or until smooth.

One serving contains:

Nutrients	Food group servings
392 calories	3 fruit servings
76 grams carbohydrate	1 other carbohydrate serving
20 grams protein	1 nonfat milk serving
2 grams fat	2 very lean protein servings
4 grams dietary fiber	

Lemon Lime Zinger Sport Drink

To fuel and hydrate your body, drink this power booster within two hours before exercise. It is also a great fluid replenisher during or after exercise or anytime during an active day.

1-inch piece of fresh ginger

2 cups cold unflavored sparkling water

1 tablespoon lemon juice

2 teaspoons lime juice

2 tablespoons sugar

scant 1/8 teaspoon salt

Grate the ginger and squeeze out the juice. Blend the ginger juice with the remaining ingredients in a blender for 20 seconds. Serve immediately.

One serving contains:

Nutrients	**Food group servings**
109 calories	7 other carbohydrate servings
28 grams carbohydrate	
0 gram protein	
0 gram fat	
0 gram dietary fiber	

Power Breakfasts

Indian Breakfast Salad

This delicious salad is served as a side dish in India but makes a fast and fabulous breakfast. It is spiced with cardamom, but because of cardamom's price, unless you use it in other recipes, you may prefer to use cinnamon.

½ teaspoon butter

2 tablespoons slivered almonds

2 medium bananas, thinly sliced

4 tablespoons low-fat plain yogurt

3 tablespoons light sour cream

1 tablespoon honey

⅛ teaspoon ground cardamom (or ¼ teaspoon ground cinnamon)

1. Melt the butter in a small nonstick skillet over medium heat. Toast almonds, stirring frequently, until golden, about three minutes.
2. Meanwhile, in a medium bowl, mix bananas with yogurt, sour cream, honey, and cardamom. Add almonds and enjoy. Makes 2 servings.

One serving contains:

Nutrients	Food group servings
250 calories	2 fruit servings
42 grams carbohydrate	1 other carbohydrate serving
6 grams protein	1 lean protein serving
8 grams fat	1 fat serving
4 grams dietary fiber	

Breakfast Parfait

Make this artistic, high-powered breakfast portable by using plastic drinking cups with lids.

2 cups low-fat strawberry yogurt

1 cup low-fat granola

1 cup fresh berries (whatever is in season)

1. In two 16-ounce glass or plastic cups, layer the ingredients by adding ½ cup of the yogurt, ¼ cup of the granola, and ¼ cup of berries.
2. Repeat step 1, reserving a dollop of the yogurt for the top. Makes two servings.

One serving contains:

Nutrients	**Food group servings**
458 calories	1 bread serving
94 grams carbohydrate	1 fruit serving
14 grams protein	1 nonfat milk serving
5 grams fat	3½ other carbohydrate servings
5 grams dietary fiber	½ lean protein serving
	½ fat serving

Peach Melba Yogurt Pops

These delicious pops can be prepared the night before to make a great light breakfast that you can easily hit the road with on a warm summer morning. If you don't want to bother with adding the sticks, just poke a fork into the pop when you are ready to eat.

1 cup sliced canned peaches in light syrup

1 cup low-fat raspberry yogurt

1 cup orange juice

1. Blend ingredients until smooth. Pour into four 10-ounce plastic cups. Place in the freezer.

(continued)

Peach Melba Yogurt Pops (continued)

2. When mixture is partly frozen, insert sticks or plastic spoons.

Makes two servings.

One serving contains:

Nutrients	**Food group servings**
280 calories	2 fruit servings
64 grams carbohydrate	1½ other carbohydrate servings
6 grams protein	1 nonfat milk serving
1 gram fat	
3 grams dietary fiber	

Orange Cinnamon French Toast

This toast takes only slightly longer to prepare than the standard version that pops out of the toaster.

2 large eggs, lightly beaten

2 tablespoons orange juice

¼ teaspoon ground cinnamon

vegetable cooking spray

4 slices whole wheat bread

1. In a shallow bowl, combine eggs, orange juice, and cinnamon.
2. Spray a nonstick skillet and heat over medium heat for one to two minutes, until hot. Dip bread into the mixture to coat both sides. Place bread slices in the skillet, pouring any extra egg mixture over them. Cook for about two minutes on each side or until browned. Makes two servings.

One serving contains:

Nutrients	**Food group servings**
220 calories	2 bread servings
28 grams carbohydrate	1 medium-fat protein serving
12 grams protein	
7 grams fat	
4 grams dietary fiber	

Pineapple Cheese Danish

4 slices raisin bread

4 tablespoons canned unsweetened crushed pineapple, drained

½ cup (4 ounces) part-skim-milk ricotta cheese

1 teaspoon brown sugar

dash ground cinnamon

1. Spread each slice of bread with one ounce of cheese and top with pineapple. Combine brown sugar and cinnamon and sprinkle on top of the pineapple.
2. Broil in a toaster oven or under the broiler until sugar starts to bubble, about two minutes. Makes two servings.

One serving contains:

Nutrients	**Food group servings**
246 calories	2 bread servings
35 grams carbohydrate	⅓ fruit serving
11 grams protein	½ medium-fat protein serving
7 grams fat	½ fat serving
3 grams dietary fiber	

Fruit 'n' Cheese

1 small red apple, cored and sliced

1 small D'Anjou or Bartlett pear, cored and sliced

2 ounces thinly sliced cheddar cheese

4 slices whole wheat toast

Place apple and pear slices on bread and cover with cheese to make open-face sandwiches. Place under broiler or in toaster oven for two to three minutes or until cheese melts and bubbles. Makes two servings.

(continued)

Fruit 'n' Cheese (continued)

One serving contains:

Nutrients	Food group servings
332 calories	2 bread servings
47 grams carbohydrate	1 fruit serving
13 grams protein	1 medium-fat protein serving
12 grams fat	1 fat serving
7 grams dietary fiber	

Pump Up Your Power Drink

You can create your own designer drink by adding certain natural ingredients and nutritional supplements. Here's a rundown:

Fiber. With a goal of 25 to 35 grams per day, getting in enough fiber is often difficult. Commercial juices and smoothies are usually devoid of fiber, but they don't have to be. Increase the fiber content of your power drinks by using fruit, fruits with skins or seeds, and wheat germ. You can also eat whole wheat crackers or breads with your drink to easily increase fiber.

Protein. Protein powders boost the protein content of your drink when you don't want to increase any other nutrients. Nonfat dry milk powder and whey powder are easy ways to supplement drinks with protein, carbohydrate, calcium, and riboflavin.

Energy. To pack in energy and nutrients, instant breakfast powders work well. If you are lactose intolerant, choose a lactose-free energy-boosting supplement powder.

Creatine monohydrate. If you participate in power sports or strength train, add creatine to your diet to enhance your performance. Especially after exercise, a power drink is a great way to get in one of your four daily 5-milligram doses.

References

Akermark, C., I. Jacobs, M. Rasmusson, and J. Karlsson. 1996. Diet and muscle glycogen concentration in relation to physical performance in Swedish elite ice hockey players. *International Journal of Sport Nutrition* 6: 272-284.

Allen, J.D. et al. 1998. Ginseng supplementation does not enhance healthy young adults' peak aerobic exercise performance. *Journal of the American College of Nutrition* 17: 462-466.

American Dietetic Association. 1995. Position of the American Dietetic Association: Phytochemicals and functional foods. *Journal of the American Dietetic Association* 95: 493-496.

American Dietetic Association. 1998. Position of the American Dietetic Association: Use of nutritive and non-nutritive sweeteners. *Journal of the American Dietetic Association* 98: 580-588.

Anderson, J.W. et al. 2000. Health advantages and disadvantages of weight-reducing diets: A computer analysis and critical review. *Journal of the American College of Nutrition* 19: 578-590.

Anderson, O. 1995. Burn, baby, burn. *Runner's World*, May, 38.

Andersson, B., X. Xuefan, M. Rebuffe-Scrive, K. Terning, et al. 1991. The effects of exercise training on body composition and metabolism in men and women. *International Journal of Obesity* 15: 75-81.

Antonio, J. 2000. The effects of Tribulus terrestris on body composition and exercise performance in resistance-trained males. *International Journal of Sports Nutrition and Exercise Metabolism* 10: 208-215.

Antonio, J. et al. 1999. Glutamine: A potentially useful supplement for athletes. *Canadian Journal of Applied Physiology* 24: 1-14.

Applegate, L. 1992. Protein power. *Runner's World*, June, 22-24.

Bahrke, M.S. et al. 1994. Evaluation of the ergogenic properties of ginseng. *Sports Medicine* 18: 229-248.

Balon, T.W., J.F. Horowitz, and K.M. Fitzsimmons. 1992. Effects of carbohydrate loading and weight-lifting on muscle girth. *International Journal of Sports Nutrition* 2: 328-334.

Balsom, P.D. et al. 1998. Carbohydrate intake and multiple sprint sports: With special reference to football (soccer). *International Journal of Sports Medicine* 20: 48-52.

Baranov, A.I. 1982. Medicinal uses of ginseng and related plants in the Soviet Union: Recent trends in the Soviet literature. *Journal of Ethnopharmacology* 6: 339-353.

Barth, C.A., and U. Behnke. 1997. Nutritional physiology of whey components. *Nahrung* 41: 2-12.

Bazzarre, T.L. et al. 1992. Plasma amino acid responses of trained athletes to two successive exhaustive trials with and without interim carbohydrate feeding. *Journal of the American College of Nutrition* 11 (5): 501-511.

Bean, A. 1996. Here's to your immunity. *Runner's World*, February, 23.

Bellisle, F., and C. Perez. 1994. Low-energy substitutes for sugars and fats in the human diet: Impact on nutritional regulation. *Neuroscience Behavioral Review* 18: 197-205.

Biolo, G. et al. 1997. An abundant supply of amino acids enhances the metabolic effect of exercise on muscle protein. *American Journal of Physiology* 273: E122-E129.

Bjorntorp, P. 1991. Importance of fat as a support nutrient for energy: Metabolism of athletes. *Journal of Sports Sciences* 9: 71-76.

Blumenthal, M. (ed.). 1998. *The Complete German Commission E Monographs*. Austin, Texas: American Botanical Council.

Brilla, L.R., and V. Conte. 1999. Effects of zinc-magnesium (ZMA) supplementation on muscle attributes of football players. *Medicine and Science in Sports and Exercise* 31 (5 Supplement): Abstract No. 483.

Brilla, L.R., and T.F. Haley. 1992. Effect of magnesium supplementation on strength training in humans. *Journal of the American College of Nutrition* 11: 326-329.

Brown, G.A. et al. 2000. Effects of anabolic precursors on serum testosterone concentrations and adaptations to resistance training in young men. *International Journal of Sports Nutrition and Exercise Metabolism* 10: 340-359.

Brown, J. 1990. *The science of human nutrition.* San Diego: Harcourt Brace Jovanovich, Publishers.

Brown, J., M.C. Crim, V.R. Young, and W.J. Evans. 1994. Increased energy requirements and changes in body composition with resistance training in older adults. *The American Journal of Clinical Nutrition* 60: 167-175.

Bryner, R.W., R.C. Toffle, I.H. Ullrich, and R.A. Yeager. 1997. The effects of exercise intensity on body composition, weight loss, and dietary composition in women. *Journal of the American College of Nutrition* 16: 68-73.

Bucci, L.R. 2000. Selected herbals and human exercise performance. *The American Journal of Clinical Nutrition* 72 (2 Supplement): 624S-636S.

Buckley, J.D. et al. 1998. Effect of an oral bovine colostrum supplement (Intact) on running performance. Abstract, 1998 Australian Conference of Science and Medicine in Sport, Adelaide, South Australia.

Buckley, J.D. et al. 1999. Oral supplementation with bovine colostrum (Intact) increases vertical jump performance. Abstract, 4th Annual Congress of the European College of Sport Science, Rome.

Bujko, J. et al. 1997. Benefit of more but smaller meals at a fixed daily protein intake. *Zeitschrift Fur Ernahrungswissenschaft* 36: 347-349.

Burke, E.R. 1999. *D-ribose: What you need to know.* Garden City Park, New York: Avery Publishing Group.

Burke, L.M. 1997. Nutrition for post-exercise recovery. *International Journal of Sports Nutrition* 1: 214-224.

Burke, L.M. et al. 1998. Carbohydrate intake during prolonged cycling minimizes effect of glycemic index of preexercise meal. *Journal of Applied Physiology* 85: 2220-2226.

Butterfield, G. et al. 1991. Amino acids and high protein diets. In D. Lamb and M. Williams (Eds.). *Perspectives in exercise science and sports medicine.* Vol 4, Brown & Benchmark, 87-122.

Campbell, W.W., M.C. Crim, V.R. Young, et al. 1995. Effects of resistance training and dietary protein intake on protein metabolism in older adults. *American Journal of Physiology* 268: E1143-E1153.

Carli, G. et al. 1992. Changes in exercise-induced hormone response to branched chain amino acid administration. *European Journal of Applied Physiology* 64: 272-277.

Casa, D.J. et al. 2000. National Athletic Trainers' Association Position Statement: Fluid replacement for athletes. *Journal of Athletic Training* 35: 212-224.

Castell, L.M. 1996. Does glutamine have a role in reducing infections in athletes? *European Journal of Applied Physiology* 73: 488-490.

Chandler, R.M., H.K. Byrne, J.G. Patterson, and J.L. Ivy. 1994. Dietary supplements affect the anabolic hormones after weight-training exercise. *Journal of Applied Physiology* 76: 839-845.

Charley, H. 1982. *Food science.* New York: John Wiley & Sons, Inc.

Cheuvront, S.N. et al. 1999. Effect of ENDUROX on metabolic responses to submaximal exercise. *International Journal of Sports Nutrition* 9: 434-442.

Clancy, S.P., P.M. Clarkson, M.E. DeCheke, et al. 1994. Effects of chromium picolinate supplementation on body composition, strength, and urinary chromium loss in football players. *International Journal of Sport Nutrition* 4: 142-153.

Clark, N. 1993. Athletes with amenorrhea. *The Physician and Sportsmedicine* 21: 45-48.

Clarkson, P.M. 1991. Nutritional ergogenic aids: Chromium, exercise, and muscle mass. *International Journal of Sport Nutrition* 1: 289-293.

Clarkson, P.M. 1996. Nutrition for improved sports performance: Current issues on ergogenic aids. *Sports Medicine* 21: 393-401.

Coleman, E. 1997. Carbohydrate unloading: A reality check. *The Physician and Sportsmedicine* 25: 97-98.

Collomp, K. 1991. Effects of caffeine ingestion on performance and anaerobic metabolism during the Wingate Test. *International Journal of Sports Medicine* 12: 439-443.

Collomp, K., A. Ahmaidi, M. Audran, and C. Prefaut. 1992. Benefits of caffeine ingestion on sprint performance in trained and untrained swimmers. *European Journal of Applied Physiology* 64: 377-380.

Convertino, V.A. et al. 1996. ACSM position stand. Exercise and fluid replacement. *Medicine and Science in Sports and Exercise* 28: i-vii.

Coyle, E.F. 1991. Timing and method of increased carbohydrate intake to cope with heavy training, competition and recovery. *Journal of Sports Sciences* 9 Spec No: 29-51.

Coyle, E.F. 1995. Fat metabolism during exercise. *Sports Science Exchange* 8: 1-7.

Coyle, E.F. 1997. Fuels for sport performance. In D. Lamb and R. Murray (Eds.). *Perspectives in exercise science and sports medicine.* Carmel, Indiana: Cooper Publishing Group.

Craciun, A.M. et al. 1998. Improved bone metabolism in female elite athletes after vitamin K supplementation. *International Journal of Sports Medicine* 19: 479-484.

Dalton, R.A. et al. 1999. Acute carbohydrate consumption does not influence resistance exercise performance during energy restriction. *International Journal of Sport Nutrition* 9: 319-332.

Davis, J.M. et al. 1999. Effects of branched-chain amino acids and carbohydrate on fatigue during intermittent, high-intensity running. *International Journal of Sports Medicine* 20: 309-314.

DeMarco, H.M. et al. 1999. Pre-exercise carbohydrate meals: Application of glycemic index. *Medicine and Science in Sports and Exercise* 31: 164-170.

Deschenes, M.R., and W.J. Kraemer. 1989. The biochemical basis of muscular fatigue. *National Strength and Conditioning Association Journal* 11: 41-44.

Dias, V. 1990. Effects of feeding and energy balance in adult humans. *Metabolism* 39: 887-891.

Dimeff, R.J. 1993. Steroids and other performance enhancers. In R.N. Matzen and R.S. Lang (Eds.). *Clinical preventive medicine.* St. Louis: Mosby–Year Book, Inc.

Dimeff, R.J. May 19, 1996. Drugs and sports: Prescription and non-prescription. Presented at Sports Medicine for the Rheumatologist, American College of Rheumatology, Phoenix, Arizona.

Dorant, E., P.A. van den Brandt, R.A. Goldbohm, et al. 1996. Consumption of onions and a reduced risk of stomach carcinoma. *Gastroenterology* 110: 12-20.

Dowling, E.A. et al. 1996. Effect of Eleutherococcus senticosus on submaximal and maximal performance. *Medicine and Science in Sports and Exercise* 28: 482-489.

Dulloo, A.G. 1999. Efficacy of a green tea extract rich in catechin polyphenols and caffeine in increasing 24-h energy expenditure and fat oxidation in humans. *The American Journal of Clinical Nutrition* 70: 1040-1045.

Editor. 1996. The new diet pills: Fairly but not completely safe. *Harvard Heart Letter.* 7: 1-2.

Editor. Winter 1997. Ergogenic aids: Reported facts and claims. *Scan's Pulse Supplement*: 15-19.

Editor. 2000. Performance athletes' natural supplementation translates into high dollar sales. *AOL News*, June 9.

Editor. 2000. Smart waters™. BevNet. Internet Web site: bevnet.com/reviews/smartwater/index/asp.

Editor. 2000. Vitamin drink. *Nutritional Outlook* 3: 70.

Engels, H.J. et al. 1997. No ergogenic effects of ginseng (Panax C.A. Meyer) during graded maximal aerobic exercise. *Journal of the American Dietetic Association* 97: 1110-1115.

Essen-Gustavsson, B., and P.A. Tesch. 1990. Glycogen and triglyceride utilization in relation to muscle metabolic characteristics in men performing heavy-resistance exercise. *European Journal of Applied Physiology* 61: 5-10.

Evans, W. 1996. The protective role of antioxidants in exercise induced oxidative stress. Keynote address, 13th Annual SCAN Symposium, April 28, Scottsdale, Arizona.

Fawcett, J.P., S.J. Farquhar, R.J. Walker, et al. 1996. The effect of oral vanadyl sulfate on body composition and performance in weight-training athletes. *International Journal of Sport Nutrition* 6: 382-390.

Ferreira, M. et al. 1997. Effects of conjugated linoleic acid supplementation during resistance training on body composition and strength. *Journal of Strength and Conditioning Research* 11: 280.

Fogelholm, M. 1992. Micronutrient status in females during a 24-week fitness-type exercise program. *Annals of Nutrition and Metabolism* 36: 209-218.

Fogt, D.L. et al. 2000. Effects of post exercise carbohydrate-protein supplement on skeletal muscle glycogen storage. *Medicine and Science in Sports and Exercise* 2 (Supplement): Abstract No. 131.

Foley, D. 1984. Best health bets from the B team. *Prevention*, April, 62-67.

Food and Nutrition Board. 1989. National Research Council: *Recommended dietary allowances*. 10th Edition. National Academy Press.

Frentsos, J.A., and J.R. Baer. 1997. Increased energy and nutrient intake during training and competition improves elite triathletes' endurance performance. *International Journal of Sport Nutrition* 7: 61-71.

Frey-Hewitt, K.M., K.M. Vranizan, D.M. Dreon, and P.D. Wood. 1990. The effect of weight loss by dieting or exercise on resting metabolic rate in overweight men. *International Journal of Obesity* 14: 327-334.

Friedl, K.E., R.J. Moore, L.E. Martinez-Lopez, et al. 1994. Lower limit of body fat in healthy active men. *Journal of Applied Physiology* 77: 933-940.

Gerster, H. 1989. The role of vitamin C in athletic performance. *Journal of the American College of Nutrition* 8: 636-643.

Gerster, H. 1991. Function of vitamin E in physical exercise: A review. *Zeitschrift fur Ernahrungswissenschaft* 30: 89-97.

Gillette, C.A., R.C. Bullough, and C.L. Melby. 1994. Postexercise energy expenditure in response to acute aerobic or resistive exercise. *International Journal of Sport Nutrition* 4: 347-360.

Gillman, M.W., L.A. Cupples, D. Gagnon, et al. 1995. Protective effect of fruits and vegetables on development of stroke in men. *Journal of the American Medical Association* 273: 1113-1117.

Giovannuci, E., A. Ascherio, E.B. Rimm, et al. Intake of carotenoids and retinol in relation to risk of prostate cancer. *Journal of the National Cancer Institute* 87: 1767-1776.

Goldfarb, A.H. 1999. Nutritional antioxidants as therapeutic and preventive modalities in exercise-induced muscle damage. *Canadian Journal of Applied Physiology* 24: 249-266.

Gornall, J., and R.G. Villani. 1996. Short-term changes in body composition and metabolism with severe dieting and resistance exercise. *International Journal of Sport Nutrition* 6: 285-294.

Green, A.L., E. Hultman, I.A. MacDonald, D.A. Sewell, and P.L. Greenhaff. 1996. Carbohydrate ingestion augments skeletal muscle creatine accumulation during creatine supplementation in humans. *American Journal of Physiology* 271: E821-E826.

Green, N.R., and A.A. Ferrando. 1994. Plasma boron and the effects of boron supplementation in males. *Environmental Health Perspective Supplement* 7:73-77.

Greenwood-Robinson, M. 1999. *Natural weight loss miracles*. New York: Putnam.

Gross, M. et al. 1991. Ribose administration during exercise: Effects on substrates and products of energy metabolism in healthy subjects and a patient with myoadenylate deaminase deficiency. *Klinische Wochenschrift* 69:151-155.

Haff, G.G. et al. 1999. The effect of carbohydrate supplementation on multiple sessions and bouts of resistance exercise. *Journal of Strength and Conditioning Research* 13: 111-117.

Haff, G.G. et al. 2000. Carbohydrate supplementation attenuates muscle glycogen loss during acute bouts of resistance exercise. *International Journal of Sport Nutrition and Exercise Metabolism* 10: 326-339.

Harberson, D.A. 1988. Weight gain and body composition of weightlifters: Effect of high-calorie supplementation vs. anabolic steroids. In W.E. Garrett Jr. and T.E. Malone (Eds.). *Report of the Ross Laboratories Symposium on muscle development: Nutritional alternatives to anabolic steroids.* Columbus, Ohio: Ross Laboratories, 72-78.

Hargreaves, M. 2000. Skeletal muscle metabolism during exercise in humans. *Clinical and Experimental Pharmacology and Physiology* 27: 225-228.

Hartung, G.H., J.P. Foreyt, R.S. Reeves, et al. 1990. Effect of alcohol dose on plasma lipoprotein subfractions and lipolytic enzyme activity in active and inactive men. *Metabolism* 39: 81-86.

Hasler, C.M. 1996. Functional foods: The western perspective. *Nutrition Reviews* 54 (11 Part 2): S6-S10.

Hassmen, P. et al. 1994. Branched-chain amino acid supplementation during 30-km competitive run: Mood and cognitive performance. *Nutrition* 10: 405-410.

Health, M.K. (Ed.). 1982. Diet manual, including a vegetarian meal plan, 6th edition. Seventh Day Adventist Dietetic Association, P.O. Box 75, Loma Linda, CA 92345.

Heaney, R.P. 1993. Protein intake and the calcium economy. *Journal of the American Dietetic Association* 93: 1259-1260.

Hegewald, M.G. et al. 1991. Ribose infusion accelerates thallium redistribution with early imaging compared with late 24-hour imaging without ribose. *Journal of the American College of Cardiology* 18:1671-1681.

Heinonen, O.J. 1996. Carnitine and physical exercise. *Sports Medicine* 22: 109-132.

Hemila, H. 1996. Vitamin C and common cold incidence: A review of studies with subjects under heavy physical stress. *International Journal of Sports Medicine* 17: 379-383.

Herbert, V., and K.C. Dos. 1994. Folic acid and vitamin B12. In M. Shils, J. Olson, and M. Shike (Eds.). *Modern nutrition in health and disease.* Philadelphia: Lea & Febiger, 1430-1435.

Hickson, J.F. et al. 1987. Nutritional intake from food sources of high school football athletes. *Journal of the American Dietetic Association* 87:1656-1659.

Hitchins, S. et al. 1999. Glycerol hyperhydration improves cycle time trial performance in hot humid conditions. *European Journal of Applied Physiology and Occupational Physiology* 80: 494-501.

Holt, S.H. et al. 1999. The effects of high-carbohydrate vs high-fat breakfasts on feelings of fullness and alertness, and subsequent food intake. *International Journal of Food Sciences and Nutrition* 50: 13-28.

Ivy, J.L. 1998. Effect of pyruvate and dihydroxyacetone on metabolism and aerobic endurance capacity. *Medicine and Science in Sports and Exercise* 30: 837-843.

Ivy, J.L. et al. 1988. Muscle glycogen storage after different amounts of carbohydrate ingestion. *Journal of Applied Physiology* 65: 2018-2023.

Jackman, M., P. Wendling, D. Friars, et al. 1994. Caffeine ingestion and high-intensity intermittent exercise. Abstract. Personal communication with Larry Spriet, University of Guelph, Ontario, Canada.

Jacobsen, B.H. 1990. Effect of amino acids on growth hormone release. *The Physician and Sportsmedicine* 18: 68.

Jennings, E. 1995. Folic acid as a cancer-preventing agent. *Medical Hypotheses* 45: 297-303.

Ji, L.L. 1996. Exercise, oxidative stress, and antioxidants. *The American Journal of Sports Medicine* 24: S20-S24.

Kalman, D. et al. 1998. Effect of pyruvate supplementation on body composition and mood. *Current Therapeutic Research* 59: 798-802.

Kalman, D. et al. 1999. The effects of pyruvate supplementation on body composition in overweight individuals. *Nutrition* 15: 337-340.

Kanarek, R. 1997. Psychological effects of snacks and altered meal frequency. *British Journal of Nutrition* 77 (Supplement): S105-S118.

Kanter, M.M. et al. 1995. Antioxidants, carnitine and choline as putative ergogenic aids. *International Journal of Sport Nutrition* 5: S120-S131.

Kanter, M.M., L.A. Nolte, and J.O. Holloszy. 1993. Effects of an antioxidant vitamin mixture on lipid peroxidation at rest and postexercise. *Journal of Applied Physiology* 74: 965-969.

Keim, N.L., T.F Barbieri, M.D. Van Loan, and B.L. Anderson. 1990. Energy expenditure and physical performance in overweight women: Response to training with and without caloric restriction. *Metabolism* 39: 651-658.

Keim, N.L., A.Z. Belko, and T.F. Barbieri. 1996. Body fat percentage and gender: Associations with exercise energy expenditure, substrate utilization, and mechanical work efficiency. *International Journal of Sport Nutrition* 6: 356-369.

Keith, R.E., K.A. O'Keefe, D.L. Blessing, and G.D. Wilson. 1991. Alterations in dietary carbohydrate, protein, and fat intake and mood state in trained female cyclists. *Medicine and Science in Sports and Exercise* 212-216.

Kendrick, Z.V., M.B. Affrime, and D.T. Lowenthal. 1993. Effect of ethanol on metabolic responses to treadmill running in well-trained men. *Journal of Clinical Pharmacology* 33: 136-139.

Kerksick, C. et al. 2001. Bovine colostrum supplementation on training adaptations II: Performance. Abstract presented at 2001 FASEB meeting, Orlando, FL.

Kirkendall, D.T. 1998. Fluid and electrolyte replacement in soccer. *Clinics in Sports Medicine* 17: 729-738.

Kleiner, S.M. 1991. Performance-enhancing aids in sport: Health consequences and nutritional alternatives. *Journal of the American College of Nutrition* 10: 163-176.

Kleiner, S.M. 1999. Water: An essential but overlooked nutrient. *Journal of the American Dietetic Association* 99: 200-206.

Kleiner, S.M. 2000. Bodybuilding. In C.A. Rosenbloom (Ed.). *Sports nutrition: A guide for the professional working with active people*. (3rd edition). Chicago: SCAN, American Dietetic Association.

Kleiner, S.M., and M. Greenwood-Robinson. 1998. *High performance nutrition*. New York: John Wiley & Sons, Inc.

Kleiner, S.M. et al. 1989. Dietary influences on cardiovascular disease risk in anabolic steroid-using and non-using bodybuilders. *Journal of the American College of Nutrition* 8: 109-119.

Kleiner, S.M. et al. 1990. Metabolic profiles, diet, and health practices of championship male and female bodybuilders. *Journal of the American Dietetic Association* 90: 962-967.

Kleiner, S.M. et al. 1994. Nutritional status of nationally ranked elite bodybuilders. *International Journal of Sport Nutrition* 1: 54-69.

Kraemer, W.J. et al. 1998. Hormonal responses to consecutive days of heavy-resistance exercise with or without nutritional supplementation. *Journal of Applied Physiology* 85: 1544-1555.

Kreider, R.B. 1999. Dietary supplements and the promotion of muscle growth. *Sports Medicine* 27: 97-110.

Kreider, R.B. 1999. Protein: Is it all the same? *Muscular Development*, December.

Kreider, R.B. 2000. Nutritional considerations of overtraining. In J.R. Stout and J. Antonio (Eds.). *Sport supplements: A complete guide to physique and athletic enhancement.* Baltimore: Lippincott, Williams & Wilkins.

Kreider, R.B., R. Klesges, K. Harmon, et al. 1996. Effects of ingesting supplements designed to promote lean tissue accretion on body composition during resistance training. *International Journal of Sport Nutrition* 6: 234-246.

Kreider, R.B., V. Miriel, and E. Bertun. 1993. Amino acid supplementation and exercise performance: Analysis of the proposed ergogenic value. *Sports Medicine* 16: 190-209.

Kreider, R. et al. 1998. Effects of conjugated linoleic acid (CLA) supplementation during resistance training on bone mineral content, bone mineral density, and markers of immune stress. *FASEB Journal* 12: A244.

Kreider, R.B. et al. 1998. Effects of creatine supplementation on body composition, strength, and sprint performance. *Medicine and Science in Sports and Exercise* 30: 73-82.

Kreider, R.B. et al. (Eds.). 1998. *Overtraining in sport.* Champaign, IL: Human Kinetics.

Kreider, R.B. et al 1999. Effects of calcium b-hydroxy b-methylbutyrate (HMB) supplementation during resistance-training on markers of catabolism, body composition and strength. *International Journal of Sports Medicine* 22: 1-7.

Kreider, R.B. et al. 1999. Effects of protein and amino-acid supplementation on athletic performance. *Sportscience* 3: sportscie.org/jour/9901/rbk.html.

Kreider, R.B. et al. 2000. Nutrition in exercise and sport. In T. Wilson and N. Temple (Eds.). *Frontiers in nutrition.* Totowa, NJ: Humana Press, Inc.

Kreider, R.B. et al. 2001. Bovine colostrum supplementation on training adaptations I: Body Composition. Abstract presented at 2001 FASEB meeting, Orlando, FL.

Laaksonen., R. et al. 1995. Ubiquinone supplementation and exercise capacity in trained young and older men. *European Journal of Applied Physiology* 72: 95-100.

Lamb, D.R., K.F. Rinehardt, R.L. Bartels, et al. 1990. Dietary carbohydrate and intensity of interval swim training. *The American Journal of Clinical Nutrition* 52: 1058-1063.

Lambert, C.P., M.G. Flynn, J.B. Boone, et al. 1991. Effects of carbohydrate feeding on multiple-bout resistance exercise. *Journal of Applied Sport Science Research* 5: 192-197.

Lambert, M.I. et al. 1993. Failure of commercial oral amino acid supplements to increase serum growth hormone concentrations in male body-builders. *International Journal of Sport Nutrition* 3: 298-305.

Lands, L.C. et al. 1999. Effect of supplementation with cysteine donor on muscular performance. *Journal of Applied Physiology* 87: 1381-1385.

Lane, L. 1999. Nutritionist calls for tighter regulation of supplements. *CNN.com News*, September 17.

Langfort, J. et al. 1997. The effect of a low-carbohydrate diet on performance, hormonal and metabolic responses to a 30-s bout of supramaximal exercise. *European Journal of Applied Physiology and Occupational Physiology* 76:128-133.

Lefavi, R.G., R.A. Anderson, R.E. Keith, et al. 1992. Efficacy of chromium supplementation in athletes: Emphasis on anabolism. *International Journal of Sport Nutrition* 2: 111-122.

Lemon, P.W.R. 1991. Effect of exercise on protein requirements. *Journal of Sports Sciences* 9: 53-70.

Lemon, P.W.R. November 11-12, 1994. Dietary protein and amino acids. Presented at Nutritional Ergogenic Aids Conference sponsored by the Gatorade Sports Institute, Chicago.

Lemon, P.W.R. 2000. Beyond the Zone: Protein needs of active individuals. *Journal of the American College of Nutrition* 19: 513S-521S.

Lemon, P.W.R. et al. 1992. Protein requirements and muscle mass/strength changes during intensive training in novice bodybuilders. *Journal of Applied Physiology* 73: 767-775.

Lemon, P.W.R. et al. 1995. Do athletes need more dietary protein and amino acids? *International Journal of Sport Nutrition* 5 (Supplement): S39-S61.

Liberti, L.E. et al. 1978. Evaluation of commercial ginseng products. *Journal of Pharmaceutical Sciences* 67: 1487-1489.

Lowe, B. 2000. Powerful products. *Nutritional Outlook* 3: 37-43.

Ludwig, D.S. et al. 2001. Relation between consumption of sugar-sweetened drinks and childhood obesity: a prospective, observational analysis. *Lancet* 357: 505-508.

Lukaski, H.C. 2000. Magnesium, zinc, and chromium nutriture and physical activity. *American Journal of Clinical Nutrition* 72 (2 Supplement):585S-593S.

Malm, C. et al. 1996. Supplementation with ubiquinone-10 causes cellular damage during intense exercise. *Acta Physiologica Scandinavica* 157: 511-512.

Manore, M.M. 2000. *Sports nutrition for health and performance.* Champaign, IL: Human Kinetics.

Manore, M.M., J. Thompson, and M. Russo. 1993. Diet and exercise strategies of a world-class bodybuilder. *International Journal of Sport Nutrition* 3: 76-86.

Manson, J.E., W.C. Willett, M.J. Stampfer, et al. 1994. Vegetable and fruit consumption and incidence of stroke in women. *Circulation* 89: 932.

Maughan, R.J., and D.C. Poole. 1981. The effects of a glycogen-loading regimen on the capacity to perform anaerobic exercise. *European Journal of Applied Physiology* 46: 211-219.

Mazer, E. 1981. Biotin—The little known lifesaver. *Prevention*, July, 97-102.

McNaughton, L.R. et al. 1997. Neutralize acid to enhance performance. *Sportscience Training & Technology:* www.sportsci.org/traintech/buffer/lrm.htm.

Mero, A. 1999. Leucine supplementation and intensive training. *Sports Medicine* 27: 347-358.

Meydani, M. et al. 1993. Protective effect of vitamin E on exercise-induced oxidative damage in young and older adults. *American Journal of Physiology* 264 (5 Part 2): R992-998.

Miller, W.C., M.G. Niederpruem, J.P. Wallace, and A.K. Lindeman. 1994. Dietary fat, sugar, and fiber predict body fat content. *Journal of the American Dietetic Association* 94: 612-615.

Morris, A.C. et al. 1996. No ergogenic effect of ginseng ingestion. *International Journal of Sports Nutrition* 6: 263-271.

Most Americans require supplements. 1995. *USA Today Magazine*, October.

National Research Council. 1989. *Diet and health: Implications for reducing chronic disease risk.* Washington, D.C.: National Academy Press.

Nazar, K. et al. 1996. Phosphate supplementation prevents a decrease of triiodothyronine and increases resting metabolic rate during low energy diet. *Journal of Physiology and Pharmacology* 47: 373-383.

Nicholas, C.W. et al. 1999. Carbohydrate-electrolyte ingestion during intermittent high-intensity running. *Medicine and Science in Sports and Exercise* 31: 1280-1286.

Nissen, S., R. Sharp, M. Ray, et al. 1996. Effect of leucine metabolite beta-hydroxy-beta-methylbutyrate on muscle metabolism during resistance-exercise training. *Journal of Applied Physiology* 81: 2095-2104.

Oakley, G.P., M.J. Adams, and C.M. Dickinson. 1996. More folic acid for everyone, now. *Journal of Nutrition* 126: 751S-755S.

Olney, J. Transcript from December 29, 1996, airing of *60 Minutes*, CBS, New York.

Parrott, S. 1999. Herbs said harmful before surgery. *AOL News*, October 14.

Pieralisi, G. 1991. Effects of standardized ginseng extract combined with dimethylaminoethanol bitartrate, vitamins, minerals, and trace elements on physical performance during exercise. *Clinical Therapeutics* 13: 373-382.

Poortmans, J.R. et al. 2000. Do regular high protein diets have potential health risks on kidney function in athletes? *International Journal of Sport Nutrition and Exercise Metabolism* 10: 28-38.

Reilly, T. 1997. Energetics of high-intensity exercise (soccer) with particular reference to fatigue. *Journal of Sports Science* 15: 257-263.

Robergs, R.A. 1998. Glycerol hyperhydration to beat the heat? *Sportscience Training & Technology:* www.sportsci.org/traintech/buffer/lrm.htm.

Rolls, B.J. et al. 1988. The specificity of satiety: The influence of foods of different macronutrient content on the development of satiety. *Physiology and Behavior* 43: 145-153.

Sarubin, A. 2000. *The health professional's guide to popular dietary supplements.* The American Dietetic Association, pp.184-188.

Schabort, E.J. et al. 1999. The effect of a preexercise meal on time to fatigue during prolonged cycling exercise. *Medicine and Science in Sports and Exercise* 31: 464-471.

Seaton, T.B., S.L. Welle, M.K. Warenko, and R.G. Campbell. 1986. Thermic effect of medium and long chain triglycerides in man. *The American Journal of Clinical Nutrition* 44: 630-634.

Seidle, R. et al. 2000. A taurine and caffeine-containing drink stimulates cognitive performance and well-being. *Amino Acids* 19:635-642.

Shugarman, A.E. 1999. Trends in the sports nutrition industry. *Nutraceuticals World* 2: 56-59.

Simko, M.D., and J. Jarosz. 1990. Organic foods: Are they better? *Journal of the American Dietetic Association* 90: 367-370.

Singh, A. et al. 1994. Exercise-induced changes in immune function: Effects of zinc supplementation. *Journal of Applied Physiology* 76: 2298-2303.

Sizer, F., and E. Whitney. 1994. *Nutrition concepts and controversies.* Minneapolis/St. Paul: West Publishing Company.

Slavin, J.L. 1991. Assessing athletes' nutritional status. *The Physician and Sportsmedicine* 19: 79-94.

Somer, E. 1996. Maximum energy: How to eat and exercise for it. *Working Woman*, May, 72-76.

Speechly, D.P. et al. 1999. Greater appetite control associated with an increased frequency of eating in lean males. *Appetite* 33: 285-297.

Spiller, G.A., C.D. Jensen, T.S. Pattison, C.S. Chuck, et al. 1987. Effect of protein dose on serum glucose and insulin response to sugars. *The American Journal of Clinical Nutrition* 46: 474-480.

Spriet, L.L. 1995. Caffeine and performance. *International Journal of Sport Nutrition* 5: S84-S99.

Stanko, R.T. et al. 1996. Inhibition of regain in body weight and fat with addition of 3-carbon compounds to the diet with hyperenergetic refeeding after weight reduction. *International Journal of Obesity Related Metabolic Disorders* 20: 925-930.

Steinmetz, K.A. et al. 1996. Vegetables, fruit, and cancer prevention: A review. *Journal of the American Dietetic Association* 96: 1027-1039.

Stewart, A.M. 1999. Amino acids and athletic performance: A mini-conference in Oxford. *Sportscience Training & Technology:* www.sportsci.org/jour/9902/ams.html.

Stone, N. 1996. AHA Medical/Scientific Statement on fish consumption, fish oil, lipids, and coronary heart disease. Internet Web site: www.americanheart.org.

Szlyk, P.C., R.P. Francesconi, M.S. Rose, et al. 1991. Incidence of hypohydration when consuming carbohydrate-electrolyte solutions during field training. *Military Medicine* 156: 399-402.

Tarnopolsky, M.A. 1993. Protein, caffeine, and sports. *The Physician and Sportsmedicine* 21:137-146.

Tarnopolsky, M.A. 1998. Influence of differing macronutrient intakes on muscle glycogen resynthesis after resistance training. *Journal of Applied Physiology* 84: 890-896.

Tarnopolsky, M.A. et al. 1992. Evaluation of protein requirements for trained strength athletes. *Journal of Applied Physiology* 73: 1986-1995.

Tarnopolsky, M.A. et al. 1997. Postexercise protein-carbohydrate supplements increase muscle glycogen in men and women. *Journal of Applied Physiology* 83:1877-1883.

Thomas, D.E. et al. 1991. Carbohydrate feeding before exercise: Effect of glycemic index. *International Journal of Sports Medicine* 12:180-186.

Thornton, J.S. 1990. How can you tell when an athlete is too thin? *The Physician and Sportsmedicine* 18:124-133.

Tiidus, P.M. et al. 1995. Vitamin E status and response to exercise training. *Sports Medicine* 20: 12-23.

Trumbo, P. et al. 2001. Dietary reference intakes. *Journal of the American Dietetic Association* 101(3): 294-301.

Tullson, P.C. et al. 1991. Adenine nucleotide synthesis in exercising and endurance-trained skeletal muscle. *American Journal of Physiology* 261(2 Part 1): C342-347.

Tyler, V.E. 1987. *The new honest herbal: A sensible guide to the use of herbs and related remedies*. Philadelphia: George F. Stickley Co.

U.S. Department of Agriculture and U.S. Department of Health and Human Services. 1995. Nutrition and your health: Dietary guidelines for Americans. Washington, D.C.: GPO.

Van Zyl, C.G. et al. 1996. Effects of medium-chain triglyceride ingestion on fuel metabolism and cycling performance. *Journal of Applied Physiology* 80: 2217-2225.

Wagner, D.R. 1999. Hyperhydrating with glycerol: Implications for athletic performance. *Journal of the American Dietetic Association* 99: 207-212.

Wagner, D.R. et al. 1992. Effects of oral ribose on muscle metabolism during bicycle ergometer exercise in AMPD-deficient patients. *Annals of Nutrition and Metabolism* 35: 297-302.

Wagner, J.C. 1991. Enhancement of athletic performance with drugs: An overview. *Sports Medicine* 12: 250-265.

Walberg, J.L. et al. 1988. Macronutrient content of a hypoenergy diet affects nitrogen retention and muscle function in weight lifters. *International Journal of Sports Medicine* 9: 261-266.

Walberg-Rankin, J.L. November 11-12, 1994. Ergogenic effects of carbohydrate intake during long- and short-term exercise. Presented at Nutritional Ergogenic Aids Conference sponsored by the Gatorade Sports Institute, Chicago.

Walberg-Rankin, J.L. 1995. Dietary carbohydrate as an ergogenic aid for prolonged and brief competitions in sport. *International Journal of Sport Nutrition* 5: S13-S28.

Walberg-Rankin, J.L. et al. 1994. The effect of oral arginine during energy restriction in male weight lifters. *Journal of Strength and Conditioning Research* 8: 170-177.

Walton, R.G., R. Hudak, and R.J. Green-Waite. 1993. Adverse reactions to aspartame: Double-blind challenge in patients from a vulnerable population. *Biological Psychiatry* 34: 13-17.

Ward, R.J. et al. 1999. Changes in plasma taurine levels after different endurance events. *Amino Acids* 16 (1): 71-77.

Wardlaw, G.M., P.M. Insel, and M.F. Seyler. 1994. *Contemporary nutrition.* St. Louis: Mosby–Year Book, Inc.

Washington State Department of Agriculture. 1995. Organic food standards. Organic Food Program, Food Safety and Animal Health Division.

Weak potions for building strong muscles. October 1992. *Tufts University Diet and Nutrition Letter* 10:7.

Wesson, M., L. McNaughton, P. Davies, and S. Tristram. 1988. Effects of oral administration of aspartic acid salts on the endurance capacity of trained athletes. *Research Quarterly for Exercise and Sport* 59: 234-239.

Williams, C. 1995. Macronutrients and performance. *Journal of Sports Sciences* 13: S1-S10.

Williams, M.H. 1989. Vitamin supplementation and athletic performance. *International Journal for Vitamin and Nutrition Research, Supplement,* 30: 163-191.

Williams, M.H. et al. 1998. *The ergogenics edge.* Champaign, IL: Human Kinetics.

Williams, M.H. et al. 1999. *Creatine: The power supplement.* Champaign, IL: Human Kinetics.

Wilmore, J.H., and D.L. Costill. 1994. *Physiology of sport and exercise.* Champaign, IL: Human Kinetics, 392-395.

Winters, L.R., R.S. Yoon, H.J. Kalkwarf, J.C. Davies, et al. 1992. Riboflavin requirements and exercise adaption in older women. *The American Journal of Clinical Nutrition* 56: 526-532.

Yaspelkis, B.B. et al. 1999. The effect of a carbohydrate-arginine supplement on postexercise carbohydrate metabolism. *International Journal of Sports Nutrition* 9: 241-250.

Zawadzki, K.M., B.B. Yaselkis, and J.L. Ivy. 1992. Carbohydrate-protein complex increases the rate of muscle glycogen storage after exercise. *Journal of Applied Physiology* 72: 1854-1859.

Index

About the Authors

Susan M. Kleiner holds a PhD in nutrition and human performance from Case Western Reserve University and currently serves as a nutrition consultant to GNC and to the Seattle SuperSonics. She has consulted numerous other strength and bodybuilding athletes, including sports teams in the NFL and NBA. She serves on the advisory boards for *Shape* and *Let's Live Magazine/Physical,* and she is the nutrition column editor for *Athletic Therapy Today.* She writes frequent columns and features for magazines ranging from *Muscle & Fitness* to *Parenting.* Kleiner has published *The Power Eating and Fitness Log*, which can be purchased by calling 800-448-8212. She is also building a Web site at **www.powereating.com**, where she can be contacted for more information.

A registered dietitian, Kleiner is a fellow in the American College of Nutrition, who honored her with a Young Investigator Award in 1987 for her work on the influence of diet and anabolic steroids on competitive male bodybuilders. She is an Associate Member of Sigma Xi, a scientific research society, and a member of the American College of Sports Medicine; the National Strength and Conditioning Association; the American Dietetic Association; and the Sport, Cardiovascular and Wellness Nutritionists.

Kleiner lives in Mercer Island, Washington, with her husband Jeffrey Kanter and their two daughters. In her free time she enjoys skiing, strength training, and spending time with her family in the great outdoors of the Pacific Northwest.

A certified nutrition counselor, **Maggie Greenwood-Robinson** has authored or coauthored 19 books in the health and fitness field. She writes the Natural Dieter column for *Let's Live* magazine and the Body Shop column for *Christian Single.* She is also a member of the advisory board for *Physical* magazine.

Greenwood-Robinson's articles have appeared in *Women's Sports and Fitness, Working Woman, Great Life, MuscleMag International, Ironman, Muscle and Fitness, Female Bodybuilding,* and many other publications. She has conducted seminars on strength training, exercise motivation, diet and nutrition, fat loss, and couple's fitness; she has also taught bodyshaping classes at the University of Southern Indiana.

Greenwood-Robinson has a PhD in nutrition counseling from LaSalle University. She and her husband Jeff live in Destin, Florida, where she enjoys weight training and walking the beach.